NO REMORSE

A FATHER'S MURDEROUS RAGE

by Kirstie McLellan

Published by: K-Jules Productions Inc.
e-mail: kjulesproductions@home.com
tel: 403.234.8566

Printing by: Quebecor World Printpak
Calgary, Alberta

For Paul and Gabi

ACKNOWLEDGEMENTS

The author gratefully acknowledges special contributions from: Liba and my family for giving me two years of support and room to write, my parents for their constant encouragement, my husband for his wealth of ideas, Lana Libke, Kathy and Heather Erhardt, Jiri Srom, Nick Kyska, Wally Purcell, Sandy Harder, John Cantafio, Colin Glabus, Dahl Chambers, Merv Harrower, Father John Bastigal, John Orme, Dr. Paul Martyn, Dr. Jill Teschke, The Calgary Herald, The Calgary Sun, Andy MacIntosh, Warkworth Correctional Institute, Dr. Robin Reesal, Dr. Thomas Dalby, Dr. Arboleda-Florez, Dr. John Butt, Julie Sinclair, Tara Halerwich, Laura O'Grady, The Calgary Public Library Business and Research Section, The Toronto Star, Alberta Office of the Chief Medical Examiner, Patrick Nelson, Josef Dolejs, Gabriela Docekalova, Darlene Cook, Gerald Chipeur, John Bascom, Wayne Logan, Jamie Polley, Donald Young, Balfour Der, Alberta Law Society, Olga Vyskocil, Bill Hushion, Arnold Gosewich, Editor- Larry Day, Proof readers - Jill Foran and Joan McLellan, Book Cover - Karo Design, W. Edward Johnson and Quebecor World Printpak.

Liba would like to thank: All RCMP involved, Dr. Brian Smith, Lana Libke, Rick Pegoraro, Heather Erhardt and family, Gordon and Dorothy Johnson, Dan MacGregor, Bill Deagle, Carol Monson, Kerry Hilderman, Manfred Lukas, Rose Salnikowski, Dr. Reesal, Peter Martin, John Bascom and last but not least my husband, for his strength and patience.

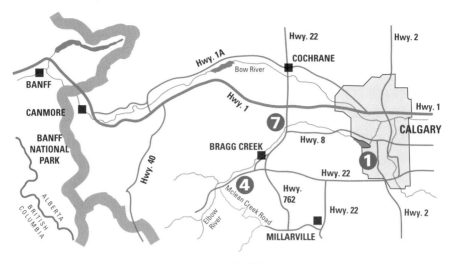

LEGEND

1. **July 27, 1986** – 9:00 a.m.
Children picked up in Calgary

2. **July 27** – 1:30 p.m.
Neil White fishes with children at Allen Bill Pond

3. **July 27** – Approx. 2:30 p.m.
Ruth Lindmark and family encounter speeding Ramcharger

4. **July 27** – 4:00 and 5:30 p.m.
Gooseberry Info Center; Al's two calls to Liba

5. **July 28** – 9:45-10:00 a.m.
Gooseberry Campground. On-duty Kananaskis
employee sees Al emerge from bathroom

6. **July 28** – 11:00 a.m.
First reported sighting of Al's truck

7. **August 7** – 7:15 p.m.
Clem Gardner Bridge.
Cst. Deheer finds Al 1/4 mile north of bridge

8. **Early September**
Liba's solitary search for the children

9. **June 4, 1987**
Al finally reveals where he killed the children
and RCMP investigate and find children's remains

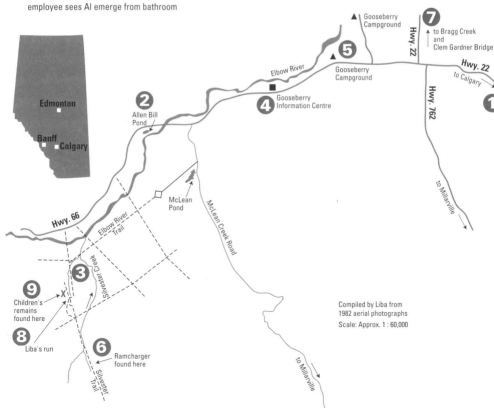

CHAPTER ONE

THE KIDS

Although she awoke with her usual smile, Gabi Dolejs now sat gloomily on her bed. Slowly she pulled the straps of her blue jean overalls up over her long-sleeved shirt. Then she wiped all the smudges off her large, pink-framed glasses with the bottom of her favorite kangaroo sweater, the navy one with the red and white striped pouch at the front. It was 8:00 AM Sunday morning, July 27, 1986. Too early. She wanted to sleep in, but Daddy was coming to take her and her big brother, Paul, fishing. Gabi stood up and yawned. Fishing? She wondered what the heck Daddy was up to now.

She gathered up her babies, Little Pink Elephant, her brown bunny (the one Mommy found in Fish Creek Park while on a picnic), her big blue dog that wore her old sundress and Vorisek, the stuffed puppy from Woolco. Gabi remembered buying Vorisek. He was cradled in her arms and the pretty checkout girl said, "Vorisek, what a nice name."

Mommy had laughed in surprise. "Hello," Mommy said. "My name is Liba Dolejs," and started speaking to the girl in Czech.

Gabi shoved all of them under her sheets, then pulled each up by its ears so its head rested comfortably on her pillow. She glanced across the room at Paul's Winnie the Pooh and stuffed tiger. He had tucked them in the same way. They looked happy beneath his green striped Ikea duvet comforter that matched her own. His burgundy patterned polo pajamas were lying in a heap near the bottom of the bed beside Mommy's good leather hiking boots. He got to borrow them because the weather was so rainy and they would probably be doing some hiking. Gabi could hardly wait until she was big enough to borrow Mommy's stuff.

Paul was always up early. He'd been watching cartoons since 5:00 AM. She shut her eyes and listened. Downstairs she could hear Newton, the Centaur, exclaiming, "That's me! That's me!" followed by the wicked cackle of Daedalius, the villain, on one of Paul's favorite cartoons, Hercules.

She shuffled into the bathroom across the hall, closed the door with a creak and a whump and stared at her reflection in the mirror above the marble vanity. She laid her glasses carefully up against the wall to protect them from water spots as she washed her face. Her short-cropped hair was standing up at the crown like Dennis the Menace. She narrowed her big brown eyes so she could focus more clearly. She knew she was a cutie. At least that's what everyone told her. They also said she was a real character. Her Mommy called her a motor mouth.

"But when you were born, Elunka," her Mommy would croon gently, as she sat on the edge of Gabi's bed rubbing her long, downy back before sleep, "You were my little pink angel."

Gabi leaned forward to get a closer look at her teeth. She wore a retainer at night to help straighten the spacing between them. Better than braces like some of her friends. Her lips turned up at the corners and when she smiled she looked so impish, she made others smile. She cocked her head to the side examining her face. Her dark eyebrows winged out toward her temples like birds in flight and she had a little turned up nose. Her gymnastics coach, Lana Libke, once said Gabi looked so much like her Dad she had to pull her chin up off the ground the first time she met him.

Gabi had only seen Daddy six times since Easter Sunday. That was the day Daddy had taken her and Paul up to Banff Hot Springs to go swimming. He'd been mad at Paul again. While they were swimming, Daddy held him under water quite a few times, almost drowning him and Paul had cried. Paul didn't cry too often now that he was twelve. While they were getting changed, Paul ran away and found the RCMP, just like their mother had taught him to do. After that, Mommy took them to the

Sheriff King Women's Emergency Shelter. They stayed ten days and Daddy had to move out of their house.

Gabi was glad about that. No more yelling and hitting Mommy. But she kind of missed Daddy and felt sorry for him because he was all alone. Paul took pity on him too and that's why they agreed to go fishing with him.

Suddenly, the bathroom door swung open and Paul barged in, full of vinegar. He jostled playfully for position at the sink and turned on the tap splashing water all over his face and getting Gabi's glasses wet on purpose.

"Paulie!" she yelped, snatching up her glasses and shaking them at him. "Look what you've done! I just cleaned them!"

"Oops. Let me see." He frowned, seizing them from her hand and holding them under the tap.

"No!" She shrieked and made a grab for his outstretched hand. "Paulie! Give them to me or I'll tell Mommy!" She pressed her lips together and made as if to summon her mother. "Mmmmmmmmaaa."

"Okay." Paul chuckled and handed back her dripping frames. He opened the door and casually started for the stairs. "I guess I'll just go and eat breakfast now. But I noticed there's only one orange Flintstones vitamin left, and I think it's Dino. I hope you get to it before I do." With that, he bounded down the stairs and Gabi took off after him.

Paul Dolejs was mature beyond his twelve years and as good as a kid gets. He felt it was his job to look after Gabi and protect his Mom. He wasn't jealous of his ten-year-old sister, even though he realized his dad didn't like him and loved her. It was quite a marked contrast. It was as if he felt Gabi could do no wrong. Mommy said Gabi had Daddy wrapped around her baby finger from day one.

What did bother Paul was despite his primogeniture, everything he did seemed to make his dad angry. Until last year, his dad mainly just used insults to show it. Coming from Czechoslovakia in his twenties, his dad never really mastered English. Paul was a straight A student so he knew his dad's grammar was atrocious. Alois Dolejs was a carpenter and on the construction sites where he worked almost everyone was from a different part of Europe so they created their own language. Most of it would turn the air blue and at home a lot of it was directed at Paul.

His dad was always calling him a fag. "I'm raising a fag," he'd sneer, especially if Paul allowed a scoring chance on his own goal playing defense in one of his hockey games.

Maybe it was his looks. His Mom told a story about being in Eaton's when he was only two. He was in a stroller and all dressed in red. A lady came up, peered at Paul's long black lashes and fine, beautiful features and pronounced him a gorgeous little girl.

"Well, actually he's a boy," his mother replied. To which the lady said, "What a shame! Such beauty wasted on a boy."

But it was a stupid thing for his dad to call him anyway, because Paul really liked girls, especially Heather with her long brown hair. She was a gymnast and he sat near her in Mr. Orme's class. Paul's cheeks felt hot, as he recalled agonizing over what to get Heather for Easter. He knew his Mom would help, but he'd felt awkward as he approached her in the kitchen.

Paul's Mom, Liba, was an energetic dynamo, short and sturdy with a soft brown pixie cut, lovely white teeth, pink cheeks and intelligent green eyes behind large thick glasses. She had been stirring soup in the kitchen and noticed the tips of Paul's ears were bright red and he had an odd, self-conscious look on his face as if he were about to confess to some wrongdoing. She waited for him to speak.

"Mommy, I'd like to ask you something," he said, "but don't laugh at me or anything."

Liba managed to keep her expression neutral. "You know I would never do that, Paul. You can ask me absolutely anything."

"There's this girl at school named Heather. She's very nice and I was wondering would it be okay if I bought her an Easter Egg at the Co-Op? I'll use my own money," he hastened to add.

Liba suppressed a smile. "I don't see why not. Would you like me to drive you over there?"

Paul looked unsure. "Sure. Right now?"

Liba looked at her watch and chewed her bottom lip. Al would be angry if supper was late. Then she looked at her son's eager face. "Okay. Get in the car."

Garish looking cartoon rabbits with big grins adorned the windows of the store. Mother and son had no trouble finding the large Easter display with its plastic picket fence.

Liba stood and watched as Paul maneuvered his long, lean body gracefully through the open gate and bent to study each egg very carefully.

Finally, he chose one made of milk chocolate. It was wrapped in bright fuchsia foil and covered with painted flowers. Purchase price, $1.99. He picked it up with a triumphant grin. "I think she'd like this one."

Back in the car, Paul was silent for a moment, then he blurted out, "I don't want to give this to her at school, but I know where she lives."

Liba turned the ignition key. "Fine, let's drop it off then."

They drove to Southwood Elementary, the school both Paul and Gabi attended. From there, Paul directed Liba down a couple of alleys and around a corner. He pointed to a house and said, "That's it."

Liba pulled up in front. "I guess you'd better take it to her."

Paul's knees wobbled as he made his way up the walk. He rang the bell and Heather's mother answered. To Paul's tremendous relief, she accepted the egg, and explained Heather was at gymnastics.

Liba's heart was bursting with love as she watched him fairly skip back down the walk and get in the car, a big grin plastered all over his face. "She wasn't home!" he announced happily, "so I left it with her mother."

When Paul turned twelve, his dad started getting meaner and rougher. One day he reached across the supper table and slugged Paul at the top of his spine with a closed fist. It made a terrible squeaking sound and before Paul knew it, Mommy was standing in front of him, confronting his dad. Although his father was very angry and towered over her by a good six inches, she faced him down. She spoke slowly and softly, but with grim resolve, "If you want to get to him, you'll have to go through me." The only thing that kept Paul's tears at bay that night was the pride he felt at Mommy's courage.

Paul went to a chiropractor soon after that incident because his back hurt so much. His dad labeled him a sissy. Slaps across the head and shoulders became more and more frequent. Then, there was the incident at Banff.

It happened on Easter Sunday. Mommy was working as a realtor holding an open house, so his dad took him and Gabi to Banff. It was supposed to be a treat, but while they were in the swimming pool, Daddy started playing really rough. It wasn't really even play. His dad just wanted people to think it was. It started with his dad pushing him under the water. When Paul complained, his dad called him a crybaby and 'little girl.' Then his dad held him under water until Paul felt his lungs would explode. He struggled hard to come up, but his dad was too strong. Just when he thought he would drown, his dad let go.

Finally, his dad lunged for him, twisting his arm behind his back and pulling him close. Paul could smell the stink of his dad's cigarette breath on his ear as he hissed, "You big baby. You Mama's boy. I'm going to arrange it so that you will never see her again. I'm going to take you far, far away, where she'll never find you." With that, he pushed Paul under water and held him there even longer.

In the locker room, Paul's hands shook as he hurriedly pulled his jeans over his wet body. He could see his dad's and Gabi's feet as they dressed in an adjacent cubicle. His own feet slid around in his runners as he ran toward the exit, frantically yanking on the sweatshirt stuck to his midriff.

Paul knew he couldn't stay on the road from the Hot Springs. His dad would see him when he drove down the mountain toward town. So he decided to take a shortcut through the woods. His heart raced as he scrambled down the slippery path through the forest. When he reached the old Banff Hospital, he asked for directions to the police station. Seeing his distress, they offered him a ride, but Paul suddenly felt embarrassed and confused.

"No, I was just curious, that's all," he lied.

He fled the building and ran across the bridge. He felt terribly vulnerable in the open and when he spotted the RCMP station just one street over, he headed straight for it.

Liba got a phone call from the RCMP toward the end of the afternoon. They informed her they had Paul at the Detachment in Banff and he was insisting he did not want to be with his father. He was saying his father had threatened to take him away from her so that she would never find him again. Apparently, he'd made the threat before, but Paul was convinced this day, his father meant business.

Liba instructed them under no circumstances should they hand him over to his father. "I'll come to Banff. Just keep him there. I'll come and get him." When she hung up, Liba found herself panting. The phone rang again. It was Social Services. She started to panic as visions of the government agency taking both kids away from her played out in her head. Frightened, she told the Social Worker her plan to retrieve Paul and agreed to meet later.

Al had taken her compact Datsun because it was cheaper on gas, so she jumped in their rusty 1977 Ram Charger 4X4. About fifty kilometers out of the city on Highway 1 near Chief Chiniki Gas Station, there was a loud bang in the truck and Liba started losing oil pressure and power. Obviously, something was terribly wrong. Spotting no oncoming traffic, she steered the truck toward the south side of the highway, across the grass median, and rolled into the gas station under the large, black Indian headdress logo at the side of the building.

The on-duty mechanic took a quick look at it, shook his head and announced gravely, "You've blown the block. The piston shaft has gone right through the bottom."

Liba, a trained mechanical engineer, grasped the situation. It was unfixable. She needed a new engine. To hell with it. She had bigger things on her mind. "Is there anybody here? I have to get to Banff," she pleaded. "I'll hitchhike or whatever, it doesn't matter."

A grizzled old trucker, heading for a tow truck that had seen better days, overheard their conversation. He looked her up and down. "I have to go to Banff to pick something up. I guess I can take you there and help you out."

Liba swallowed. His boots were muddy and his overalls were stained with grease. He looked like he hadn't bathed or shaved in days. She forced a smile. "That would be great. I'll pay you." She hopped in and slammed the faded green door bearing the name, Bow River Corridor Tow Truck Service. On the way, she explained her situation. "I have to pick up my son and I have to take him back to Calgary tonight." The trucker offered to return her home, but apologized, saying he'd have to charge gas money. Liba gratefully accepted.

When she entered the RCMP station Paul ran into her arms and they held on to each other for a very long time. One of the officers told her how, upon emerging from the changing cubicle at the Hot Springs, Mr. Dolejs searched for Paul. He and Gabi drove around Banff, then gave up and reported him missing. The RCMP informed him Paul was there, but refused to release him. According to the officer, Al just shrugged his shoulders, took Gabi's hand, and left.

But that had been months ago. Now that his parents were separated, things were different. His dad was making more of an effort to be friends.

Like a lot of people of European descent, Mommy served rye bread, sliced tomatoes and cold cuts with mustard for breakfast. Paul liked his with a little butter, no mayonnaise. Neither child drank milk. So Mommy gave them liquid calcium supplements in their juice. Cereal was just for snacking on, dry.

Paul stuffed a baggie full of Fruit Loops into the pocket of his blue jeans, for later, then wandered back into the living room.

The weather was awful. Wet, rainy and cold. Paul traced his name in the condensation on the pane of the front room window, then quickly removed it with his shirtsleeve. Mommy worked hard enough without having to wash windows. Everyone kept saying it was the worst July in Calgary ever. Yet, his dad wanted to take them fishing. "Why fishing?" Paul wondered. They didn't even have rods.

A few minutes later, he watched the Ram Charger pull up. Mommy went to the door and opened it a little. His dad came up the walk and stood before her. She let the door go and he caught it with the toe of his boot.

"Are the kids ready?" Paul heard him ask.

"I'll get them," Mommy replied coolly. She looked across the foyer into the living room and motioned to Paul with a slight nod.

Paul started toward her, then froze in his tracks when he heard his dad's next comment. "Make sure they bring their swim suits. We're going swimming up at the Hot Springs."

His Mother's head snapped up and Paul paled visibly. Panic swept over him as his mind raced back to Easter Sunday and the incident. He forced his feet forward and met Mommy on the stairs. They exchanged glances. Neither of them wanted to make a fuss or say anything, because they knew Al would take it out on Paul later. "Come on, we'll get your swimsuit," Mommy said. She gently guided him up the stairs with the back of her hand.

Mommy dug around in Gabi's drawer until she found a pink Strawberry Shortcake one-piece. She rolled it up in a square-shaped, flowered swim towel and started back down the stairs. She turned and looked at Paul. "Are you sure?"

He nodded. She patted him, then left the room.

Trembling, Paul located his Speedo and rolled it into his Magnum P.I. towel. He stared at Tom Selleck, one of his favorite actors. Boy he liked that show. Someday he would either be an NHL player or a cop and help people like Magnum or the RCMP officers at Banff did. He'd written an essay for Mr. Orme about how they had fed him a hamburger and really listened to him. He won the Sergeant-For-A-Day competition at school. The prize was a whole day with Police Sergeant Vic Norman. One of the best days of his life.

He didn't have much time for TV, due to hockey and gymnastics and piano, but the tube had been on every minute his dad lived with them. In fact, that's basically all Daddy did, sit and stare at the television. Especially shows about crime. He always ridiculed the bad guys when they got caught. They were fags and idiots too.

Paul opened his closet and removed his ball glove from the shelf. He tossed it in the air all the way down the stairs to the kitchen. Maybe his dad would soften up if they played catch.

Mommy was standing by the front door hugging Gabi. When they went out with their friends, she brushed their cheeks with a kiss and told them to be good. But whenever they left with Al, she knew they'd be on their best behavior. They were too afraid of his sour moods and bad temper to do otherwise. This time she leaned over and held Gabi's sweet face in her hands and kissed her. "I love you, Elunka," she murmured.

"Love you too, Mommy." Gabi smiled and skipped out the door in front of her Daddy.

"Wait!" Mommy called after her and held up her red winter coat with the fur trim. "It's cold."

Al gave Liba a rare smile and took it from her. "When I come back, I'll have another surprise for you," he said.

Liba blinked and looked at Paul. They had a lowball offer on their house that Liba had been trying to get Al to sign. Was he saying he would?

"Okay," replied Liba. "You'll have them home by four, right?"

Again Al smiled. "By four," he agreed and followed Gabi out to the car.

Paul turned to face his mother, trying to hide the anxiety he felt. "Bye," he said.

Liba hugged him hard and buried her nose in his freshly mown brush cut. She could feel his heart pounding under the suede panels of his kangaroo jacket. "I love you, Pavel," she whispered.

"Me too," he answered and before he left, she kissed him tenderly on the cheek.

CHAPTER TWO

DREAMS

The night Gabi was born, Liba awoke in a panic. She just had the most awful dream. Perhaps the worst ever. She was in a densely wooded forest some place off-road, near a narrow clay footpath. As she stepped onto the path, she could smell the earth and feel the coolness of the loam beneath her feet. She began walking. A male figure approached her. He told her Paul killed a man.

She shook her head. "But he couldn't have done such a thing! He is a small boy. He's only two years old."

"I'll show you," said the fellow. And he led her further down the path to some thick undergrowth. Just beyond, in a small clearing, she could see Al. He was lying on the ground, his arms splayed and his head back. There was blood everywhere, stemming from gaping holes all over his body. Someone had killed him with an ax or a sharp tool. Horrified, Liba turned to the messenger. "I am telling you, Paul couldn't have done this. How could he? He is two!" But the man just stared at her. When she turned back to look at Al's body, she realized with a sinking feeling that Paul was guilty.

She could not rid herself of the aftermath of the dream, so she got up out of her hospital bed and paced the quiet linoleum floor outside her room. The clock over the nurses' station told her it was 2:00 AM.

She found her way to an area with a sink and a coffeepot. She opened a cupboard looking for some grounds, then changed her mind. She couldn't drink coffee this late. She'd never sleep. She left the alcove and headed back to her room. The dream, with its horrendous act, replayed in her head. Never had she felt so anxious. She couldn't seem to shake it. It left her cloaked in a feeling of dread. She lost track of where she was or what she'd done since she awoke. She found a sink and coffeepot, but when she reached for the grounds, she chided herself. "I've just done all of this."

Back in bed, fear bit into her chest and throat so that she could hardly breathe. She ached to hold her little boy and wondered if Al was taking good care of him. Since Paul's birth two years before, all they seemed to do was argue. She used to work out regularly and participate in sports. She tried to get back to it when Paul was a few weeks old by joining a judo class. When she told Al he became angry. "What about Paul?" he snarled.

"He'll be in bed. Besides, it's only two evenings a week for heaven's sake," she replied.

His eyes turned cold, like marbles. "Well, you are going to be here at home with him those evenings!"

She ignored him and went to the classes anyway. Paul was always asleep in his crib, just the way she'd left him, when she returned. But for days after, she had to endure Al's crankiness and snarky remarks.

She lay awake the rest of the night, afraid to go back to sleep. Ironically, in the future, sleep would be her only escape from the nightmares that gripped her while she was awake.

The next time she felt that same surge of panic was on July 27, 1986, three days after Gabi's tenth birthday. The day of the fishing trip. At 3:45 that afternoon, she was sitting on the big couch against the wall of the living room in her Woodbine home, the one she so badly needed to sell.

The signs she placed on the lawn indicated it was an Open House. Liba had her Realtor's license, mainly to save commission on houses she and her husband built and sold. But after sixteen years of physical and emotional abuse, she'd finally left Al. Money was very tight and even though she had three jobs, a drafting business, house cleaning and work as part-time realtor, she had trouble keeping up with all the bills. Besides, it was totally unnecessary for her and the two kids to live in such a big home. It was over two thousand square feet for goodness sake.

Unfortunately, the bottom had fallen out of the housing market in Calgary and the only offer they'd had was a poor one. It had cost them $160,000 to build the house and the first couple who wanted it offered $123,000. Al flatly refused.

Nothing happened for a couple of months until another couple came along with an even lower offer, $105,000. Liba had counter-offered and it had gone back and forth four times. She felt their most recent offer of $114,000, was acceptable. It would be such a load off. If only Al would agree to sign the offer! What did he mean by his remark that morning about having another surprise for her?

As she sat contemplating this, a bad feeling came over her. Suddenly she felt as if she were being torn to pieces. She began shaking all over. Her tongue and vocal cords became paralyzed. Inside she felt a loud rumbling, as if she were a volcano about to erupt. Then physically, emotionally, mentally, everything fell apart. She thought she was splintering.

A huge fear for the safety of the kids overwhelmed her, and the colors around her faded. The walls and the leaves on the trees looked like they'd been washed in bleach. Everything became distant and esoteric. Objects in the room looked translucent, as if they were holograms. It appeared to her that her hands could glide through the furniture.

She vaguely became aware of her own body, but felt immured in this strange state. She focused on the clock and thought to herself, "You idiot, don't be stupid. The kids will be home in 10 minutes."

At 4:00 the phone rang. She grabbed at the receiver. It was Al.

"Where are you?" she challenged.

"On the way." His voice sounded cool and businesslike. "I'll be there shortly. Get the offer ready."

"How are the kids?" The terrible feeling and Paul's tortured expression that morning still haunted her.

"Fine." He hung up.

Liba got up and gathered the papers together. He had probably called from the basement suite he rented. They should be home in fifteen, maybe twenty minutes.

At 5:52, the phone rang again. That bastard. She'd bent over backward to accommodate him. Why had they all felt so sorry for him? How dare he keep the kids this late? She'd be damned if he would ever do this to her again! This was it! She had a restraining order. She'd call her lawyer tomorrow morning.

"Where are you? Where are the kids?" she demanded.

"I'm keeping the kids. You will never see them again." His voice was calm.

Liba felt panic rising in her throat. But she refused to sound frightened because she knew that was exactly what he wanted. "You can't do that." She said matching his tone.

"Yes I can," he said harshly.

Liba tried to swallow the worry and anger she felt building inside of her. "But why?"

"It's no good seeing the children like this, under all of these conditions. "It's better...nothing!"

He was angry now, but she felt she could get him to back down. He was a coward and a bully and would pounce on any sign of weakness from her. What did he mean, 'it's better nothing?' Such strange wording. She swallowed hard trying to put a shrug in her voice. "If it's all the same to you, then you don't have to see them at all."

His thin, nasal voice turned even colder and more sarcastic at that point. "That's not what I meant. And anyway," he continued, "I have to do it now, because you won't let me see them again after me telling you this."

He was taunting her. She knew he wanted her to grab at his words so he could repeat his threats about the children and frighten her more. It had been a long time since he had the upper hand and he was making the most of it.

"I'm still coming over to sign the offer," he quickly assured her.

She thought he was lying, but she was desperate to believe him. "Will the kids be with you?" Again she tried to make her voice sound casual.

"No!" He was emphatic and he added a creepy little laugh. She felt confused. It didn't make sense. How could he come over without the children? Then he said something really bizarre.

"I better stop talking. Your phone is probably bugged." This hit her like a rock because it indicated he was feeling paranoid beyond reason. Why would he feel so threatened? Why would he worry she had the phone bugged?

Hundreds of questions formed in her mind. Are the kids still with you? What have you done with them? Have you left them somewhere? Are they safe? Can I speak to them? Instead she said, "Why should it be bugged? Is yours?"

He simply replied, "No," and hung up.

She stood gripping the receiver tightly and staring at it until the high-pitched squeal of the open line forced her to replace it on the hook.

She was having trouble breathing. He had to be bluffing. Where were the kids?

CHAPTER THREE

MAMI AND TATI

At eleven years of age, Liba Novak looked like a preteen Lauren Bacall. She had light, slanted eyes, fine-boned features and sun-streaked hair. Her mother, Emily (pseudonym), tried to make her wear her hair long but Liba hated the way the humid weather caused it to frizz up. At the beginning of grade six, Liba defiantly went to the barber and got it chopped off.

She held her books tightly against her thin chest and ran down the dirt road toward home. Her heart raced as she anticipated her mother's anger. She'd stayed late after school dropping the thickly buttered slices of bread her mother had made for her lunch off the bridge near the house. She knew it was wrong, but the butter made her gag and it wasn't really wasteful if she fed the fish. Raising the heel of her right palm to her nose she inhaled the sweaty scent of chalk from the gymnastics equipment at school. Her mother said no to most things, like going to the Sunday movies with a bunch of girls, or joining something, or playing somewhere, but she did allow Liba to take gymnastics.

Liba arranged her life accordingly and didn't ask her mother's permission to do things. If it was important enough, like the haircut, she just did it. The scent of the resin seemed to give her courage. She would need it to face her mother's angry looks, banging pots and, worst of all, nighttime.

Mami took great pride in a clean kitchen. The white ceramic floor tiles which also lined the bottom half of the walls were scrubbed meticulously and, due to her non-stop washing, the top part of the walls had to be painted frequently. In Czechoslovakia, where house painting is a trade, the painter would bring his roller, which had a stamp that repeated a pattern. Mami always chose a leaf pattern in soft green with pale yellow, as a base color underneath. Liba loved the strong smell of the oil paint even though it gave her a splitting headache. She would sit fascinated as the painter ran his roller down the kitchen walls, making a perfect path of little leaves like rabbit footprints in the snow.

Their house was unusual. Originally, it was a gorgeous villa that belonged to a wealthy miller. But when the Communists took over after the war, they confiscated all his property. Soon after, a fire broke out in the flourmill and the top two stories burned down. The Communists charged the miller with arson. They said he set the fire out of spite. He was sentenced to serve time in jail and spent eight years in the uranium mines doing hard labor. Even his son who was in electronic engineering at the university, wasn't allowed to finish his degree. While the miller labored in the mines, the house fell into disrepair.

In the spring of 1952, Liba's family moved in, two years before the miller's return. The house was divided into several suites. Her family had the maid's quarters.

After suppers, Mami would send Liba and her younger sister, Alana (pseudonym), directly to bed. The bedroom was adjacent to the kitchen and was only separated by a French door, with the upper part made of glass, so you could see and hear through it. The whole family shared the bedroom. In it were two separate mattresses on one frame. Liba and Mami and Alana slept on one mattress and her father on the other.

There was also a tiny pantry that was originally the maid's bedroom. The entrance to the kitchen door went into the hallway of the villa. It was a huge receiving hall with a cathedral ceiling. All the rooms in the house had doors to this entry. On the other side of the hallway, Liba's family had one more room. That was where the china was kept and the books and extra blankets. No one really ever used it. It was too cold in the winter.

Last year, just after she turned eleven, Liba's Dad, Tati, packed his suitcase and moved his things out of the bedroom and into the cold room across the hall. In Czechoslovakia in 1961, the population was so dense you couldn't find an apartment or any place to rent, even in the little mountain town of Teplice Nad Olsi (pseudonym). Her parents had no choice but to live under one roof, even though they were separated.

When the dishes were done, Mami would sit at the table alone, talking to phantoms. Whispering, actually. You couldn't quite catch what she was saying although sometimes you could hear her scolding Tati with bad language. She talked to herself like this for hours. Then she'd start crying. Her sobs would grow from tiny hiccups to loud wails.

While all this was happening, Liba would lie numb in the big double bed, pretending to sleep. Finally, Mami's keening would give way to hoarse coughs of despair. Her chair would scrape back and Liba could relax enough to sleep.

Their parents' separation was very confusing for Liba and Alana because nothing was said to them about it. And due to Mami's temper, they didn't dare ask. She believed children didn't need explanations. However, one day when Liba was home with the flu, Tati snuck into her room and sat on the edge of the bed.

He said, "You've probably noticed things between Mother and me are not going well and I'll probably have to leave soon." Liba burst into tears, but she did not blame him. She knew how unbearable Mami could be. He said not to cry. "I love you just as much as ever." That remark made her cry harder because, as bad as things were, she wanted everything to stay the same. The idea of change terrified her.

Tati bought a coiled metal hot plate for his room so he could cook his own meals. He left for the steel mill at 4:00 AM and did not return until after school each day. If Mami was out, Liba would sneak home early to catch a glimpse of him when he came through the door. He was always glad to see her. They whispered in case her mother came home early and caught them speaking. She and Tati could talk about sports, school, where she liked to go and what she was doing. She talked to him about her friends and about hikes and what the weather was like. Liba loved these good relaxing conversations.

Tati was born a farm boy, but had trained as an apprentice baker. In 1948, it became clear the Communists were going to take over Czechoslovakia. He couldn't start his own bakery, so he went to work in a factory and re-apprenticed as a welder.

Liba was born that year, so she knew he baked only because people sometimes asked him to make wedding cakes. That's when he gave off the aroma of wine, like bread baking. Otherwise, when she pressed her nose against his wool sweater, he smelled of burnt steel from the mill. One time at Grandma's farm during hay time, he smelled like fresh hay and sweat because he worked in the fields the whole day.

The only other time she got hugs was from her agnate Grandma. She was also allowed to sit on Grandma's lap.

Liba and Tati were close because they did things together. Tati had really wanted a boy. Until the second grade, he'd take Liba skiing and skating and bike riding. Luckily, all of these things appealed to Liba's rough and tumble nature. When he tried to do the same things with Alana, she threw tantrums and refused to go.

Liba's father, Tati or Rudy Novak (pseudonym) as everyone else called him, loved hockey. He coached and refereed. It was one of his favorite topics of conversation. He told his Liba all about Canadian hockey players. He knew everything there was to know about them. He talked about Stan Mikita, a Czech who played in the NHL, Frank Mahovlich, Gordie Howe, Bobby Hull, all the greats. Canada was the Promised Land. Canada was a non-aggressive country. Canada had never, ever invaded anybody. Canadian soldiers were very brave during the war.

And the beauty of the countryside! It had mountains just like Teplice Nad Olsi. And bears! And the plants were incredible. It was said, in the West, roses grew wild on the sides of the road.

CHAPTER FOUR

NICK

August 7, Evening

Nick Kyska looks like a homicide cop straight out of the movies. Just under six feet, thick dark hair cut funky and short. He has a tan complexion and sexy brown eyes fringed with long, dark lashes. He likes clothes and stays fit by pumping iron. His Armani suits and Hugo Boss ties coordinate perfectly. Even his socks match. Attention to detail is what makes Nick such a good investigator.

The son of Polish immigrants, Nick is the father of two teenagers, Matt and Leah. His wife, Debbie, is attractive, dark haired and equally fit. In 1986, Debbie was a nurse and Nick was a 30-year-old detective in the General Investigations Section in Six District of the Calgary Police Force. Nick and Debbie worked opposite shifts so they could care for the kids without sitters. He'd been in plain-clothes for one year. Six District is in the south part of Calgary where income levels are high and crime is low.

On August 7th, at six o'clock in the evening, Nick started his shift. He worked without a partner. Things were slow. He drove downtown to answer a complaint and turned his windshield wipers up a notch. The weather was bad.

At 8:30 that night, after getting the particulars on the case, Nick's pager went off. Staff Sergeant Bill Gaskarth was summoning him to Headquarters.

RCMP Corporal Frank Peter DeHeer was working out of Cochrane on Highway Patrol when he came across a man walking in the pouring rain across the Clem Gardener Bridge. As Frank drove by, the man kept his head tucked into the collar of his rain-soaked jacket and trudged along. He looked like a drowned rat. Frank was on his way to another call, but he rolled down his window and waved the man over. "What's up? Do you need help?"

In broken English, the man talked about having his 4x4 vehicle stuck in the bush in the McLean Creek area and said he needed a tow truck. He said his name was Alois Dolejs. Frank tried to pronounce it a couple of times, but gave up. Alois told Frank he was unemployed.

Frank looked at him. He was filthy and unshaven. "Do you have any money?"

The man reached into his pocket and pulled out a roll of bills. "Yeah. I have around sixty dollars."

So Frank called in and ordered a tow truck. "Are you going to wait here for it?"

The man nodded. As Frank drove off he queried Dolejs on the Canadian Police Information System as a matter of routine. About a mile down the road, Frank stomped on the brakes, turned his cruiser around and sped back toward the stranger.

Nick first laid eyes on Al in a room used by identification technicians for mug shots and fingerprints. It looked like he had been in the bush for a few days. He was soaking wet.

His clothes were filthy and he stunk. Nick had him put in the interview room and they sat facing each other across a small table. Nick noticed Al had curious looking fine scratches all over his hands, face and neck.

Nick was concerned. The monsoon-like weather gave no sign of letting up. Twelve-year-old Paul Dolejs and ten-year-old Gabi had been missing for eleven days and it was getting dark again. There was talk of sending up a fixed wing aircraft or a helicopter to look for them in the

McLean Creek area where Al said his truck was stuck. But the airport reported a low ceiling. Nick re-read Liba's statement. He knew Al was unhappy about his limited access to the children. So he decided to play along.

He leaned close and looked Al straight in the eyes. "I want to speak with you about the welfare of your children." He said huskily, "The most important thing here is not your marital difficulties or the charges against you, but the well being of your children. Wouldn't you agree?"

Al's shoulders were hunched and his face remained impassive. "Yes," he replied.

"Can you tell me where the children are?"

Al stared at the floor. Nick rephrased the question a couple of ways, but still got no response. Nick pulled the kids' school pictures out of a manila envelope and slid them slowly across the table toward Al. "Al, the only thing I want to do is satisfy myself that the children are okay."

Al pushed the photos back toward Nick.

Nick shook his head. "In my opinion Al, you're not acting like a parent who loves his children. A concerned parent would resign himself to the fact that this situation is not good for you. A concerned parent would tell me where I can find the kids."

Again, Nick pushed the pictures toward him. Again, Al pushed them back to Nick.

"Al, do you love your kids?" Nick asked.

"Of course," Al mumbled.

Encouraged by his response, Nick continued. "Do you consider yourself a good father?"

"Yeah." Al stared at the floor.

"Well, I'm not passing judgment on your marital situation or any problems you've had with your wife. If you hate your wife..."

Al interrupted suddenly. "I don't hate my wife."

Nick was slightly startled, but he continued. "What I was going to say is, a loving father wouldn't want any harm to come to his children. I don't is, a loving father wouldn't want any harm to come to his children. I don't know what kind of circumstances you've left them under, but let's face it, if they're in the country, a caring father would be worried about them."

"They're okay."

"Is someone else looking after them?"

"No."

Al was silent a few minutes. "They're okay. I don't want to say anything until I talk to a lawyer. The RCMP said I could talk to a lawyer."

Nick sat back and spread his hands expansively. "By all means. You should talk to a lawyer. Would you like to contact one?"

Al looked up at him. "Could you do it for me?"

Nick's eyebrows shot up in surprise. "You want me to contact a lawyer on your behalf?"

Al shrugged. "Well you must know a lot of lawyers."

Nick shook his head. "That's not the issue Al. I don't want to be put in the position where I'm recommending a particular lawyer."

"If you let me talk to a lawyer, I'll tell you everything you want to know."

Nick stared at him a moment, debating. "Well your right to a lawyer goes beyond that Al, but if you want to make a gentleman's agreement, that you'll tell me where the kids are after consulting with a lawyer, let's shake on it." Nick reached across the table and Al took his hand and shook it.

CHAPTER FIVE

PUBERTY

Liba knew her mother was going off the deep end. Her temper seemed to worsen after Liba started her period, at fourteen.

Mami had never even mentioned menstruation or things like wearing a bra. When somebody's parents were not at home, Liba and her friends would sneak down the house medical book and look at the pictures in an effort to unfold the mysteries of the human body. Another source of sex education was dirty jokes. They'd watch each other surreptitiously to see who laughed at what and try to make sense of things.

When Liba started developing breasts, she found it painful to run and embarrassing to wear certain blouses. She knew she couldn't possibly ask her mother to get her a brassiere. But her friend Jane had three! Jane recognized Liba's dilemma during gym class one day and offered to lend her one.

The following morning Liba quickly slipped the thing on and pulled her white blouse over it. Her fingers flew over the buttons at superhuman speed. But Mami, whose back was turned making the bed, had eyes at the back of her head. She swiveled around sharply.

"Where did you get that?" she demanded.

Liba swallowed. "I borrowed it from Jane," she replied meekly.

Mami's lips hardened into little, thin, angry lines. "You don't borrow underwear," she spit out.

When Liba got home from school that day, a stiff, new, white bra was laid out on the bed.

Maybe it all had to do with Mami's hard life. Liba's Grandpa, Antonin Koubek (pseudonym), was a hard and terrible man. When he returned home from the First World War he was greatly changed. The once sweet boy had become an abusive brute and he beat Grandma Marie unmercifully. She married him anyway and had three children, Walter, Emily and George. Grandpa died when Liba's mother, Emily was fourteen. It was 1940, and they were living in Peter's Forest, a region very close to the Polish border. At that time, the Second World War was raging, and Poland and any land near it, was occupied by the Germans. The Czech people living in the area were given a choice: either declare themselves Polish, or leave. The Koubeks were patriotic. Both were involved with the Czech Church. They were prominent figures in the town's society. There was no way they could declare themselves Polish.

It was November and the temperatures often dropped to ten degrees below freezing. Forced to leave with nowhere to go, the family followed a road south out of town with their most valued possessions in tow. They stopped in a field and arranged all their furniture in a circle around them. Grandpa Antonin threw up a tarp and that became their makeshift house. They stayed there for two weeks.

Grandpa got pneumonia and a kidney infection simultaneously, and died. The youngest child, George, developed strep throat and died a week later. Grandma was left with the oldest, Walter, about sixteen at the time, and Emily. People from another town, who belonged to the same church, took them in and put them up in barns. And that's how Liba's mother came to live in Teplice Nad Olsi.

Liba's Grandma, a widow with two kids, had absolutely no outside skills of any kind. She was a homemaker so all she could manage was to get work doing laundry and heavy duty housework for the richer ladies. Wages were mingy. Sometimes she earned only potatoes or cabbages.

She pinned all of her hopes on Walter. She believed that he soon would marry and take on the responsibility of supporting her. Grandma knew he'd need an education. She saved every penny and put him through school. He became an engineer and after graduation entered the army. All boys in the country were required to serve two years. Then he met and married Nadia, or 'The General in Skirts' as the rest of the family called her. But as Grandma had predicted, he did support her for the rest of her life.

At the time, Emily had just completed Grade Eight and had to fight to continue to Grade Nine. It was accepted she would marry eventually and do housework like her mother. Why would she need an education? Emily had a high IQ and knew education was her only means of escape from poverty and a life she detested. She begged her mother to change her mind. But it was not meant to be.

When that avenue was cut off, it closed the doors and covered the windows to her soul. She no longer felt hope and had no one she could trust. She became bitter. Even when she became a mother, she was no longer capable of forging emotional bonds. She'd lost all empathy.

By the time Liba was five, it dawned on her that she could not rely on her mother. One day, Mami was in a good mood, which was very rare. She promised to take Liba and baby Alana, for a walk. Liba's heart raced with excitement. Perhaps Mami would hold her hand and smile at her and tell her the names of all the different trees and animals they saw. She would show Mami what a big girl she was, how she could run and skip and even climb trees.

While she waited for Mami to get ready, she wandered into the Halata family's farmyard next door, to play on the swing they had in their barn. But first, she checked with Mami, asking her to call when it was time for the walk.

After several swings, Liba began feeling anxious. Too much time had passed. What was taking so long? She ran back home. The small apartment was deserted and Alana's stroller was gone. Mami had gone on the walk without her.

Liba's heart sank far down into her chest and a large lump formed at the base of her throat. Small children are the greatest optimists. They hold onto hope for a long time, but it would be the last time she ever expected anything from Mami.

There were many times Mami didn't speak. The only livable room was the kitchen and Liba would sit hunched over her homework at the big square oak table for hours. Her Mother would not say one word to her the whole time. When Mami did say something, it was an order. "Bring more coal." or "Bring more wood." or "Get water." God help you if you crossed her in some way because she would stop talking to you altogether. And that was worse than if she had used physical violence.

One time Mami angrily greeted Liba's return from school with an accusation. "You lost a kitchen knife."

Liba knew she hadn't. "I didn't," she insisted. "I made sandwiches for a hike and that was it."

"No!" Mami was adamant. "You lost the kitchen knife, you lost it on the mountain somewhere." That winter Liba was fourteen and it was the last thing Mami said to her for two months. One day Liba entered the coal and wood cellar for fuel to start a fire. She decided to do a little reorganizing and when she moved a large log she found the knife. She brought it to the kitchen and slapped it down on the counter. "Well here it is. I found it in the wood." Mami offered no apologies, but she did start speaking again.

Ninety percent of the time Liba wasn't aware of the reason Mami was angry with her. But shortly after Liba turned sixteen, Mami stopped speaking to her for a year. Absolute total silence. At first Liba pleaded with her.

"What have I done? Please Mami, just tell me. Maybe I can explain." But her daughter's pleas were ignored. Liba got no answer, no explanation. Things still had to be done in the house. So Mami would take the daily newspaper and write commands on the white borders around the articles. Instead of, "Liba, please go and get bread and butter or milk or do this or do that." They would read, "Get milk. Get butter. Bring water."

The grammar of the Czech language is different from English in many ways. So the commands she wrote don't translate the same. In English the infinitive form and the command form of the verb are the same. In Czech, the forms are different and Mami's harsh commands were a slap in the face.

At the end of her second year in technical school, Liba's mechanical engineering class went on an excursion. Because it was part of a school program Mami couldn't say no. They visited a factory with a guide who covered technological problems and showed them the practical applications of things they learned at school. Part of it was just a sightseeing trip and social event. Some guys in her class played guitar, so they sat by a fire singing and a few beers were passed around.

Liba and her class were away for three days and she came back without incident, but she was tired from the travel and the fun. The next morning she slept in an extra half-hour. She didn't hear Mami's approach, but she felt the hard punch across her face.

"Get up!" Mami snarled.

Liba shot out of bed. Dazed and confused, she staggered and fell back on the bed. Later she tried to sort out what happened, but Mami refused to explain and again ignored her for months.

Liba's younger sister, Alana, didn't know what to do. The entire flat was perhaps four hundred square feet and no one had his or her own bedroom to escape to. She felt torn. If Mami wouldn't speak to Liba, then maybe she shouldn't as well. She was between a rock and a hard place. Both girls were very close to going crazy.

To keep her sanity, Liba looked at maps. She spent stolen hours pouring over old atlases. Her mother, though compulsively clean, never threw things away. She still had Tati's geography books from school and when Liba discovered them, it was like entering a new world. She galloped the globe in her imagination and always ended up staring at the big pink part of the British Commonwealth, just across the North Atlantic. Canada.

CHAPTER SIX

THE LAWYER

August 7, Late night

When he left Al in the interview room, Nick placed a late night call to the finest defense lawyer he knew, John Bascom.

John Bascom looks like Wild Bill Hickok. Hard brown eyes, high cheekbones on a lean, handsome face and a bushy brown mustache. He wears his shoulder length sandy hair tucked behind his ears with a hint of curl. The only thing he's missing is a pair of six guns. All his life John has crusaded for right. He is a brilliant criminal lawyer and could easily charge more than three hundred dollars an hour. Yet he continues to devote twenty five percent of his practice to legal aid work.

In 1986, when John was billing more than two hundred dollars an hour, Legal Aid was paying forty.

John's father, Steven, was in the Air Force, Provost Core, so John grew up in Ottawa. Back in the '50s and '60s during the Cold War, Steven was involved in spying and covert operations. In those days each branch of the forces had its own intelligence organization. Steven was part of counter intelligence.

Steven's father, Horace Bascom, was a doctor who became a lawyer. He had eleven children. Steven, the youngest, was born when Horace was in his sixties. Horace received a commission from F. W. Borden, Minister of the Militia and Defense, in 1903. Borden later became the Prime Minister of Canada. Today, that Commission hangs on his grandson's wall.

On the night Alois Dolejs was arrested, John was sound asleep in his house in the suburbs. It was his habit to go to bed early, and get up at 5:00 or 6:00 AM with his new baby, Alexandra. He grabbed the phone on the first ring. Nick explained the situation and John replied that he would talk with Al on the phone, but didn't see the need to drive all the way downtown that night.

"I'll see you guys tomorrow morning at 8:30," he promised.

Nick gave the phone to Al and left the room.

At midnight, Bascom's phone rang again. RCMP Sergeant Mervin Harrower was on the other end. He identified himself as the Inspector in charge of the case.

"Mr. Dolejs refuses to speak with anyone until he sees you in the morning and we have two kids missing tonight. If you do not have transportation to police headquarters I will send a car for you. Now."

John rubbed his eyes. "Well if you put it that way, I'm on..." The line went dead. John sighed and got out of bed.

"What's up John?" murmured his wife, Tannis. A doctor, she was usually the one rousted in the middle of the night.

"An RCMP Sergeant has just... requested my services downtown."

"Do you have to go now?" she asked.

"No, but if I stay here, we'll be making hors d'oeuvres for several Mounties in an hour or so."

At headquarters, John was greeted by Nick Kyska and RCMP Officer Wally Purcell. John had just wrapped up a case with Wally involving a fellow who was having sexual relations with his common-law wife's children. It was a really nasty case. And John thought Wally had done a good investigation. John pled the bad guy guilty. Both men respected each other.

Wally Purcell is a big bear of a man. Six three, two hundred and fifteen pounds. But despite his size, he's more teddy bear than grizzly. His face is as Irish as a potato. He has a big friendly grin, an innocent, wide-eyed stare and he genuinely likes people. Most perpetrators find themselves opening up to Wally just because he's so darn likable.

Nick took John aside to explain the situation. "We think the kids could be somewhere out in the Bragg Creek area alive. They may be injured or wandering around. We need you to determine where these children are."

John felt there was no belief by the authorities that the children were dead. They weren't using him to hang a murder rap on this guy. He was there for the purpose of giving Dolejs legal advice, finding out where the kids were and getting them back home. He knew the rules of legal ethics very well. He took part in the Code of Conduct and was Vice-Chair Conduct for two years. Still he had his own interpretation of certain rules. He knew he would breach solicitor/client privilege if he thought it was important enough.

In this case, solicitor/client privilege didn't yet exist and if it involved a continuation of a further criminal offense, such as abduction, he would have to tell the police where the kids were. But he was obligated to let Al know his intentions up front.

Nick entered the interrogation room and had Al remove all of his clothing. Then handed him some green overalls. Nick noted the little scratches that covered Al's face and hands also covered every inch of his body. Al caught Nick's stare and assured him he would keep their agreement and tell Nick everything once he had talked with his lawyer, Mr. Bascom, in the morning.

Nick smiled. "No need to wait, Al. He's here now." Nick closed the door on the startled prisoner and went to fetch the lawyer. John went in and closed the door.

Half an hour later, the door opened and John emerged. Nick gaped at him. John was white as a sheet. The normally tough lawyer had a look of shock on his face Nick had seen only once before, on an officer who'd just shot a guy.

"I've been retained by Mr. Dolejs. I'll see you at 8:30 AM," John told them grimly. Then he left the station. Nick and Wally exchanged glances. The situation didn't look good.

CHAPTER SEVEN

GETTING OUT

Liba was determined the political climate would not break her spirit as it had her mother's.

In August, 1968, when Liba was nineteen years old, Russia invaded Czechoslovakia. Within four months of the occupation, it became apparent that there was really no hope for the country. The politicians who were considered liberal or progressive resigned or quietly disappeared. They were replaced by Communist Party hard liners. Censorship was rampant. Russians were everywhere.

Liba and her friends were outraged. They compared what was happening to what the Russians did in Hungary in 1956. They knew it took about twenty years before things loosened up enough in Hungary to give the people even a semblance of freedom of speech or some form of expression. At nineteen, twenty years is eternity. They were not going to waste their lives on the faint hope that when they were forty things might be better. To them, forty was ancient. Life would be over then.

Liba knew she would not be able to close her eyes to the injustices around her. Her rebellious nature would eventually compel her to speak up. She decided to leave and her lover, Stan Zak, wanted to join her.

———————

Stan was a handsome engineering student who shared Liba's love of outdoor sports. He was from her hometown, Teplice Nad Olsi. The girls all admired his muscular build and used to giggle when he was around. He had a deep tan in the summer and his blonde hair, though short, was always sun kissed. They'd grown up together and had been dating for a year and half.

Liba knew the women in his family had catered to Stan all his life. His father was seventy-three, quite old compared to Tati who was only forty-seven. Stan had not been a planned pregnancy. His sisters were fifteen and seventeen years older than he.

Stan's father was a binge drinker and once in a while he would go out with his friends on a payday and get falling down drunk. Normally a mild man, he was a mean drunk. He'd stagger home and yell and scream at Stan's mother. He always gave her a three-day ultimatum: either they started doing things his way or she could leave. Mrs. Zak would pack an overnight case for herself and little Stan and they would walk to one of his sisters. By then, the sisters were all married with children of their own. Stan and his mother would stay until Mr. Zak sobered up and realized what he had done. Thoroughly ashamed of himself, he would track down his wife and beg her forgiveness. Tears running down both cheeks, he'd swear off liquor and promise he'd never treat her that way again. Stan's mother always went back.

By November, Liba and Stan finalized their plans. Secrecy was crucial. It was now four months since the occupation. The borders were intensely guarded. Unlike the first three weeks, you couldn't just walk across. You now needed a passport and visa and a valid reason to travel. You also needed to guarantee you would return.

They started trying to sign up on some tours because it was impossible to travel privately. The rules were stringent. As insurance against citizens defecting, everyone was allowed to exchange the equivalent of only twenty dollars. Anyone going abroad to visit a western country had to have proof that someone there was waiting for him or her. That somebody would have to feed and house them and be financially responsible for them. This required a private invitation. And the private invitation had to come from a close relative.

The second way to get out of the country was to sign up for a tour with a travel agency and then everything was prepaid, accommodation, meals and transportation. Of course, all travel was done within a group. Liba and Stan decided to sign up for a trip like that, but it took them until May the following year because the newspapers would advertise them in the morning and by noon they were full.

Teplice was so small it didn't have a travel agency so Liba had to travel by train to a big city 40 kilometers away. By the time she got there, the spaces were always gone. Liba refused to give up and after at least twenty such trips she found success. She left their names on a waiting list for a trip to Denmark. Fortunately, a few people dropped out and they were notified by mail to get ready for a 10 day excursion in August.

Preparation was nerve wracking because it was so difficult to get a passport. Permission to leave the country could be obtained only on the recommendation of a boss or some official in authority. Liba's boss in the drafting department was a stern, uncompromising Communist named Josef Stefek. He was always on the lookout for some infraction. But Liba was careful. She did her work and kept her mouth shut.

The trip was organized by a student travel bureau. Liba and Stan were told to meet at the train station in Teplice at noon. As the train pulled away, Liba got up out of her seat and stood by one of the windows at the front. Her elbows rested on the wood frame.

"This is possibly the last time I'll ever see my home town," she thought. But she knew she could not afford tears. If she acted sad as they embarked on this holiday, it would look very suspicious. She glanced at Stan. He was lost in thought. Liba knew he was thinking about his family too. They all loved him so much.

In East Germany, they were loaded on a train to Copenhagen for the weekend. This leg of the trip was supposed to last two days, but during a sight seeing excursion, they slipped away and found a police station where they asked for asylum. The police in Copenhagen were pragmatic. When they found out the two Czechs still had one night of accommodation and food owing from their tour, they ordered them to go back to the group and come back the next day.

Liba and Stan did what they were told. It turned out they weren't alone. Six more people from the same group of twenty had the same idea. They all met at the police station the next day.

Copenhagen is a seaport. It was humid, so although Liba's skin glowed, the dampness in the air made her nose run and chilled her to the bone. She let her hair grow longer because Stan preferred it that way, but it was curlier and more out of control than ever.

She didn't find the sound of the waves crashing along the shoreline soothing. In fact, it got on her nerves and gave her headaches. And the fishy smell that clung to the salty air was offensive to her. Again and again she would complain to Stan that she was not a water person.

Stan was feeling lost and lonely. He missed his family much more than he had anticipated. He began to cling to Liba, relying on her for everything. He could barely stand to be without her. Although she found this a little stifling, at twenty, she also felt flattered by his constant attention and willingness to do anything she asked.

At nights after making love, they'd lie huddled under the feathered tick loaned to them by the government and talk about where they wanted to settle. Liba was adamant they move to Canada. Tati's love of the country had influenced her greatly. One night as she lay cuddled in Stan's arms, she checked off the pros and cons trying to determine just where in Canada they should settle.

"I don't like big cities or the ocean. I don't want to learn French. The Maritimes are poor. I would die on the prairies. So we're basically left with either central British Columbia or Alberta. And it's tough to find a job with our training in central British Columbia so that leaves Alberta. And Calgary is a lot closer to the mountains than Edmonton is. It has an oil industry too. I think that it is the best place for us."

She turned her head to look at him, but he was already asleep. She patted him gently on the arm and carefully removed it from around her waist. Quietly, she crept to her own narrow cot and settled into the cold sheets. When she closed her eyes, Liba saw the majestic Rockies looming in the distance and felt warm Chinook breezes ruffle her hair. She let the scent of pine trees fill her imagination as she trekked up glorious mountain paths on cross-country skis to vast undiscovered ice fields. But her stoic nature kept such romantic thoughts locked inside her head. Voicing them to Stan might make her appear foolish and weak.

In September, 1969, Liba and Stan paid their first visit to the Canadian Consulate in Copenhagen and came away with the understanding that Canada didn't want single girls emigrating alone. They decided they should marry before officially applying for their Landed Immigrant status. They had a second interview scheduled in another couple of months and if they got through that one, there would be one more. If all went as planned, the Canadian Government would loan them money for plane fare and the Canadian Immigration Department would look after them until they found work.

Autumn in Copenhagen is generally very cold and that year was no exception. On her wedding day in November, Liba wore a white blouse with white embroidered flowers beneath the collar. She wore a short brown skirt, white nylons and her new brown winter boots. Stan was dressed as usual, in a white shirt with a brown pullover wool sweater, brown dress pants and his good black dress shoes. His hair was buzzed in something resembling an army cut.

There was an older Czech couple they'd met in the hotel who were also getting married. They decided to sign the papers together. After the small ceremony, the tiny group took a taxi to a Chinese restaurant. They ordered stew and rice and toasted each other with a glass of red wine.

It was mid-afternoon when Liba and Stan boarded a bus and went back to the hotel. Liba was feeling rotten and, sensing her mood, Stan didn't say anything. A sense of disbelief settled upon her. What had she just done? Was this really her wedding day? It was so different than she'd ever imagined. She didn't even love Stan.

At first back in Teplice, she'd felt infatuated. Now there were things about him she couldn't stand! He was ridiculously romantic. She remembered standing with him on a corner under a street lamp one night back home and he'd made some silly speech about how, if they ever parted, he'd revisit that corner again and again because part of their love would be embedded there forever. The moment was so melodramatic she'd felt like laughing.

And then there was the wedding ring issue. Liba liked things simple, but Stan was determined she would wear a large thick ring. Liba suspected it was a symbol of ownership, not partnership. She sighed. Perhaps it would work out okay in the future.

But she was wrong. The warning signs continued. She met a new Orienteering coach in Denmark. It was a sport she enjoyed very much at home. When she started training again shortly after they got married, Stan kicked up a real fuss.

"You're not starting that again! You are a married woman now. You have other obligations." She should be waiting on him hand and foot. She should only do what he wanted to do.

Their Canadian visas came through in February and Liba gathered together her meager possessions and her prickly new husband and boarded a plane for Calgary. They found a little suite in an old house near downtown where the rent was reasonable. The Immigration Department would be responsible for their well being for one year. They were given $180 a month to live on and two months of English lessons.

Pierre Elliot Trudeau was Prime Minister and the country was swept up in Trudeau-mania. Coming from a Communist country, Liba and Stan weren't fazed by his invoking the War Measures Act in 1970 with its extraordinary powers of arrest, detention and censorship. The action was triggered by the kidnapping of Quebec Cabinet Minister Pierre Laporte and British Diplomat James Cross by terrorists fighting for Quebec separatism.

Liba and Stan were more concerned about the weak Canadian economy and high unemployment. Even oil rich Alberta was suffering and Saskatchewan was in a terrible slump. One day on their way to get groceries, Liba remarked that every other car seemed to have green and white Saskatchewan plates.

"That's part of our problem," Stan complained. "We'll never find a job, because those guys speak English and we don't."

After two months, it was obvious neither Liba nor Stan could get along well enough in English to land work, so they appealed to the Immigration Department for more help and were awarded two more months of English lessons.

During the lessons, Liba and Stan befriended a quiet, dark-haired newcomer from their homeland. He was four years older than Liba, the same age as Stan. He was pleasant looking, with large soft brown eyes and a fine straight nose on the smallish side. But his most attractive feature was his generous mouth with white teeth that bowed into a slight overbite.

He introduced himself as Alois Dolejs, but said everyone called him Al.

CHAPTER EIGHT

WALLY

Friday, August 8, Early morning

Searchers are still looking for two Calgary children, Paul and Gabi Dolejs, in the Elbow Falls area west of Bragg Creek. The children were kidnapped by their father, Alois Dolejs, on July 27. Steady rain brought out swarms of mosquitoes and turned back roads into molasses, hampering the efforts of 20 RCMP officers from Cochrane and a handful of Calgary City Police. Today Dolejs was charged with two counts of first-degree murder. The search was called off before 8:00 PM due to heavy rain.

Wally Purcell and his partner, Brian Phillips, decided ahead of time Brian would be the note-taker and Wally would do the talking. Nick told Wally how Al had reacted to the photographs of Paul and Gabi. This struck a chord with Wally who had a six-year-old daughter, Lisa, and a ten-year-old son, Scott.

Wally pulled their pictures out of his wallet as he entered the interview room.

He positioned Al on a stationary chair, then took a rolling chair and moved it beside him. Wally is an expert at the technique of getting into a person's space. He knows when to back off, when to go in and how close you can get. Each person has a different sphere that they allow people into. Sometimes you get in by talking and being very friendly and very gentle, even though they don't want you there initially.

Wally studied the slumped figure in the green overalls. Al's dark complexion indicated his background was European. Slavic European. And he seemed pretty calm for a guy being investigated for probable homicide of his kids. He seemed cold. Almost in another world. Far away.

Instead of going right to the crime, Wally asked Al about himself. How he came to Canada and found work. Wally was reassuring, frequently touching Al's arm or shoulder or knee. Then he calmly and quietly placed Lisa and Scott's pictures on the table beside Al.

Al didn't like looking at the photos. He kept covering up the picture of Lisa with the picture of Scott. Wally explained later, "I knew he was bothered about the girl," so he concentrated on Gabi.

"She's cold, Al. She needs to be taken care of. It's not right a little ten-year-old girl out in the cold, dark woods at night. There's bears in that country, big time. There's cougars. I'm a hunter myself, Al. I know that territory. I know about wildlife. Coyotes. Coyotes are going to go after them."

After the first hour and a half, Wally found himself making headway. He was in. Al was feeling comfortable and believing at that point that Wally was a friend. Wally suspected the kids were dead, but he held hope they might be alive. He thought about how resilient the human body is. How you hear of stories about people lost in the bush for twenty days and surviving.

"Where are the children?"

No reply.

"Where are they? Do you miss them right now?"

Al swallowed hard.

Wally pushed the pictures of his kids on the table closer to Al. "These are my kids. Lisa and Scott. I miss them right now because of the simple fact I'm working tonight and can't be with them. Are you going to miss your children?"

Al said, "I have already screwed up my life. Try always the best. Never works. I left the country, the family. Go to freedom, better life, better everything. Come with high, high hopes. Didn't work, yeah."

"Al, you are a father. I am a father." Wally pointed to the pictures of Lisa and Scott. "A parent cares for his children, loves his children. It's our job, our job to make sure they are safe. They have to be recovered. They have to be found. If they are not alive, it's your job to take care of their bodies."

Al sat immobile. Then Wally asked, "How old are the children?"

Al replied, "Ten and twelve years of age."

Wally nodded. "Do you believe in God?"

"Yes, I do," Al replied.

"Well, it's important that they go to heaven, Al. They have to have a proper burial for that."

Al was mute once more.

Wally tried another tack. "Would you describe the children to us?"

"What do you mean?" Al asked.

Wally shrugged. "You know, their height and weight."

Al replied, "Paul is approximately chest height. Brown hair. Gabriela is waist height. Brown hair also. Haircut is somewhat short. Almost like a boy's haircut. She wears glasses with plastic frames. Both have brown eyes." Al went on to say that both kids and his wife excelled in sports.

"How could a person leave these kids out in the cold, Al? It's been what? Ten days? They can't survive without food and shelter."

Al was silent, then, "Always trying the best. We have enough money for their upbringing and physical needs."

Wally sat close to Al and in a soft voice said, "Do you think they should have a funeral?"

Al replied, "Don't want to speak about God or question God in any way."

Wally once again pushed the pictures of his kids toward Al. This time, Al picked them up and examined them very carefully. Then he raised his head and looked Wally in the eye and smiled. "Mine are better," he said.

Wally chuckled. "Every parent thinks their kid is the best. Will you take me and show me where they are so we can give them a decent funeral and they can be with God?"

"Yes," Al replied. He got up out of his chair and walked to the door. Wally immediately got a rush of adrenaline. He was going to solve the crime. Having a suspect take you to a body is the best evidence there is. Then suddenly Al came back and sat down. He'd built up his barrier again. And it was like a brick wall. Wally had just spent hours throwing little pebbles at that brick wall and now he had to start all over again.

Wally continued to question Al through the night. Al got up and went to the door twice more before morning. Each time, Wally was sure he would lead them to the children. The third time Al grasped the door handle and opened the door before he sat down again. After that Wally gave up hope, thinking, "You can only go to the well so many times."

CHAPTER NINE

CALGARY

Liba loved Calgary and was adapting fast. In her third month of English lessons she found she could communicate with Canadians while buying food or even looking for a job. Stan on the other hand was miserable. He couldn't pick up English no matter how hard he tried and he became terribly frustrated at not being able to even ask directions on the street. Liba noticed he was becoming even more possessive, but understood his frustration at having to rely on her. She told a friend in English class about her plight.

"He was brought up sort of thinking of himself. The man is the king of the castle in my country so, you know, he's got this kind of an upbringing and suddenly he's dependent on a woman to translate everything that's being said. It doesn't sit well."

Stan was jealous of Liba's quick mastery of the language. She knew she was picking up English a lot quicker than everybody else in the class and attributed it to learning German back in Czechoslovakia. When the teacher asked her how she was managing to learn so rapidly, she explained, "German is an Anglo-Saxon language as well. So a lot of things are similar."

When someone in the class needed something they would come to her and ask her to translate. She enjoyed the challenge and ended up going many places with her friends to help them out. Stan didn't like it.

She and Stan befriended another couple of Czechs from the class, Jana and Peter Sura. At just nineteen, Jana was newly pregnant and Peter, her elder by three years, was charming and protective of her. None of them had two cents to rub together, so almost every day was spent at Fish Creek Park.

The Alberta Government was rather innovative in establishing a Provincial Park right on the edge of Calgary. That way, all the residents had quick access and even those without vehicles could escape the city. But in 1970, it was just some wild land that sat beyond a small town called Midnapore.

Alois had his own car, a cream colored Austin that he had purchased from Farmer Jones, a discount used car dealer on 9th Avenue. The 'J' in Jones was turned backward on the sign and out front on the sidewalk there was a freestanding sign bearing the slogan, 'Stupid salesman on duty!' The salesmen at Farmer Jones were always eager to make a deal. Any deal. Peter and Jana soon visited the lot as did Liba and Stan.

Stan became curt and abrupt and began sulking. It got to the point where he would not let Liba leave the house without him. They lived two blocks from a Safeway store and one day while making cookies she called to Stan.

"I'm just going to pick up some butter at the store." He leaped up off their black leatherette couch and insisted on coming along. As they walked out the door together, Liba swallowed her thoughts. She was starting to feel suffocated.

Soon after, she came home to find a rope hanging from the ceiling in the foyer. There was no question to its meaning. If she left him, he would hang himself.

A few weeks later, the little group was enjoying a picnic at Fish Creek. Liba and Jana lounged under a tall poplar, watching a zephyr rustle the leaves in a lazy fashion. Nearby, the men kibitzed in a small brook that ran through the park and joined up with the Bow River a mile away. Liba heard shouting and looked up to find Stan and Al wrestling in the water.

Stan was the aggressor and Al was trying to defend himself. Peter tried unsuccessfully to step in between the two, but they were thrashing about so wildly it was impossible. Finally, Peter caught hold of Stan's shirt and held on until Al could pull himself free.

Stan stomped angrily out of the water and told Liba they were leaving. She threw Jana a look of total bewilderment and followed him to the car. When they arrived home, Liba sought refuge in her garden while Stan moped about inside. After a little while she heard the bang of the screen door and the clump of his footsteps on the wooden porch. She looked up to see him glaring at her.

"I'm giving you an ultimatum," he stated. "Either you quit your independent ways and behave like a normal loving wife or get out. You've got three days to decide."

Liba looked at him. It was if he were playing out some scene in a B-Movie. "I don't need three days," she said. "I'll leave now."

The marriage hadn't lasted six months and, although Jana was big with her baby, she and Peter insisted Liba stay on their couch. They still had their own bedroom and the extra seventeen dollars a month plus food helped.

Two days later, as Liba stood in the kitchen helping Jana and Peter clean up after supper, they were startled by a sound. It was Stan. He stood in the doorway looking sheepishly at her. Liba frowned.

"What are you doing here?" she asked. He hadn't any business in Jana and Peter's apartment without knocking.

He cleared his throat. "We need to talk."

Jana and Peter exchanged glances. "You can go in there," Peter said with a nod toward the living room.

"Thanks," Stan said quietly. Liba felt she had no choice but to follow him in.

She sat in the middle of the couch with her back toward the window as he paced around the room.

"Have you made your decision?" He asked.

"Yes." She replied

"Well?" He looked at her expectantly.

"Well, what do you think? What does it look like?" she replied.

Suddenly he was on his knees in front of her. "I can't live without you! Please, please come back." He began to cry.

Liba stared at him. This was a game he had learned from his father, but nobody had given her the rules.

"Darling. You are my whole life. I was a fool. I was totally wrong in the way I treated you. You mean everything to me." He was still weeping, and in a dramatic gesture he flung his arms around her knees. Liba shifted uncomfortably and looked around. His movements were so theatrical it was almost as if he were playing to an audience.

"I told you. I'm not coming back. It's over Stan. It's actually been over for sometime. We just aren't suited. You want some little woman who will cook and clean and devote her life to you. And with me...well, that's just not going to happen. Ever."

Stan stood up and wiped his eyes with the backs of his hands. "All right." he said sadly. "I can see there is no use." Head hanging low, he shuffled out of the room and she heard the door to the suite softly close.

––––––––––

Al was a frequent visitor at Jana and Peter's. He would find his way over to the little suite and take Liba for walks. She was severely depressed. One day, as they strolled toward the Stampede Grounds which housed Calgary's world famous rodeo each year, he casually threw his arm around her shoulders and mentioned it wouldn't be much longer before Jana had her baby.

"I know." Liba sighed. "I just don't know what I'm going to do. When the baby comes they'll have no room for me."

"Maybe we should pool our money together." He lifted his eyes and looked directly at her. "It will be easier because we both have so little."

A married couple received $180 a month from the Immigration Department. Liba and Stan split that in half when they went their separate ways. Al was single so he got one hundred and twenty dollars a month. Together, they could just barely scrape by. Alone, Liba had no chance. Her means of support were non-existent. Her home had been erased.

Although she was only twenty-one years old, Liba considered herself second-hand merchandise. She looked at her separation from Stan as a personal failure. That, combined with her mother's open displeasure with her, convinced her that she was worthless. She didn't find Al particularly attractive or interesting. In fact, he was pretty quiet. Too quiet. But he was nice to her and his offer seemed to make financial sense so that was good enough.

"Al I'm... you know what kind of a situation I'm in. I'm not interested in a relationship or anything."

He nodded. "Okay. It's fine. We'll just be roommates."

While they kept their eyes open for a suitable place, Liba surveyed her belongings. She had nothing but a few changes of clothes. No pots, pans, knives, forks, plates, towels, nothing. She decided to head over to Stan's and collect a few of her things. She was greeted by his new Slovak roommate.

"Stan isn't here," he growled.

"Fine." Liba tried to smile. "I just want to get some of my things."

"Yeah, well he said you'd be here eventually, and I'm supposed to watch what you take."

The Slovak sat on a stool with his arms crossed and his lips drawn into hard tight lines as she opened drawers and collected the rest of her clothes. But, as she reached for her photo album, he stopped her.

"Don't touch that!" he ordered. "Stan says the pictures are his!" He wouldn't allow her to take anything other than personal items. She didn't want to get into an argument with this bull-headed man so she closed the box and left.

When she relayed her experience over coffee to one of her former English teachers, she was told in no uncertain terms that since she and Stan were not formally separated, she had as much right to their common property as he. So one afternoon, when she was sure Stan and the Slovak were out, she and Al drove up to the front of the house. Using her old key, they removed a mattress, a couple of plates, some bedding and her precious photo albums.

Soon after, Liba and Al found a one-bedroom basement suite, on the west edge of the city near the Army Barracks. They agreed on rent with the landlord, $110 dollars a month. At the beginning of September, they loaded Liba's mattress on the roof of Al's car and then carried it down the stairs to their new life, together.

They had barely any furniture because the room where Al had boarded was furnished. Thankfully, Liba had retrieved a few dishes from Stan's, but for night tables they used cardboard boxes. They kept their clothes in a little wooden dresser, which also belonged to Liba during her marriage to Stan. Al designed a couch out of two wooden apple crates and over that he tied some foam and cloth. Their coffee table consisted of two apple crates stacked on top of each other. They ate off it as well. Eventually Al picked up some planks from a construction site and nailed together a little shelf for a few books. They bought a second-hand black and white TV set and that was it.

Every time Liba felt down about her impending divorce, Al was surprisingly supportive. He tried to get her to do some positive thinking.

"It's not the end of the world, Liba." He'd smile. "You're young, you still have your whole life ahead. Think of it as a small mistake."

Al seemed to know what he was talking about. He knew a lot more about happy families than she did. He often mentioned his parents, older sister Gabriela and younger brother Josef. He told a funny story about Josef. Once when his brother was little, his parents bought him a pair of shoes he didn't like. Josef dragged his feet along the ground for a week and managed to ruin them. The next week he got to choose a new pair that were more to his liking.

Al's sister was named after her mother. Gabriela Sr. was a Business College major which was quite remarkable for someone her age. Very few women over forty had been to university back home. His father, also named Alois, was a lawyer who specialized in tax law before the 1948 takeover by communists. They had been very well-to-do until then. The whole family was smart. Gabriela and Josef both attended the university in Prague. They lived in residence there. Al graduated from a technical school, but had hated it. His mother insisted he study to be an engineer. Liba assumed her decision was a financial one. Maybe she thought the other two were more academic so it was worth the financial strain for them to live in Prague. Going to the technical school meant Al could live at home which saved a lot of money.

Al preferred working with his hands. He liked construction and an outdoor environment. In Canada, he had to start at the bottom, not only because his English was lacking, but also because he had no training. He could have learned his craft in Pardubice, his hometown, but his mother felt carpentry wasn't a lofty enough profession. Her son would be a white-collar worker, not a blue-collar worker. Even though Al said he didn't give a damn about engineering, he did manage to graduate so Liba gave him credit for having brains.

Liba was a little concerned about Al's parents. Their status as successful professionals intimidated her and she worried about whether they would accept his living with a woman who was married to someone else. She sat down and wrote them a heartfelt letter admitting she had been married to Stan. She said she didn't want to get into details because it was not her intent to smear him. She told Al's family their son had befriended her and helped her learn to trust again.

Gradually, Liba's self esteem began to rise. Al seemed to find her attractive and she didn't feel so much like used goods when she told him Stan hadn't even been her first lover. Al said he didn't care. What happened before they met didn't matter, he said.

She asked Al about his previous relationships and he told her there weren't any. After he graduated from engineering he'd gone straight into mandatory army duty for two years, and hadn't had time to get a girlfriend.

On their first night together in the basement suite they became intimate. Although she wasn't especially attracted to Al, he turned out to be a considerate and gentle lover. His chest was hairless and like other Czechs who weren't Jewish, he was uncircumcised. He had dark chestnut hair, brown eyes and was fairly slim. His skin was darker than most central Europeans. He attributed his coloring to his Italian grandmother whom his grandpa had brought over in the First World War. Later Gabriela confessed to Liba that their grandma was really a gypsy and they just passed her off as an Italian.

Liba didn't feel any passion for Al as she had for Stan. But she found him a lot easier to live with. Her feelings for him deepened somewhat, even though she knew she wasn't in love. Far from it.

Stan moved to Ontario. He was bitter about their breakup, claiming Liba left him for Al. "She liked him better," he said. Liba was aware he would refuse to come back for a divorce hearing so she would not be able to obtain a legal divorce for three years. This suited her fine. She was in no hurry to remarry.

Liba was tenacious in her search for a job. She finally landed one at The University of Calgary, cleaning classrooms. Her shift was from eleven at night until seven in the morning.

Meanwhile, Calgary's economy began to pick up a little and Al continued to find work as a carpenter on construction sites. He worked all day and she worked all night. Liba was philosophical about it. "It is pure survival. We have to do what we have to do."

But because of her traumatic nighttime experiences as a child, she had never learned to sleep at the best of times so sleeping during the day was impossible. She became habitually tired, so tired she felt sick. But she never complained because, as she said later, "That's the way it was. And if that's the only job you can get, that's the only job you can get."

Liba and Al saved what they could and used it to go hiking and camping in the Rockies on weekends. They had very little, but whatever they had, they shared. Sometimes they would go to a movie, although not very often. There were no signs of anything being wrong with him.

Every night for the four months Liba worked as a cleaner, Al would drive her to the University for the start of her shift. By the time he got home it would be close to midnight. Though he started work at dawn, he seemed happy to do it.

Liba would fetch a heavy tin bucket, cart it over to the janitorial sink, then fill it to the last groove with ammonia and water. She pulled it behind her as she slapped a heavy cotton broom along the floors of the university. Unfortunately, she was unable to brush up on her English because her co-workers were all immigrants. "But," she laughingly told Al, "I'm picking up a lot of Italian words."

She spent her days, traipsing to Manpower, a Canadian federal employment agency that tries to match people with job skills. Liba said she'd take anything, in the daytime. Finally, one of the job counselors, a plump, middle-aged matron who had the same black hair and perm that Mami had, took pity on the exhausted-looking waif with the oversized glasses and shy smile. She left a message with Liba's landlord saying there was an opening at an office downtown which entailed working with maps. Training would be provided to the successful candidate.

It turned out to be a field title service that updated land lease maps for the oil industry. The Human Resource Officer, Frances DeBodo, was a lovely, tall and slim, freckled redhead from Britain. She was married to a

Hungarian and understood the plight of new immigrants. She saw promise in Liba and hired her on the spot.

At minimum wage, Liba actually made less than she had cleaning, but she felt there was far more opportunity in her new job. And working days rather than nights made it possible to sleep again.

Liba knew Al was falling in love with her. English people seemed to say, "I love this, I love that. Oh, I love you. Do you love me?" But Czech people didn't say such things. Stan was theatrical, but even he didn't often go on about love. Her culture, she observed, was a little more reserved. You gathered how someone felt through his or her actions. She knew she was incapable of returning Al's love. She was just too emotionally beat up.

As soon as she got her first paycheck from her new job, she confessed to Al she found living in a basement suite depressing.

"Would it be all right, do you think, if we moved into a normal apartment above ground?" she asked.

Al didn't hesitate. But he suggested that since they'd have to spend an extra fifteen to seventeen dollars a month for a ground level suite, they might as well move closer to downtown so she could walk to work. This delighted Liba, she loved exercise of any kind.

Things got a little better financially because every few months she received a little raise. Al got small salary increases too. They traded in his old beater of a car and bought something in a little better shape.

On their second Christmas together Liba and Al decided on a twenty-dollar limit for gifts. Al bought her nice simple earrings each with a little gold leaf cradling a pearl. Their friends, Jiri Srom, who they'd met in English classes and his Canadian wife, Terry, gave them a glass bowl that resembled an octopus with thick opaline tentacles sticking out all over. When she opened it, Al said, "That thing is really ugly as hell," but Liba just laughed. "I think they're getting rid of some unwanted wedding presents."

A month or so later, Al came home from work in a dither. "This stupid bastard at work screwed up in his measuring and I had to re-frame an entire window!" He stood in the kitchen his jaw clenched and his hands clamped. He was tense, but he seemed very much in control.

"I want to...I want to break something. I want to break something." He repeated. His eyes swept their little apartment. "What can I break?"

Liba was amused. Surely he wasn't serious. She pointed waggishly to the glass bowl Christmas present that sat on their apple box table. "Well, if you want to break something, break that thing."

He picked up the bowl and smashed it on the floor. The cheap glass shattered everywhere. Liba's jaw dropped, but relief filled Al's face and she saw his posture relax. He moved to the broom closet and calmly cleaned up the shards.

Liba shook her head and thought, "This is too bizarre. I don't believe what I just saw." But that was it. There was no aftermath. Al went back to being perfectly normal. As bad as things had been with her mother, she'd rarely witnessed physical violence. Feelings were always controlled. "Maybe too controlled," she thought, so she just let it go.

Field Title Services farmed her out as a temporary worker to other companies. Liba befriended a girl named Linda Simpson. They worked on the same floor and had an occasional coffee together. One day Linda asked Liba about her previous training.

"You're a draftsman, aren't you?"

Liba nodded.

"Well," she continued, "my dad's company, Midwest Surveys, is looking for one. You should apply."

Liba jumped at the opportunity. The job interview seemed to go well, but when she didn't hear anything she figured they had hired someone else. She'd been with Field Title Services for a little over a year and, though she picked up some of the technical terminology, she found it pretty boring. Socializing with co-workers was frowned upon except at lunch and coffee breaks. She spent most of the day picking up and transferring documents. Someday she hoped to apply her hard-earned knowledge of mechanical engineering to something challenging.

Two months after she applied for the job at Midwest Surveys, they called and offered her the job. She felt nervous and elated at the same time. It was a drafting job, but it was not in her field so she would have to re-train and her knowledge of English was still fairly limited.

For the first time in her life, Liba had a car and a little money, but neither she nor Al were into buying things. They preferred exploring the countryside, usually the mountains. Liba's new job as a land survey draftsman exposed her to topographical maps of Alberta and sparked her curiosity about the province. One weekend, she suggested they try camping east of Calgary in the opposite direction from the mountains, in the Badlands where dinosaur bones are plentiful. She heard there was a campsite at Dinosaur Provincial Park by a small town called Brooks. Nearby there was supposed to be a half-excavated dinosaur under a glass cage.

Al sulked during the two-hour drive. The scenery wasn't spectacular. It was flat prairie farm land, but the sky was blue and the wheat fields flew by the open car windows in golden waves. When they pulled up at a campground, Liba got out and started unloading. Al reached in the trunk and angrily tossed all the camping equipment on the ground.

"What's wrong?" Liba asked.

He began yelling at her. "Look around! Look at this lousy place. Nothing is green, there is not a flower in sight. Thanks to you, we are spending a weekend in the middle of a desert!" He kicked at the ground in frustration. "It's so ugly and so plain!"

Liba was taken aback. "How was I supposed to know?" she defended herself. "I wanted to see the dinosaurs. I was curious about the geology on this piece of the country. Same as you I have never been here before. I don't have any idea ahead of time what it's going to look like. So we are here, we are here." She shrugged. "We'll never have to come back here again. But let's have a nice weekend."

He glared at her. "No! I'm not staying here!" He chucked everything back in the trunk. "We are going home!" he declared as he slammed the lid down.

Moving stiffly, Liba got back in the car. He didn't speak for most of the drive, but as they neared the outskirts of Calgary, he seemed to calm down. He cleared his throat.

"I'm sorry, I think I wrecked the day."

Liba was looking out the window on her side. She rolled her eyes and thought, "That's an understatement." But again she said nothing.

Mother Dolejs sent Liba a Namesday card. Czechs consider Namesday just as important as a birthday. Every day on the calendar year is dedicated to a saint. When the saint's day bearing your name comes up, you have cause to celebrate. Mother Dolejs asked a curious question in her note. Was Lola, her pet name for Al, still treating her as nicely as he had been when they met? Because she would be glad to prompt him to mind his manners.

Liba wrote a polite thank you letter, glossing over an incident that took place on a recent hike in the mountains.

"We were running together in a field and throwing snow at each other and when it was time to come down I leaped over a creek. When Al tried to do the same he landed in the middle of it. I was laughing all the way down, but he was mumbling angrily, insisting someone grabbed his sleeve from behind." Then she added, "You were wondering if Al is still as nice as he was. Don't worry, you don't have to say anything to him. Sometimes he is tired from work and in a bad mood, but that could happen to anyone and usually he gets over it. I know he is a good person and when he resents me momentarily it doesn't mean he has changed."

CHAPTER TEN

WHERE ARE THE BODIES?

August, 8:00 AM

As a criminal defense lawyer, John Bascom deals with bad guys all the time. He shakes their hands, talks with them, and makes eye contact. Physical proximity can't be avoided but he never puts the legal part aside.

A judge once told him, "We don't punish the person, we punish their acts. People who have done horrific things can be extremely charming individuals."

John agrees. "I acted for this guy who was truly a sociopath. He pled guilty to two first-degree murder charges. And this guy was absolutely a charmer. I guess at some point in his life, he decided to become a contract killer. The guards liked him because any time they were having trouble with someone in the Remand Center they put the troublemaker into the hitman's cell. If it was a young punk mouthing off, Bart (pseudonym) would smile and in a quiet voice say, 'I'm here on two first-degree murder charges. And here's how I like it in my cell. I like it quiet here and I don't want anybody to disturb me.'

"You could joke with him. I remember he picked up my pen once and it was sort of a square pen. It had a very sharp edge and he said, 'Oh this would be a perfect pen.' And we're sitting in this relatively small area and there's no table or desk between us. And he held the pen hard in his grip and looked at me. 'Now I could take this pen and shove it into your throat and kill you.' And I said, 'Now Bart, you only kill incompetent lawyers.' The moment passed and he laughed. Then we both laughed."

As promised, John arrived at Calgary Police Headquarters at 8:30 the next morning. Al was still in the interrogation room. Wally and Brian's interview, initiated eight hours earlier, would resume just after John left and wrap up forty-five minutes later. But by then, Wally was no longer asking about the kids. He was asking about the bodies.

John says real life questioning of a suspect in Canada is not like what you see on television. "As soon as you ask for a lawyer the police can say, 'Oh well that's very nice, yeah, we'll get you a lawyer in a minute, but...' and then they can keep on questioning."

John reminded Al about his constitutional rights against self-incrimination. "In Canada you have one right, and really just one right, and that's to keep your mouth shut." Legally, John could not inflict his morals on Al. He could not advise him to tell the police where the children's bodies were.

Some people didn't agree. When it was revealed John had informed his client, a man accused of murdering his own children, of his rights, he was bombarded with nasty phone calls and hate mail. John understands why this happened.

"We've got to look at this in perspective. It's 1986. Calgary is on the verge of becoming a big city. A thing like what happened with Dolejs and the death of his two children, I think we always felt that this was something that could only happen in the United States. This would never happen in a neighborly hometown like Calgary. The shock that all of a sudden we're a big city and these things can occur here, the reaction was quite different than the way people react today."

Twelve years later in 1998, John defended Ian Gordon. Gordon, a 43-year-old math tutor, pleaded guilty in September 1998 to second degree murder for bludgeoning to death his two daughters, 14-year-old Kayla and 9-year-old Liane, and his common law wife, Linda Kriske.

Coincidentally, Nick Kyska was the chief investigating officer on the Gordon case.

"I received no phone calls from the public criticizing my actions," John recalls. "This may be an indication that due to the proliferation of violent acts that have occurred in this city over the past decade the public has become desensitized."

"The calls I received when I was defending Mr. Dolejs were from individuals who said, 'This man should have no rights. What are you doing? You're just as bad as he is. You're a dirty son-of-a-bitch.' Or words worse than that. They didn't seem to understand that no matter what a person is charged with there's supposed to be a presumption of innocence.

"My secretary started screening the calls because people wouldn't give their names. She'd say, 'Who's calling?' And of course, they'd just say, 'Well give Bascom this message. He's an asshole.' Or something along those lines.

"Two people that I remember specifically gave their names so she put them through to me. And they started off ranting and raving. I said, 'Okay, now if you want to hear my side.' So they listened. At the end of it they said, 'Oh. Well we understand now.'"

"An important part of our democracy is a free and independent bar who are able to criticize Government actions which affect the rights of our citizens. I'm a child of the '60s. Part of that rebellious anti-government feeling that a lot of us had was that we were not like our parents. We refused to follow everything the government said. We questioned. We criticized. Some of us went into more active aspects of anti-government protest while others like me joined up and said we can change it from inside. We can oppose the government when they are trying to take our individual rights away. And that's part of the entire fight.

"I think at this particular stage, we are seeing individual rights slowly eroding. The unfortunate thing is our Constitution is perhaps the only thing we've got left. There is always the question by members of the public why individuals are entitled to State run defenses. Many of the citizens look at individuals like Mr. Dolejs as not deserving any defense at all. I was shocked when people would phone me up and threaten me.

"Even members of my own profession expressed concern about what I was doing. As a result of an editorial in the newspaper, I received a call from an official of the Law Society of Alberta who indicated to me that he didn't think I had done anything wrong. My reaction was, not only have I done nothing wrong, I have done the only proper thing, which was to maintain solicitor/client privilege."

John Bascom had a duty to protect Al's rights. That morning, they talked until 8:55. Al hadn't eaten yet, but the RCMP had given him water. He was hungry. Wally agreed to get him breakfast, but first he persuaded Al to run a comb through his hair. Wally kept the comb for hair samples. Then Wally made a few attempts to prick Al's finger with a pin for blood samples. Finally, Wally got Al to shove his hand down his pants and retrieve some pubic hair.

John Cantafio is now a Sergeant in Major Crimes with the RCMP. His area runs south of Edmonton right down to the US border. He belongs to an eight-man team. John looks like a work by Michelangelo. Thick black hair, large dark eyes, sculptured mouth, strong, square jaw and chiseled chin. He doesn't like to be photographed because he still does a fair bit of undercover work.

Wally Purcell called him at 5:30 the morning of August 8.

"We have a guy in custody who kidnapped his kids and was last seen on July 27 when he'd made some kind of comment to his wife like, 'You'll never see the kids again.' There's blood on his pant leg and his lawyer is John Bascom. The children's names are Paul and Gabi. Paul is twelve, Gabi, ten."

This information hit John in the gut. In 1986, his son Matt was four and baby Jodi was two. He and Susan, a dark haired beauty, had married at twenty, eight years before, and their world revolved around the kids.

The first time John saw a dead child he was on the job. He'd been with the RCMP just a couple of years and there was a motor vehicle accident. A little fellow, no more than four, was lying dead on the road. Later he told Susan, "It really pissed me off because he wasn't wearing a seat belt."

John was immediately teamed with polygraph operator Danny Lyon. Polygraph operators are amongst the best interviewers any police force has and Sergeant Danny Lyon was no exception. At 8:55 AM, Cantafio and Lyon waited outside the interrogation room for John Bascom to leave. The plan was for Wally to finish up with Al and then the two of them would take a crack at him.

The door opened and the lawyer emerged. Like Nick Kyska the night before, Cantafio was struck by John Bascom's pallor. They'd worked together before and the man usually looked so vigorous. Cantafio figured whatever he heard in the room with Al must have been pretty shocking.

CHAPTER ELEVEN

PAUL

Liba and Al had been relying on the IUD Liba's doctor back in Czechoslovakia had placed in her uterus. Her period was always very regular so when she missed it, she went to see her Calgary gynecologist, Dr. Johnson (pseudonym). He gave her a pelvic examination and told her she was pregnant. He knew she wasn't married, so he asked her what she wanted to do. She was 26 years old.

"I might as well keep it. I'm old enough to take care of a baby."

A few days later she told Al. He asked, "What do you want to do? Do you want to get married?"

Liba contemplated this. "Well, I would prefer if the baby had a father."

Al smiled. "Okay, let's get married." They got married in October.

Liba had a miserable pregnancy. It began with a lot of bleeding for the first four months. She was losing so much blood, she constantly felt light-headed, but Dr. Johnson insisted they leave her IUD in place.

Dr. Paul Martyn, President of the Alberta Society of Obstetricians and Gynecologists, says the IUD could have been a factor responsible for the ongoing bleeding, but Liba thinks there was another reason.

"Maybe some higher power or some higher wisdom already knew what was going to happen and it was trying to abort itself and it didn't quite succeed. As if he should have never been born. I don't know."

Al was pretty scared. He didn't know what was going on and he wasn't used to seeing his usually strong, independent wife in such a weakened state. Getting pregnant was not something Liba ever thought would happen. Unlike other girls, it was never her dream to be married and have a family. But fate decided that she have a child, so she would have a child and do the best she could.

She was so sick it was all she could do to get out of bed and get dressed. Her short-term memory all but disappeared. Had she eaten that morning or not? When she started passing blood clots the size of golf balls, she became frightened and went back to the doctor. He was very concerned and told her they had to do something. "You can't go on like this anymore."

He gave her some pills to take and told her within four days she would begin to experience cramps in her abdomen. "When that happens, go to the hospital." He told her she would miscarry.

According to Dr. Martyn, the pills were most likely some sort of an abortifacient. "Perhaps he gave her aminopterin, which was a folate antagonist that would sometimes cause babies to abort. Folic acid is an essential vitamin that's necessary for growth and development of babies. They need lots of it. Without it the fetus dies."

She was in her third month of pregnancy when she took the four tiny pills on a Tuesday. But Friday came and nothing happened. So she returned to the doctor's office. He examined her and shook his head in amazement. "I can't believe it, but the fetus actually grew. I've never seen anything like it in my life. I don't want to abort it this way. Let's do the best to carry you through."

He began giving her iron shots instead and gradually, she started feeling well again. She was due in April, but they lived close to downtown so she walked to work even on the coldest days. Toward the end of her pregnancy her stomach got so big she couldn't bend over. A fellow from work befriended her. His name was Gordie Johnson. He watched one day as she struggled with the zipper on her boots.

"May I do that for you?" he gallantly offered.

Liba blushed. "I feel totally embarrassed, but would you mind?"

Gordie knelt down in front of her and zipped them up. "Don't worry about it." He laughed. "My wife Dorothy and I have four kids. I've done this before." Liba was grateful and began spending time with him during her breaks.

Al was proud she was carrying his baby and showed concern for her suffering. On April 9th, Liba went into labor. She had no idea that something could hurt so much. The baby's head was banging against her cervix but she wasn't dilating so there was no way for her to push the baby out. She felt reduced to an animal. Dr. Johnson consulted with two other doctors at the hospital. They decided she could still deliver vaginally.

She signaled the delivery team at the start of each contraction and they took turns examining her to see how she was progressing. Her labor continued for twenty-two hours. Al made an effort to help by trying to hold her hand, but she didn't want him there. She didn't want anything or anybody. She was given shots of Demerol despite her protests.

"I don't care if the pain kills me!" she yelled. "I just want it to be over with!"

Paul was finally born at 5:00 PM the next afternoon, April 10. Dr. Johnson was reassuring. "He's not very big, but he's okay."

He weighed five pounds, ten ounces and he wasn't okay. He was placed in an incubator in Intensive Care for eleven days. His temperature kept dropping and he would turn blue. Small babies don't have any subcutaneous fat so they can't regulate their temperatures as well.

Liba knew absolutely nothing about babies. She'd never even held one. They put him across her stomach for a fleeting moment and then whisked him away. She didn't expect him to be brought in for the feeding immediately because she knew they had to clean him up. But worry began to overtake her twenty-four hours later when a nurse brought the other babies into the ward and she still hadn't seen hers.

Liba asked, "Where's my baby?"

The nurse looked at her. "I'll check."

Fifteen minutes later the nurse returned. She stared at Liba. "There is no Baby Dolejs."

When Liba objected, the nurse pooh-poohed her concern. "Oh, don't worry, I'll find out."

This time the nurse didn't return for over an hour. Then she poked her head in the door and said. "I found him. He's in Intensive Care."

"Can I see him?" Liba asked in a faltering voice.

The nurse sighed, "Okay, but it's in a different wing," and proceeded to give Liba a complicated set of directions. The Calgary General was a decrepit old hospital, an architectural maze of old wards and new annexes. Finding her baby was not going to be easy.

Eventually, Liba got there. She approached the desk and gave her name. The attending nurse barely glanced up. Consulting a chart, she said, "Incubator number four."

Liba walked through another set of doors and waded through a series of eerie looking little coffin-like boxes with windows. She found number four, but was totally unprepared for what she saw. A baby, all hooked up to monitors and tubes, skinny as a rail. He was quite long, twenty-one inches, but only five pounds. His head was bruised and misshapen from the arduous labor he'd endured. They'd shaved off all his hair and his hands and his ankles were tied with a towel so he couldn't yank out the tubes.

Liba stared at her infant son for a moment, then fainted.

CHAPTER TWELVE

THE RIDE

August 8, Morning to late afternoon

At 10:28 the morning of August 8, Wally Purcell introduced Al to Danny Lyon and John Cantafio. After advising him of his rights, the first thing Lyon did was tell him they were going to start fresh on the investigation. Al wanted to know when he could eat and sleep. They told him they'd get him something soon. They then questioned him for awhile, but he refused to cooperate. So an hour later, they loaded him in their cruiser and after stopping at Wendy's for a burger, drove him out to Bragg Creek.

Bragg Creek is a small community on the edge of the Rocky Mountain foothills west of the city, near where Al was walking when he was picked up. They drove to Allen Bill Pond. Al pointed to an area near a footbridge and told the officers he had taken his kids fishing there.

The officers ran different scenarios by Al. After he talked with Liba, maybe the children wanted to leave and he lost his temper and decided not to take them back. Maybe one of the children objected and he got mad and killed one and had to kill the other to cover up. Maybe one was killed and the other ran away and he spent the next couple of days in the bush looking for the child. Maybe he planned this and took them somewhere and tied them to a tree and they starved to death or died of exposure. Maybe he'd thrown them in the river. Maybe he buried them. Al didn't react to any of these suggestions.

But when Cantafio suggested, "Maybe you sexually assaulted the children," Al became visibly upset, his color heightened and his jaw tightened. They'd found a button.

"Is impossible for anyone to do that to their children," he protested. "And furthermore I am not capable of doing such as that. All you have to do is ask my wife! She will say to you same thing!"

At four o'clock, they drove to the Cochrane RCMP Detachment. Cantafio waited with Al while Lyon left the room. Al confided to the Italian detective that he liked him.

"If we were having beer. We could be friends. But I don't want to talk about nothing else."

———————

The officers in the detachment decided to try something new. They knew through Liba that Al was raised a Catholic, so they called the diocese and found a priest who could speak Al's language.

Father John Bastigal was a parish priest at Ascension Parish in Calgary. His parents came from Slovakia back in the early 1920s. They settled in Drumheller, a coal-mining town in Alberta now famous for its frequent archaeological finds of dinosaur bones. They insisted he learn their native tongue. Every once in a while his mother would say, "Okay now, you're going to sit down and write a letter to your grandparents." John would groan as he picked up his pen and slowly and laboriously waded through the difficult words. But as he got older, he began to appreciate knowing more than one language.

When he became a priest, he would say mass for the Catholic Slovak community. A lot of the older generation had died off but he found a whole new generation of Slovaks anxious to preserve their language and their culture.

Father John's seminary education included philosophy and theology. Following that, he did graduate work in New York in sociology, both the MA and Ph.D. programs. People found John easy to talk to. Perhaps because of his gentle looks, unimposing with large sympathetic eyes under bushy strawberry blonde brows and a head of matching wavy hair.

His deep voice was mild and soft and he listened intently to others without interrupting.

When the police called for his help, he didn't hesitate. They gave him a little bit of background. No one but Al knew what had happened to the children. But they had suspicions. Would he appeal to Al? Father John was cognizant that priests in Europe carry a lot of weight. He dressed carefully, wearing black pants and a clerical shirt. Perhaps it might help Al open up a little bit.

When he arrived Danny Lyon showed him a picture of the kids. Father John sat for a moment. He found it painful trying to process how a person could even think about harming his two children.

"Can you help us Father?" asked Danny.

Father John leveled with him. "If he should choose to appeal to the confidentiality of confession I can't say anything to you."

As Father John entered the room and sat down, Al directed his cold stare toward the wall. Father John moved his chair in front of Al, but like a cobra, Al's hooded eyes slid away. Father John introduced himself and said he was a Slovak so he could probably understand if Al wanted to speak Czech. Al shook his head.

"Okay, " said Father John. "Let's speak English then. Is there anything I can do for you Al? Anything specific?"

Al looked at him, his eyes showing no emotion. "No. Maybe I would like to read scripture."

"Scripture?" Father John nodded. "We'll get you a Bible, of course."

"A Bible," mused Al, "will give me strength."

"Indeed. Indeed it will," agreed the priest. "As I understand it, Al, you were arrested last night?"

Al nodded.

"The police suspect you have something to do with your missing children. Is that correct?"

"Yes," Al said.

Father John studied Al a moment. He looked haggard and exhausted. Al picked up the sympathy in Father John's expression. He yawned. "Need sleep and food."

"Have you eaten since your arrest Al?" queried Father John.

"Wendy's," came the reply.

"How are they treating you?"

Al considered a moment. "Good. One or two of them especially. They're good. Concerned for me."

"Al," Father John said in a confidential tone. "Do you feel a desire for the sacraments? Particularly the sacrament of reconciliation? Anything you confess will remain strictly between us, as you know."

Al shook his head. "I need a time to…prepare myself for that," said Al.

"Ah, I understand. A person does not approach the sacrament lightly. You need time." The priest's tone was hushed and respectful.

They continued discussing the sacraments for a few moments when Danny Lyon interrupted them. He informed them Al was to be taken before a Justice of the Peace. He was being charged with first degree murder.

Twenty-four hours after his arrest Al ate and showered. They locked him in his cell with Constable John Stephen Wells, an undercover officer posing as another inmate. Wells was instructed to take a passive role in listening and observing anything Al might say or do. Wells told Al he'd been stopped for a traffic infraction on Highway 1 near Cochrane and it was discovered he hadn't paid an outstanding drunk driving fine of one thousand dollars. Wells was lying on one of the bottom bunks in the cell. Al took the one opposite and scooped up a magazine. Wells was wearing a wire.

"What are you in for?" Wells asked Al.

"Don't ask," came the answer. "Whatever you did is nothing compared to me." And he slept.

August 9, Morning

The search for Paul and Gabi Dolejs was called off for the day at 9:00 PM. Scuba diving teams dragged ponds near McLean Creek campground, an area where the children were last seen. All together, thirty-two people spent the day combing the mosquito-infested area south of Elbow Ranger station. Four all terrain vehicles and dog tracking teams, combined with park rangers, forestry workers and one helicopter made up the team. They covered twelve to fourteen kilometers of bush, concentrating on back roads and trails.

The next morning John Cantafio teamed up with Corporal Brian Phillips. Phillips was on hand taking notes for Wally the first night of Al's incarceration. Al was the exact opposite of what he had been the day before and Phillips was amazed.

Cantafio commented, "He is so eager to talk, he has diarrhea of the mouth."

Nodding and gesturing with his hands, Al had a story ready. He said he picked up the kids on Sunday, the 27th of July. He was driving his Dodge Ram Charger, black and silver in color.

"I got tools in truck. I'm carpenter. I like House of Tools, Heritage Drive. I stop at Canmore one hour. Buy kids breakfast at Esso. Five bucks each. Buy tickets, day passes, two bucks, for Hot Springs. We go to upper Hot Springs. We are there for a while and then go into town site and walk around. It's nice, you know?

"Then to Canmore from Banff. Buying gas at either Esso or Shell using Chargex card. Get to Bragg Creek between 2:00 or 3:00 PM. Next at 6:00 PM make a call to my wife. Talk about my house, about selling it. We have buyer for one hundred twelve thousand."

Al was excited and talking so fast Cantafio had trouble taking notes. "Kids are with me at Gooseberry campground. Then to Elbow Falls, look around there. Eat buns at parking lot at Elbow Falls." Al shrugged. "Back to Calgary Woodbine. No one home. That's 8:00 PM."

"What exactly happened when you took the kids home Al?" Cantafio asked.

"Garage door is unlocked, so is house." He looked up at Cantafio. "Typical woman," he sneered. "I'm pissed off about price. If house sells, I get thirty thousand, buy furniture." Al frowned.

"She can go to hell if I have to wait! I leave, went back west. Last I saw kids was at Woodbine home." Then he continued, "Went to Cochrane Ranch, Mountain Air Lodge. Up the trunk road. That night I sleep in truck. I have steaks, but don't eat them."

Al told the officers he used his Chargex to buy gas again in Cochrane on Tuesday. On Wednesday, he went to Bragg Creek and drove around the roads. Time gets fuzzy, but a few days after Tuesday, he gets stuck in the afternoon on a muddy trail. He tries all day to get his truck out, but no one shows up that afternoon or the next day so he decides to walk out. That's when he gets lost. He cannot find his way out of the bush. Trying for a shortcut he realizes he's made a complete circle. It gets dark. He goes down a cut line, finds nothing important there, but ends up in some swamps. Exhausted, he lies down under a tree and sleeps. Eventually he walks out on the McLean Trail, which is a major road.

"I cross creek in the afternoon. Come out the south side of the slough, then walk to a highway. Try to hitch a ride all day, but can't get picked up." He shook his head, disgusted.

"Night again. I see a tree, so I climb over the fence. Sleep under tree on a road close to Bragg Creek. Next morning, I walk to the Sarcee Indian

Reserve sign. I finally get a ride there in an old truck with a man who turns off at Richmond Road. I get out and decide to walk to Cochrane, but RCMP pick me up instead."

Al told Cantafio, "Is hell when you get lost." There is a silence while they all contemplated this. Al saw the puzzled look on Cantafio's face so he elaborated.

"I suffer in the bush; therefore, I suffered in hell."

Cantafio still didn't get it. Frustrated, Al continued.

"I suffered in hell, so I have already paid for all my sins."

CHAPTER THIRTEEN

THE BABY

They called him Pavel in Czech and Paul in English. It was a name Liba always liked. Liba stayed in the hospital for five days because she was told Paul would be coming home any day, but she ended up leaving the hospital without him. When she picked him up on day eleven, he was still swollen and bruised. His head didn't return to normal shape for two months.

He was a terrible baby. He never slept and he wouldn't feed well. She didn't know what to do with him. She was at her wits end. Would he starve to death? What was she doing wrong?

Al was still at home when his sister had her first baby, so he was a little more familiar with infants than Liba was. Liba sensed Al was somehow disappointed because his sister had a daughter and he expected to have a little girl too. She tried to talk to him.

"Right from minute one, you never bother with Paul. You don't want to have anything to do with him."

———————

It was funny, Liba expected him to prefer having a son. In the past couple of years he admitted he had nothing but trouble with the women in his family. He said his mother always wished he were a girl. She even gave him a girl's nickname, Lola. She was so disappointed she didn't attend his baptism. Instead she sent his father, Alois Sr. along with his aunt. The name his mother picked was Wensaslaus, but when Al's father and aunt arrived at the church, they decided to baptize him Alois Junior.

When they returned home with the baby, Al's mother refused to call him Alois. From that day on, she insisted the family refer to him as Lola.

Al claimed his mother was the most controlling person in the entire family. His father didn't get involved much at all so ignoring her wishes on naming the baby came as a shock to all. When Al referred to women he spoke with contempt and sarcasm. He was very bitter about an incident involving his sister and repeated it many times.

"When a woman farts out a brat, she thinks right away she knows it all and there is nobody above her. Just like when that bitch of a sister of mine gave birth to a little girl her brain turned into mush and she turned into a moron. Our parents bought coal twice that winter because according to the bitch, baby Sara (pseudonym) needed a nice warm room and fresh air, so in one corner was a red-hot stove and in the other was an open window! And she married that dummy, Olda, who stole a bike from his own brother and sold it. Of course I, like an idiot, had to build an apartment suite for them and I slaved in the heat like a mule while people walked by to go to Polabinky for a swim. When I started to object, the bitch got nervous and cooked some grub so I wouldn't change my mind."

Liba asked him why he would spend his summer building an apartment for his sister when he clearly hadn't wanted to. Al snorted, "At home, we all had to jump as soon as our mother whistled, and when she wasn't home, my bitch sister bossed us around."

Mother Dolejs was very emotional and blackmailed people with her tears. The family went out of their way to make sure she wouldn't get upset. She manipulated her daughter, Gabriela Jr., quite a bit. Unfortunately, Gabriela Jr. was somewhat dependent on her parents. At forty years of age, she was divorced and had a full-time job. Somebody had to look after her two daughters. Often the girls, Sara and Lenka (pseudonym), stayed with Mother and Father Dolejs. With the threat of no babysitters hanging over her head, she let them make most of her decisions. Her ex-husband didn't make his required alimony payments and this added to Gabriela's feelings of hopelessness. She became clinically depressed, saw her life going nowhere and according to Al, attempted suicide at least twice.

Even though the family had an iron clad policy about not divulging anything about each other, Gabriela Jr. was quite candid at times. When Liba spoke to her on the phone about their new baby and how Al refused to be left alone with him even for twenty minutes, Gabriela sighed, "Yes, it's too bad. Al has always had such a spidery personality."

When she had been seven months pregnant with Paul and sure she wouldn't miscarry, Liba wrote home and told Mami she was finally going to make her a grandmother. The only response she got was a line in a letter a month or so later, "Oh, it's a bit of a surprise. When the time comes, breathe as they tell you." When he was born, Mami did send a nice card. Now Liba wrote talking about how hyper Paul was and Mami wrote back, "Finally, you know what I went through with you."

Liba didn't mind the work that a baby creates, but she wasn't prepared for the limitation on her personal freedom and felt reduced to the role of maid. She did bond with Paul after about two months, but at first she expected he might die on her and was afraid to love him too much. Night after night, she lay awake convinced she was going to lose him.

Al began to act very strangely when it came to being alone with Paul. He objected when Liba wanted to go for a walk by herself and when she signed up for a judo class he hit the roof. She went anyway and when she returned he told her there was no way she could go again. But she insisted.

"Like it or not you're his father. He's your son and I'm going. And it won't kill you to look after him for an hour and a half."

He didn't hide his deep resentment every time she left for class. He'd scowl and stomp around and slam doors for days. As Paul grew older, it never got much better.

Liba knew Al had been an altar boy in the old country, but she had never seen him go to church. They hadn't chosen one as a couple. He wasn't practicing any religion, but he refused to baptize the kids Protestant, so they didn't christen them at all.

Liba was back at work within two months. Maternity benefits were non-existent and Unemployment Insurance ran out after six weeks. There was a daycare across the street from the Children's Hospital on 17th Avenue. A Danish lady ran it. It looked after babies from six weeks to two years of age. Paul was there until he was a year and a half. Despite being stuck for a sitter, Liba laughed when Paul got kicked out of daycare at the ripe old age of eighteen months.

"They can't handle him," she wrote her mother. "He's a very hyper child and he never sleeps. He is a little bit too inquisitive and is wreaking havoc in there."

The daycare worded it very nicely. They said he was too advanced for the other children and he was giving the other kids ideas. They said they would prefer that she find a different place for him.

Paul did everything ahead of schedule. He crawled early, he crawled a lot and he crawled fast. By the time he was ten months old, he was walking. At twelve months, he was running and trying to climb up on everything. There was no such thing as going for a walk with Paul. He was like a puppy. He'd run ahead, Liba would catch up and he'd run ahead again.

Liba was proud of how quickly Paul caught on to things. They played a lot on the floor. She would lie down and he would climb all over her as if she were a jungle gym. Sometimes they would pretend they were airplanes or choo-choos or trucks. She read with him constantly, in both English and Czech, so he was bilingual from the get go. Liba was determined to be a good mother and found herself loving the interaction with Paul.

Al ignored them as they wrestled or put together puzzles on the floor of their tiny apartment. But if they made too much noise and disturbed him while he watched television, then his usual mordant tone became even nastier. She learned that asking Al for any help would only cause her grief. Paul was one of those babies who had to be fed every two-and-a-half hours and didn't sleep through the night until he was ten months old. Feeling overwhelmed, she did everything herself and left Al alone.

CHAPTER FOURTEEN

Q&A

August 9, Afternoon

The Dolejs children in particular had a tendency to call home. John Bascom felt that without Al's cooperation, all the Court could find was an unlawful act, in that he had taken the children, had not returned them and caused their death. Maybe. At best it was manslaughter. For second degree murder, the Court had to be satisfied that he intended to kill them, or cause them bodily harm that he knew was likely to cause death. And how could that be done without the bodies?

There were cases where people hadn't turned up, or the bodies had never been recovered and people had been convicted. In 1953, at Swansea in Wales, a Pole by the name of Michael Onufrejczyk and his partner, Stanislaw Sykut, owned a farm. Their farming venture failed so Stanislaw wanted to break off their partnership and sell the farm. Micheal wanted to buy Stanislaw's share, but was in dire need of money. He tried to borrow from several people and failed. Unbeknownst to Stanislaw, he wrote friends claiming he paid Stanislaw seven hundred pounds for the farm and now owned the whole thing. He even persuaded a female friend to forge documents to that effect.

On December 14, 1953, Stanislaw took a horse to the blacksmith to be shod and that was the last he was ever seen. Michael told the sheriff's officer how a large dark car arrived at the farm that night and three men, one with a revolver, took poor Stanislaw away. Then, so he would not be the last person to have seen his partner alive, he tried to persuade the blacksmith to say Stanislaw brought his horse there on the 17th. Nearly a year later, on December 1, 1954, Michael Onufrejczyk was convicted of murder and sentenced to death.

―――――――

In Alberta in 1962, an Edmonton golf pro named Frank Willey was living with his wife and two children, though there was strong evidence his wife was having a relationship with a man named Workman. Fourteen months earlier, in February, 1961, Workman went to see a lawyer and wondered whether it was possible for a guilty party in an adulterous relationship to get a substantial part of the property of the opposite party. When he was told this was improbable he said to the lawyer, "We'll just have to kill him."

Then in July, Mrs. Willey sued her husband for a judicial separation and claimed maintenance of $800 per month. Mr. Willey counter-sued against Mr. Workman for damages for enticement and harboring.

In February, 1962, Workman's friend, William Huculak, moved to Edmonton from eastern Canada. In April, Workman and Huculak contacted Paul Osborne, a former neighbor of Huculak's. They told Osborne they wanted somebody 'worked over.' The next day Workman admitted he actually wanted this somebody killed. He said it should look like an accident. The victim should be lured out to a partially built house somewhere. "Knock him out, take him out in the country and hit him with another car." Paul Osborne told the two he wanted nothing to do with their plan.

On the same day, Frank Willey received a phone call asking for a set of ladies golf clubs to be delivered at nine that night as a present for the caller's wife. Workman had been at the address given to Willey that afternoon and asked the painters what time they would be finished for the day. The house was under construction and belonged to a bookkeeping client of Workman's.

Willey had dinner with his family, including his sister and mother who were visiting from Vancouver, then left to deliver the clubs. He never returned. That night at 11:30, Paul Osborne and his wife got a call from Mrs. Huculak. She was worried about her husband. Paul and his wife went over to the Huculak's and sat with her until her husband and Workman arrived at 3:30 AM. Workman was calm, but Osborne noted Huculak was 'in rough shape.'

"I took him to the washroom and calmed him down. He kept talking about this guy's eyes sticking out of his head and something hanging out of the back of his head and he was just all shook up."

Workman told Huculak to get rid of his shoes, which were very muddy. The Osbornes decided to leave and Huculak told them, "There's a body in a shed somewhere and we have to go out and bury it." Subsequently, on Easter weekend, Huculak told Osborne they hit this guy with a wrench and had trouble burying him deep enough because the ground was frozen. Both Huculak and Workman were convicted for the capital murder of Willey, though a body was never found.

But the Dolejs case was the first murder case in the Commonwealth involving two people who vanished simultaneously. Even though John Bascom had advised Al not to say anything, the police were interrogating him for long periods of time. In John's opinion the statements were not made freely and voluntarily, but as a result of the pressure being put on him. John felt the RCMP were quite frustrated and prepared to go the distance. He was concerned they would do whatever it took to get him to give a statement.

"They just wanted to find the bodies or what they thought were bodies. They were quite prepared to interrogate him non-stop, twenty four hours a day, or alternatively start beating him up. They wanted that information. At a certain stage, I don't think they really cared whether it was admissible or not."

Sgt. Cantafio was determined not to let that happen. Any form of violence would contaminate the case and he wanted to see Al locked up. He remembered a former case which involved an elderly farmer south of Calgary and a four-year-old girl. The farmer raped the child and when Cantafio asked him why, he replied, "Because the horses weren't let out into the pasture that day and there was nothing else around."

Incredibly, the guy had been using the horses for sex and when they weren't available he turned to a four-year-old girl. Cantafio wanted to wring his neck, but he knew it would be far more effective to send the guy to jail instead. He kept his cool then and he would keep his cool now.

Cantafio and Brian Phillips continued to interview Al on August 9th, but once Al had finished his story he grew quiet. Cantafio presented Al with a cardboard sheath they found in the truck. It had stains on it that turned out to be traces of blood. Al denied ever seeing it before. Cantafio then pulled out school pictures of Paul and Gabi and pushed them toward Al. Al barely acknowledged them. He leaned to one side of the chair with his shoulders hunched, his arms crossed over his chest and his legs crossed beneath him. He looked bored.

Later in court, Cantafio admitted he started yelling at Al at this point. "Why won't you talk to us? Don't you love your children?"

When Prosecutor Peter Martin asked him, "Why did your voice go up, other than your Italian ancestry?" Cantafio replied, "Because I got mad at him. He wouldn't talk to us. He just sat there."

Cantafio looked at the smiling photos of the two innocents and thought of Matt and Jodi. "I did not want to crunch up the pictures because they were the only two we had. I think Liba must have given them to us. So I crunched up a piece of foolscap and I said, 'This is what you think of your kids because you don't even care that they get a decent burial!' And I hucked it at him."

The balled up paper bounced off Al's shoulder. He didn't even flinch. Cantafio says Al is the coldest person he's ever met.

"This is the thing with this man. I mean I've interrogated many, many people prior to that and many people since. This guy has got a heart of stone."

CHAPTER FIFTEEN

CHANGES

Liba came to understand that Al didn't like people.

After Paul was born, Al became more vocal about it. His attitude toward everybody and everything had always been negative, but now he'd come home from work ranting.

"That foreman is so stupid, nobody on the job knows what they are talking about. They are all idiots!" His tirades would continue for hours. Earlier in their relationship, they'd at least had conversations about movies or even the weather. Now he never addressed her on a personal level except to complain.

Despite this, Liba felt a certain loyalty.

"We were never madly in love or anything like that. I didn't mind a quiet guy. You have to understand one thing. The Czech immigrant community is no different than any other. The people don't usually assimilate into Canadian society. They are this small group of people who depend on each other for a social life. Naturally, it doesn't take long for it to become Gossip City. And very much keeping up with the Jones's. When people start accumulating a little wealth, the talk begins. 'Oh, you know who bought what car?' And, 'How much are they paying? They bought a house in Lake Bonavista!' And, 'You know, they went to Mexico. They went to Hawaii. How come we haven't gone to Hawaii yet?'

"I wasn't interested in that and I didn't associate much with the Czech community because of my previous divorce. There's this shame you carry, so I didn't want anybody to find out about it. I preferred to have Canadian friends. But Al couldn't communicate with them, so we were isolated."

All Al did was watch television. But Liba needed more. Her judo lessons were a real sore point. He tried to ban all exercise not done right in their own home. Then near Christmas, she mentioned she'd like to go for a nightly run once Paul was in bed.

"He bought me an exercise bike, which would have been nice, except for the reason he bought it." She smiled at him, when she spotted it under the tree Christmas morning. But he scowled and jabbed his index finger in her direction, "Now you can exercise at home. You don't have to go anywhere!"

Liba sat on it for a few minutes, then never went near it again. "I hated the damn thing. It wasn't to improve my fitness or to help me out. He wasn't giving me something he thought I would enjoy. It was for his comfort, so I wouldn't leave the house."

She started running three to four times a week, for no more than forty minutes. She would not let Al hold her prisoner. After Paul was fed, changed and put to bed, she'd don her running shoes and jog around the block.

Al continued distancing himself and Liba found attempts to communicate with him futile. "He was like a pressure cooker. Silent, but the pressure was building up. I tried to avoid confrontation, but trying to speak with him was like pulling teeth. He wouldn't reply."

Al said he wanted to build his own house. When he spoke of it, his manner would soften and a dreamy look would come over him. Liba was leery because Al had trouble staying employed and did not bring in a regular paycheck, but she thought, perhaps this would be the thing that would finally make him happy, so she agreed.

In January 1975, they bought a lot in Parkland. It was on the southern edge of the city bordering Fish Creek Provincial Park. A couple of blocks from their property, she stood on top of a cliff overlooking the spot where she, Al, Stan and Jana and Peter Sura had spent those lazy summer days. She reflected on how much everything had changed, especially Al.

Liba drew up the house plans, then arranged for a building permit.

The bureaucracy involved in obtaining all of this irritated Al and he started complaining that people were making things difficult for him on purpose. When they went to apply for permission to do something pertaining to the building and were told to modify it in some way, he was convinced the authorities were out to get him.

Liba became the main target of his frustration. She was established in her job and paid well, $800 a month. When they applied for the mortgage, the female loans officer at the bank looked at Liba's income statement and, addressing Al, started questioning him about it.

Liba cleared her throat. "Uh, that's my income." Al was embarrassed and mocked her all the way home. "Pardon me, but I am the one who makes all the money. I am the big shot." He sneered. "My husband is nothing! He's a common laborer. He can't keep a job." Liba swallowed hard. Why did he hate her so much?

Liba and Al started building the house. Al labored on construction sites all day, then went over to the house, painting, pounding and pouring into the night. He worked with vigor. He was a perfectionist and made sure every wall was level and every doorframe perfectly square.

They only had one vehicle, so Liba took a bus to daycare with Paul, dropped him off, then continued on to work. They were broke because every penny went into buying construction materials. The bank would only release small amounts of money at a time so there wasn't always enough cash for what Al needed that day. Nevertheless, he would call Liba at work and order her to pick up a box of nails or screws or more tools. She would do as she was told, knowing it was useless to argue. Often, she'd miss meals or buy cheaper groceries. It was a challenge keeping Paul dressed and in diapers on a nickel-and-dime budget. And when the soup was a little thin or the cheap meat too chewy, Al would berate her for her terrible cooking.

"You stupid, heartless bitch! I work hard all day and I need a decent meal! I can't live on this!" Sometimes it would end up on the wall or dumped on her lap. Now he only addressed her two ways, Stupid or Hey You.

She was sure things would change once the house was built. She had to pin her hopes on something. Maybe it would be better when Paul got out of the baby stage or maybe it would be better when Al got a different job or maybe it would be better when he got that truck he said he needed.

CHAPTER SIXTEEN

THE EVIDENCE

August 9

The RCMP set up a command post at the Ranger's Station by Bragg Creek. They were convinced the bodies were near where Al's truck had got stuck. They took aerial photographs of McLean Pond, located adjacent to the McLean Creek Campground. Located in the heart of the Elbow Valley district of Kananaskis Country and flanked by the Elbow River Trail, a dirt road starts at the campground and runs four kilometers straight west until it reaches an intersection. West of the intersection, there's a cut-line called Sylvester Trail. Before these cutlines were graded into trails, they were built by seismograph crews who cut swaths through trees and brush in relatively straight lines for oil and gas exploration. Sylvester Trail is very rough and usually muddy due to the bogs. You have to ford small creeks to negotiate it. It's ideal for thrill rides in all-terrain vehicles, but cars get hopelessly stuck in the deep ruts. Al's truck was found on the trail. The wheels were mired in mud past the hubcaps.

Following Al's instructions the night he was arrested, the RCMP found the truck eight kilometers through the bush from the Elbow Park Ranger Station. It was 1:15 AM. Using flashlights and headlights, they did a preliminary search.

The grimy vehicle was full of garbage. Plastic and paper bags, bottles, paper cups and some clothing. They found one boy's damp swimsuit and a Magnum PI towel stuffed in a Safeway bag, one little girl's Strawberry

Shortcake swimsuit and flowered towel on the floor between two seats, and one male adult swimsuit, still dry, rolled up in a towel. There were all sorts of tools including a hammer, a chain saw, a router, a couple of levels, a drill and a hatchet. There was a small Hibachi barbecue, some briquettes and tongs. They also found some groceries, cookies, barbecue sauce, a bag of tomatoes, five packages of T-bone steaks gone bad, a Calgary Herald newspaper. There was a ball glove, a paper sheath with what appeared to be bloodstains about an inch from the end, paper towels with more stains shoved down between the driver and passenger seat and a map thrown carelessly on the back seat. Underneath the map lay a large carving knife.

The clothing, knife, cardboard sheath and four paper towels were sent to the crime lab in Edmonton. Nothing was found on the knife. Human blood was found on one of the paper towels. It was typed ABO Type A, RH positive. Gabi had this blood type, but so does forty two percent of the population.

The man's blue jean jacket turned out to have blood inside the right sleeve near the cuff. Type ABO Type B. Only 8 percent of the population has this blood type, including Al.

Human blood was also found on the cardboard sheath and one paper towel. It was typed ABO Type AB, RH positive. This is a very rare blood group. Only three per cent of Canadians have it. Paul Dolejs was part of that three per cent.

The discovery of the truck triggered a massive search throughout the rugged terrain. On August 10, forty RCMP officers, three tracking dogs, park rangers, fish and wildlife officers and ten members of the armed forces covered the wet, marshy ground. Swarms of mosquitoes attacked as searchers scoured the foothills, concentrating on trails they felt Al might have followed.

The RCMP took soil samples from the gas pedal of the Ram Charger and the bottom of Al's trousers to Dr. Arthur Limbird, a geology professor at the University of Calgary. Perhaps he could use them to zero in on where Al may have left the kids. They revealed the presence of calcite and dolomite. There were heavy deposits of both in The Bragg Creek and Sylvester Creek areas.

RCMP officer Colin Glabus was one of the Search Masters. The ink was still drying on his certificate in Military Achievement. He'd spent sixteen days in the bush at the armed forces survival camp earning it. Every morning of the search, Colin would kiss his wife and two young boys goodbye, pack a lunch, don big heavy boots, ripcord pants and heavy-duty gloves. He'd grab a shovel and his compass and head into the bush with thirty other qualified searchers. Some days they'd each use half a container of bug repellant. During cold snaps, they had to worry about inclement weather coming over the mountains.

Colin and his partner, Eric Mattson, had their own 4x4 and there were at least five other similar vehicles used in the search. The Sylvester Creek area was extremely boggy. The vehicles were creating huge ruts in the roads and searchers often had to tow each other's trucks out of the muck.

They were instructed to search for mounds which might indicate burial sites. One day Colin and Eric came upon a mound that looked suspicious. They were hesitant to dig because of what they might find. Shivers ran up and down Colin's spine and an eerie feeling came over him. Eric's eyes were wide. He was thinking the same thing. They'd found the kids.

The ground was solid, so when Eric attempted to dig, he made no headway. Colin took his pick ax and began chipping away at it. Suddenly the ax dug in, six to eight inches. Colin pulled it out and it came up dripping what appeared to be blood.

Colin had dealt with a great many terrible things on the job. He'd taken a statement from an eleven year old girl on the highway who'd just seen her father and brother die in front of her in a head-on collision. He remembered a woman dying in his arms while a car full of skiers pulled up beside him demanding he re-open the highway so they wouldn't miss half a day on the slopes. He'd even come upon a highway accident where the windshield of a car had shattered after hitting a moose and shards of glass were driven in to the driver's eyes. Every time the man moved his eyes he sustained more cuts, so Colin reached into his sockets and held his eyeballs still until the ambulance arrived.

But the horror he felt at seeing the bloody ax was beyond all that. They began digging again with trepidation. But after thoroughly dissecting the whole knoll, they found nothing but the red, gooey substance they had mistaken for blood. Later, they learned that in the Sylvester Creek area the wind and dirt blows through the forest in the fall, collecting the red autumn leaves and sap from the trees. The wind deposits its cache in low-lying areas creating these red heaps of decaying vegetation. It's a rare phenomenon and unique to the area.

Another time, Colin was riding with searcher Jim Messner. They were en route to the area where the truck was found. They could hear the dense hum of the police chopper overhead. The helicopter was equipped with FLAIR, or Forward Looking InfraRed, an attachment that seeks heat. John Cantafio says he has used it to find hydroponics marijuana growing operations. "It picks up heat from the grow lamps. Very successful. It's really slick." The pilots were hoping that Paul and Gabi were still alive and would be giving off warmth or worse case scenario, their decomposing bodies would be doing the same.

As their Suburban negotiated the difficult trails, Colin requested Jim pull over so he could relieve himself. He trekked off into the bush and as John Cantafio later put it, "Went number two." Afterward, they continued searching.

A little while later, they received a call from the helicopter, FLAIR was picking up a hot spot nearby. Colin and Jim raced to the co-ordinates given. Much to Colin's embarrassment, they were directed to his recent deposit. Needless to say, when the story got out, Colin was the target of a ton of ribbing. Even Cantafio came up with a saying.

"Does a bear shit in the woods? Not like Colin Glabus."

CHAPTER SEVENTEEN

PAUL'S TEACHER

Although the RCMP requested civilians not get involved in the search lest they mess up the crime scene, everyone who knew the kids wanted to help somehow. John Orme is a kind, decent 41-year-old, with very sad green eyes. He's a runner and each morning he takes on ten kilometers of rough, but beautiful terrain outside his hometown of Okotoks, about a twenty-minute drive south of Calgary.

John was Paul's Grade Six homeroom teacher at Southwood Elementary and, like the awful coincidences that linked John Bascom and Nick Kyska to the Ian Gordon case, John was the Grade Six teacher of bright young student, Kayla Gordon. On February 4, 1998 in Calgary, Ian Gordon, a man not unlike Alois Dolejs, killed his common law wife, Linda Kriske, as she was walking out the laundry room door with her bags packed. After months of verbal and emotional abuse, she finally summoned up the nerve to turn her back on their relationship. She hated to go because of her love for his children, 14-year-old Kayla and 9-year-old Liane.

Ian was determined Linda would never leave him and plotted to murder her on Valentine's Day. But Linda accelerated her plans and on that day in early February at 1:30 PM, as she reached for the doorknob, Ian stormed into the laundry room holding an ax high above his head. He bought the blunt end down on the back of her skull five times. Then he checked his watch. A couple more hours before he could pick the kids up from school without suspicion. A student he tutored in math was due to arrive any minute. Ian closed the laundry room door and prepared the lesson.

Ian was sweating and jittery as he and the student went over the material. The teenager's stomach began rumbling. He glanced surreptitiously toward the kitchen door. Linda would usually pop her head in to say hello and make him a grilled cheese sandwich. He wondered where she was today. Suddenly, Ian said he had to wrap things up early and the boy left.

At 2:10 PM, Ian drove three blocks to Nickle Junior High where John Orme was teaching his daughter, Kayla. John had been Kayla's homeroom teacher a couple of years previously, but now he taught her math and computer skills. She was a great kid and because of his affection for her, John was nice to Ian, even though he gave John the creeps.

Perhaps because Kayla spoke so highly of John, Ian decided he wanted to be friends, so he would phone John at home.

"He would start out on the pretext of talking about Kayla then, 'How are you doing? How are the kids? What are you doing tonight? What are you doing this weekend?' That kind of stuff. None of his business." Initially, John was polite, for Kayla's sake.

"I went out for lunch a couple times. We boated on the Sheep River in Okotoks with Kayla and Liane and my kids, Kari and Christian. We went on a bike ride with him from Calgary to Okotoks. Once, my family went to his house for dinner. That made my wife, Margaret, realize that she didn't want anything to do with this guy. She sensed that there was nothing substantial. It was just a feeling she had.

"He would push Liane away. She would try to snuggle and he would actually move her away from him. I had seen him holding hands with her, but never Kayla. They'd walk into the school holding hands. I do remember that. But I also remember him pushing them away. My wife saw he was very controlling. She noticed he had to have things his way. She's a good judge of people and usually I am too. But it took me a little bit longer to realize that maybe I was being manipulated.

"So I started distancing myself from him. But even though my responses were minimal, he kept phoning. And it was almost like, 'Why are you phoning me?' It didn't make any sense. He phoned me two, three weeks before he did this horrible thing, out of the blue one night and he was just absolutely silly. He was asking me stupid questions that didn't relate to anything else, like, 'What's going on? What are you doing right now?' I don't know what it was all about. I made that call really short. I was really quite annoyed. And I just remember thinking, 'Why did he phone me?'"

The day he killed his family, Ian arrived at John Orme's classroom around 2:15 to pick up Kayla.

"He came and talked to me for ten minutes. He was a little bit...he was a little funny. Maybe nervous. He kept looking at his watch. He wanted to get her and leave. It was more a feeling he was in a hurry. But we talked about things. I always talk about," John smiles a little. "Maybe whine a bit about the computers, something was screwing up on me, that kind of talk, and then he said to me, 'Well, you've learned a lot.'"

John squints up at the ceiling trying to remember the details of their last conversation. "He looked a little bit disheveled. His appearance was a little disorganized and he looked a little bit pale. He had bad breath, but not alcohol or anything like that. It was just more...like he hadn't taken care of himself that day."

Ian and Kayla drove back to their big house on Bonaventure Drive. Kayla could see her dad was upset. He was fidgety. She was working on a project for Mr. Orme, so she headed into the computer room and sat down. Her dad would have to go pick Liane up soon. She heard something behind her and turned. As Ian swung the ax downward toward his daughter's head, she raised her arms to try to stop the blows. But he hit her again and again until she was dead. She was found curled up on the floor in a fetal position.

Ian glanced at his watch again. Just after three. Time to get Liane. He hopped in the car and drove to the nearby elementary school. There, he calmly loaded a math program into the school computer to help the staff. Then he took Liane by the hand and led her to the car. When they got home Liane fixed herself a snack and took it to her room. She wanted to listen to her new Spice Girls CD and do her homework. She was leaning over her books when her dad snuck up behind her and struck her in the back of the head with the same bloody ax he had used to kill Linda and Kayla. He continued bludgeoning her until she fell lifeless to the floor.

Dropping the ax and kicking it under Liane's bed, Ian slunk up to his bedroom and administered some half-hearted, superficial gashes to his wrists, then called 911 and said he had killed his common-law wife because, "She was leaving me." When police arrived, he was bleeding, but very much alive.

In September of 1998, Ian was sentenced to life in prison without parole for 23 years for the second-degree murder of all three.

In the aftermath of these murders, John still suffers.

"I've had thoughts that he's going to get out some day and kill my kids because we knew him and he knows us. I imagine I've come home and he's been there already or he's there and he's killed my kids. Totally irrational."

When John heard about Paul and Gabi's disappearance, he was overwhelmed with the desire to help. He and his pretty wife, Margaret, were in their new red VW Rabbit heading back home to Okotoks from Calgary.

"On the radio it said that Paul and Gabi Dolejs were missing. I remember my wife looking at me and we just kind of knew that something was wrong."

"Paul was a great kid. The kind like you'd want your son to be. He was good looking. He was smart. He was respectful. He was open. Other kids liked him. He was a good student. I loved having him in my class. We had a good relationship."

When John turned to Margaret that day, tears sprang to his eyes. He knew how scared Paul was of his father. "Paul told me a couple of times that he was really afraid of his father. In one situation, they had gone camping in Banff and he actually ran away from the campsite and went to the RCMP. When he came back the following Monday, he recalled the story for me and said he thought his father was going to hurt him so he ran away. I asked him a couple questions about what exactly had happened. He said, 'My dad pushed me under the water and I got really scared.' Then he told me about the RCMP and I think his impression was they didn't quite believe him and they didn't do much about it. Then I reported it to the principal.

"The funny thing is both Margaret and I got it into our minds that we would start looking for them. We discussed going to Kananaskis. We were always on the lookout for these kids. We followed a van one night. This is how irrational you can get when you're emotional. You can do things that you normally wouldn't do. Shortly before we went back to school, we were in Okotoks going for a drive and following this van around for about ten minutes. In Okotoks, you can only go so many places, but he seemed to be just driving around aimlessly. So that was kind of odd. He didn't seem to be going anywhere. I guess that's why the guy was suspicious. Well, he actually stopped. I think he sensed we were following him so he stopped and we just kept on going."

John bows his head a moment. "I think the earth misses kids like the Kaylas and the Pauls. They should be here because they're really good people and it's really a shame they're not. Instead, the monsters are left. That's really hard for me to figure out. If there is a God, why does this happen?"

CHAPTER EIGHTEEN

LAST SEEN

Information was starting to come in.

Sunday, July 27, 3:30 PM

Coronation, Alberta resident Ruth Lindmark, her two teenage daughters and husband, Bruce, were out riding their four-wheel all-terrain vehicles, heading north on Sylvester Trail. It was the third summer in a row they'd chosen that spot. Few parks were designated for Quadrunners and this was one of the prettiest.

Just south of McLean Creek they crested a hill with Bruce in the lead, the girls in the middle, and Ruth at the back. A truck came at them from the opposite direction. They had to pull right off the trail as a Dodge Ram Charger came barreling through. The driver was a man with glasses. He had a stubbly beard and untidy hair. When you meet people on these secluded trails, usually they stop for a quick chat. Ruth's girls waved at the driver, but he ignored them. "Talk about unfriendly," Ruth remarked.

Almost two weeks later, Ruth heard on the television news the description of the Dodge in connection with a kidnapping and called police. She agreed to be hypnotized and made an additional observation. There were two people in the truck, the driver and a smaller passenger with glasses.

Monday, July 28, 9:45 AM

Kananaskis employee Katherine Edwards was assigned to clean the washrooms at Gooseberry campground. She knocked and got no answer, but when she tried the door, it was locked. "I'm busy!" came a surly reply.

A short while later Al emerged carrying a roll of toilet paper. He looked rumpled as if he just woke up.

"I'm sorry," she offered, but he just looked at her and walked away.

Between 11:00 and 11:30 AM, Ruth Lindmark and her family noticed the same vehicle one kilometer south of where they'd seen it the day before. It was facing south with the front wheels mired deep in the mud.

Tuesday, July 29, 1:30

Doug Milo and his common law wife, Carol Labelle, noticed a 'Blazer type vehicle' stuck in the mud on Sylvester Trail.

Wednesday, July 30

Milo spotted the vehicle in the same location. No apparent change.

Paul Viergutz, an employee of the Entheos Retreat Center, an exclusive, cedar-sided facility nestled in the forest on Number 8 highway halfway between Bragg Creek and Calgary, reported Al walked into the Center. He was nervous and dirty.

"What is this place?" He demanded. Viergutz gave a brief explanation and Al left.

Another person in the area, Ron Jackson, noted Al's vehicle stuck in the mud on Sylvester Trail.

Mackay Brown, a dirt trucker, came upon Al's truck on Sylvester Trail. He walked around it, but all the windows were rolled up and no one was around.

The calls continued. After the search for Al hit the news, more than twenty people called to report they saw the Ramcharger stuck in the mud on Sylvester Trail.

Even Frederick Bakker, the driver who picked up Al hitchhiking on August 7th, the day he was arrested, called. He said he picked him up at the mailbox entrance to Redwood Meadows on Highway 22 and dropped him off at the intersection of Richmond road and Highway 22 near the Clem Gardner Bridge.

When Al took the kids, he was working as a carpenter at a small woodworking shop called Interior Woods. He didn't show up for work on July 28. There were sixteen other employees including a shop laborer, Gerard David Bursey. Gerry had known Al a couple of years. He considered Al a loner.

"Al didn't have close friends on the job. His big interest was his kid's hockey games. He'd complain about the referees' bad calls and say his kid's team should have won." One quality Al had that Gerry marveled at was the way he worked at the same steady pace whether work was slow or the place was going crazy.

Gerry told RCMP investigators that on July 27, he was returning from a fishing trip in the Bragg Creek area. As he was leaving the area at around 1:30 PM, he saw Al entering the turn off towards McLean Creek. They passed each other on the highway. Gerry waved and said to his friends in the vehicle, "Oh, there's Al." Al didn't see him, but Gerry noted Al's little girl was seated in the front seat beside him. He'd seen them together at the beginning of the year at a company party. They seemed close.

Another part of the story came from a student about the same age as Paul. Neil White didn't care much for school. A Grade Five student at St. Dominic Elementary School in Dalhousie, a middle income area in northwest Calgary, Neil failed grade One and admitted he got "mostly Fs." Nevertheless, Neil was a likable kid who made friends easily.

On Sunday, July 27, his folks took him and his older brother, Jason, and younger brother, Kevin, fishing at Allan Bill Pond, just past McLean Creek. The family loved the outdoors and went camping in that area almost every weekend, so Neil was familiar with the area and liked to explore. That day, he left his family and headed off to the east side of the pond by a dam. He liked the fishing there better. He saw a couple of kids, so he hurried over to them and sat down on a rock by the water's edge and cast his line.

There was a boy about his age and a girl a little younger. The boy had short brown hair and was thin and athletic. The girl had short hair too and pink glasses. Neil sat closest to the boy.

"Hi," he said.

"Hi," the boy replied.

"Catch any fish?" Neil inquired.

"No." Both answered together.

Neil could see a man sitting at a picnic table about three meters away. His fishing rod was leaning up against the wooden slats of the tabletop and he had his hand resting under his chin. He looked pretty grumpy and he never took his eyes off the two kids.

"That your Dad?" Neil asked. The boy nodded.

"I'm Neil. What's your names?"

"I'm Paul and my sister is Gabriela."

Their Dad called to them in a funny language and Paul turned and answered in the same language.

Neil studied the man who was frowning. He called out, "Hi."

The man ignored him.

Neil shrugged. "What kind of bait are you using?"

Paul said, "Red salmon eggs."

"Hmm, I've never tried that. I'm using corn," Neil informed him.

"Does it work?" asked Paul.

"Oh yeah," Neil replied. Neil stole another glance at Paul's dad, then lowered his voice a little. "Where's your Mom?"

"They're divorced," Paul answered.

The boys continued to chat mostly about fishing and sports. Gabi said very little. Then Paul's line became tangled. His dad came over and untangled it. He said something to Paul, but Neil couldn't understand what it was and Paul didn't answer him.

"Where are your parents from?" Neil wanted to know.

"Czechoslovakia." Paul told him.

The next weekend as the Whites were packing up their campsite, they had their ghetto blaster tuned to a local country music station. At the newsbreak, Neil thought he heard two girls were missing in the area then he heard their names, Paul and Gabriela Dolejs.

"Dad!" Neil exclaimed. "I know them! I saw those two kids here last week!"

Neil's Dad looked at him. "The two kids you were fishing with last Sunday?"

"Yeah!"

His Dad's brow furrowed. "Neil, you better be telling the truth because you don't want the RCMP to be going on a wild goose chase."

"I swear Dad!" Neil was adamant. "Paul and Gabriel. Those were the names. We fished for about a half hour and they were with their Dad!"

Neil's family loaded up their gear and headed for the Park Ranger station.

CHAPTER NINETEEN

GABI

Liba didn't like the idea of only children and shared this with Al. "I don't think it's good for them. I don't think it's good for the parents either. Anyway I'm spending most of my time taking care of one baby, two wouldn't be much more work. If we are ever to have another, now is the time."

Al agreed. In fact, it seemed to cheer him up. Living with him became more tolerable. But as soon as they moved into the new house, Al's sourness returned. When she got pregnant again, despite his eagerness at the outset, he became physically abusive.

Liba was five months pregnant and could not believe her luck. She felt great. No morning sickness, no bleeding, she was sailing. She picked up Paul from daycare and they sang nursery rhymes in Czech all the way home. He was so clever. His favorite was Byl Jeden Domecek, Once There was a Little House.

She'd recently purchased a small Datsun so didn't have to take the bus any longer and it was heaven. She lifted her squirming little boy out of his car seat and placed him down gently on the driveway. She slipped her index finger into his little fist.

"Kde je ta ryba? Where is the fish?" he sang.

"Kocka ji snedla. A cat ate it," she replied, pleased with his excellent pronunciation.

He pulled her up the walk toward the house. It was a good day. She would make Al a nice supper and perhaps he would not get angry. He'd been flipping out over the most insignificant things lately, a lost tool, a dirty glass in the sink, a favorite shirt not yet washed. He barely looked up from the television when they entered, but that was a good sign.

She chatted happily with Paul while cutting butter into a heap of flour for cookies. She was being very careful because the counter was new. Suddenly Al barreled into the kitchen screaming.

"You stupid, careless bitch! You are slicing my counter! You are ruining my house on purpose!"

Liba swiped the counter with her hand revealing no damage. "I was using the blunt end of the knife Al. Before you start accusing people, you should check the facts first."

Her remarks enraged him. He couldn't bear to be corrected. He grabbed her wrist and started swinging at her with his free hand. She tried to back away out of the kitchen, away from Paul. She fell to the ground and curled up to prevent him from reaching her stomach. The punches landed everywhere, her head, shoulders, even in the stomach. She crossed her arms in front of her, attempting to protect her unborn child. Though his eyes were filled with hatred, he wasn't attacking wildly. His blows were calculated not to mark her face. He finally ran out of steam and after landing a few more painful kicks to her ribs he simply walked away.

They said nothing to each other for the next couple of days. Then three nights later, he crawled into bed beside her and very gently began to stroke her back. Hurt and unsure, she turned toward him. He leaned close and covered her neck with soft kisses. His actions seemed apologetic. She wanted badly to forgive him and tried to return his affection, but when his hands began to explore her body she found she couldn't bear his touch. She pushed him away and turned back on her side facing away from him.

She was overdue by a few days, not a lot, when Dr. Johnson decided it would be wise to induce labor. Al drove her to the hospital after supper. The plan was to keep her overnight then induce her the next day, but at midnight she went into labor. Gabi was born at 4:30 AM, July 24, 1976.

Liba didn't feel like talking to Al. He'd been so irritable lately. But she called him an hour or so later and told him he had a daughter.

That night she had the bad dream about Paul killing Al with an axe in the woods. Of course, she was worried about Paul at home alone with Al. Strangely, she was more worried about Paul's future than the present. She could not put a finger on anything more specific than that. She'd had accurate premonitions before and she hoped this wasn't one of them.

When they first moved to Calgary and Stan had his first job in the summer of 1970, he was helping on the construction of a warehouse in the north part of the city. It was a steel structure and he was up three or four stories under a metal roof, grinding down some metal beams with an electric grinder. The temperature where he stood was 40 degrees. You could fry an egg on the girders. He passed out momentarily and dropped the grinder while it was still running. It sliced his knee. He came to and found himself dangling on the edge of the open floor. He grabbed one of the support beams and pulled himself back up. One of the other workers took him to the hospital for a few stitches, but otherwise he was just shaken.

During Stan's close call, Liba was at home when a terrible tightening in her chest and throat suddenly overwhelmed her. She started perspiring and panting heavily. She knew something was wrong and had to sit down.

Eight years later she was married to Al. It was about two in the afternoon. She was busy drafting at work when her heart starting palpitating and the same horrible feeling came over her. She had to stop working until she could compose herself.

When she got home, she learned that Al and his co-worker, Mike Machata, had been framing a basement wall with pressure treated wood which is very heavy. It wasn't anchored and the whole wall toppled over on Al. It missed his head, pinning him from the chest down. The only thing that saved him was a small heap of wood stacked on the floor. When the wall tipped over, it hit the wood and he was trapped in a little cavity between the stack and the ground. Mike grabbed him by the armpits and pulled him out. Al twisted his ankle a bit, but that was all.

To this day, Liba wishes that wall had crushed the life out of him.

Liba had always thought Gabriela such a pretty name. She didn't mind when Al wanted to name the baby after his mother and sister because he was so delighted with Gabi. Al loved having a little girl and bonded with her immediately. He still wouldn't change diapers or wash bottles, but at least he would play with her and hold her in his arms. She was so pretty with her soft pink skin and downy blonde hair. She was everything Paul wasn't. She slept well, fed well and was a happy, contented baby. When she gooed and gahed at him, Liba could almost swear Al looked happy. Because of her limited experience with babies, Liba thought Paul was typical, so she was prepared for another rocket-powered infant.

Soon after Gabi was born, Liba felt a desperate need to get back into shape. She began to run again. Each night, she jogged along a little loop through the sub-division that took 22 minutes. It infuriated Al that she wanted him to look after the children for even that short time.

Paul always liked being outside, so the first few runs he wanted to go with her. "No, honey," she told him, "It's Mommy's turn to go outside now. I'm just going for a run and I'll be back."

Paul would be all right with this, not happy, but satisfied with her explanation. Then Al would come to the door as she was leaving and bend down beside him.

"You see Mommy's going away without you. Mommy's going away. You see, she's not taking you with her. You can't go outside. Mommy doesn't like us. Mommy's going away."

Paul would look at her, his big brown eyes filling with tears and his face would crumple. Al would flash her a self-satisfied smirk then get up and go back to the television.

At first she thought, "Al, you son of a bitch, I'm not going to get manipulated like that!" And though it broke her heart, she'd leave. But after a couple of times she couldn't stand Paul's hurt. The next time Al started in on Paul, she smiled and took him to the big clock in the kitchen. She touched the big hand and said, "You see this hand? Don't watch the little hand but the big hand. You can't tell looking at it now, but it moves. So you can play and once in a while come and have a look at it. And when the big hand reaches here," showing him a spot twenty minutes away, "I'm going to be back home."

Paul learned to ignore what his father was saying and trust that when his Mommy promised to be somewhere she meant it.

And she never let him down.

CHAPTER TWENTY

THE DEAL

August 9, Afternoon and evening

It was Danny Lyon's turn again. He entered the room at 3:00 PM carrying a Bible. "We're continuing to check out your story, Al. We have lots of leads since this thing broke and witnesses are starting to come forward. We now know your whereabouts at different times. You were seen places, Al. It won't be long before we find the kids. We have searchers everywhere in that bush. Dogs too. The pieces are slowly coming together."

He was silent a moment. "You know Al, you might have gotten away with this if your truck hadn't gotten stuck. That's where your plan failed. I just...I am convinced deep down you want to help us locate your kids, but can't for some reason."

"I don't have to say anything," Al said.

Danny pointed at him and raised his voice. "Whether you help or not, we'll find them. Even if we have to keep searching forever!" Danny went on to explain how hundreds of officers had mapped out a grid of the area and were covering every inch. "It's costing thousands of dollars a day, Al."

Al snorted, "That's not my problem. It's maybe only penny a day for a person in this country anyways. So is insignificant."

Danny presented Al with the Bible. "Swear on this, Al. Swear you didn't hurt your kids."

Al refused.

Danny pulled out pictures of Paul and Gabi, placed them on the Bible and said, "Look at them, Al."

Al stared at the photos.

"Did you hurt them?" Danny demanded. "Maybe they are alive. Tell me!"

No answer.

Danny hung his head and his voice broke. "It's not right to leave them out there."

Al looked at him. "I know you are just doing your job. No matter what you would do to me, I still won't say. You are no different than the police in Czechoslovakia. You bring in other officers and they can beat me up. I will never tell you."

On his way to see Al again, Father John passed Danny looking downcast in the hallway. Father John closed his eyes and said a silent prayer. He really needed some help. Despite his training, he was dealing with someone who was so bitter and so angry it was impossible to break through. The police had instructed him to let Al know they'd be prepared to be more lenient with him if he would cooperate.

"Alois," he implored. "If one knew where the children were, the police have assured me things will go better for you and I believe them."

No reply.

"Do you love your children, Alois?"

Something flickered in Al's eyes and there was a slight nod.

Encouraged, Father John continued. "How do you feel about their welfare? Is there anything you could do to contribute to helping them? You know it's never too late, Al. And if not them, perhaps make things right for those who are living. Your wife, your family must be terribly worried."

Al's expression turned to stone.

Father John noticed Al had a Bible on the bed next to him. "What about their spiritual welfare?"

Al grimaced. "Kids were never baptized."

"Ah," said the priest.

"What happens then when children die?" Al asked.

"If those children aren't baptized?"

Al nodded, "Or last rights?"

Father John sighed. "God is merciful, Al."

After Father John left, Danny stuck his head in the door. "Your supper is ready, Al, it's on it's way."

Al glanced at the Bible sitting next to him. "I will think. You come see me when I am done eating."

At seven o'clock, Al told a guard to fetch the officer. Danny immediately noticed a marked change in Al. He had his feet up on a chair and had adopted an attitude. His expression was smug.

"Sit down," he said to Danny. "You listen. Don't get mad. I'm going explain how I feel about this." He claimed the whole thing could have been cleared up by now if the police had just got John Bascom involved. "But it feels like you guys want to break me yourself." His tone was defiant. "Well, you can't do that. I do what I want. You guys want to be heroes. You want get praise, get ahead. Get promoted."

Danny disagreed. "Listen, we're not necessarily trying to prove you guilty, Al. We also prove people innocent."

Al sneered at him. "I think we should get back to the problem." He told Danny it didn't matter if they spent millions on the search, but on the other hand, he had to make things right for some people and look after himself.

Then he said, "Maybe we make a deal to get things done." He wanted to talk about the charges.

Danny said, "I don't know what you mean."

Al tipped back in his chair a little and folded his hands behind his head. "I can't deal with you anyways. You have bosses, or maybe lawyers can work it out."

Danny didn't want Al wiggling off the hook. "You want to talk about charges for cooperation in locating the bodies."

Al shrugged. "Basically."

Al had slaughtered his children and now he wanted a deal. He would agree to give up the bodies if they reduced the charges against him to second degree. Finally, it looked like Al was going to play ball.

Al adjusted his feet to a more comfortable position. "We could go out there six o'clock in morning when is light and be done," he sniffed derisively.

Danny told Al he would contact his boss who would then contact the Crown Prosecutor. Al snorted. The lawyers and the prosecutors had no heart and didn't care about the kids.

Danny left the room and contacted Staff Sergeant Mervin William Clare Harrower. The staff called him Munch because of his initials and his round shape. Harrower had a good sense of humor and was often teased. One time he walked into the detachment in full dress, complete with the Mounties trademark scarlet tunic. One of the fellows looked at him with a twinkle in his eye and sighed, "Munch, ya look like a keg of ketchup!" But when push came to shove, Harrower was all business. He placed a call to the prosecutor's office.

When Peter Martin graduated from law school, he articled with the Attorney General's Department. Four years later, he was prosecuting only homicides. For ten years that's almost all he did; murders, rapes or kidnappings. In 1989, Peter prosecuted a guy who murdered a young girl, Christie Mowatt, a child prostitute. His name was Donny McGregor. During the trial, Donny swore he'd kill Peter. When reporters quizzed him after court, Peter was philosophical about it. 'I guess he's right, my day will come. In the meantime, I'll just continue to pay my taxes.'"

One doesn't get the feeling Peter is afraid of anything. He's self-effacing and has a slim, athletic build. He has a merry smile, full of secret amusement on his good looking, angular face and his eyes are keen with intelligence, like a hero in a Dick Francis novel.

A 1985 Calgary Herald article entitled, Top Guns, reports he was born in West Germany and lived there six years until 1956 when he and his family immigrated to Canada. His father was a successful manufacturing executive. Peter entered law school in his hometown of Winnipeg, Manitoba, though he was tempted to join the RCMP.

In the article, Peter is hailed as a prosecutor who has, "an ability to capture images which dig deep into a juror's mind." His remarks at the 1984 trial of Wilbert Thompson, charged with murdering his estranged wife so he could live with their children and his lover, were typical.

It was a complex trial in which Thompson stood charged with splashing gasoline through his car, then setting it on fire on Deerfoot Trail with his wife in the back seat. His lover, Marilyn, had been living with him until shortly before Thompson moved back in with his wife.

"Marilyn's side of the bed isn't cold yet when his wife comes to Calgary," Peter told the jury. "The accused is trapped by the evidence which says loudly he deliberately set this fire. He had reason to. You should not let him get away with murder."

The jury was back in three hours. "Guilty."

Thompson's lawyer, Noel O'Brien, admitted with grudging admiration, "Some of his cross examinations are deadly. He picks up minor points a lot of other prosecutors would miss and blows them up to such a degree that the jury will dislike the witness."

The same article describes Peter as "a man with a flair for the dramatic...recently he startled a jury by pulling a gun from underneath his lawyer's gown to prove how the weapon could be easily hidden."

Peter's former partner, now one of Calgary's top criminal defense lawyers, Balfour Der, worked in the Crown Prosecutor's office at the time. Peter was his mentor. Balfour idolized him and strove to be like him. Balfour talks about the incident with the gun.

"He was prosecuting a fellow by the name of Gary Underwood. The charge was attempted murder revolving around a shooting in a bar and an undercover officer. It was a serious charge because of the gun involved, but it was actually Underwood who got shot. It was claimed he was shot with his own gun when it got turned around on him. The real issue was whether Underwood could have had the gun hidden on his person. So what Peter did was, during the break before his address, he took the gun, the actual exhibit, and put it in his waistband. Then, at the appropriate time in his closing speech to the jury, he pulled the gun out just to show them how easily it could be hidden. I thought that was like Peter, to make his point in a very forceful and entertaining way. Not everyone agreed with that."

On Saturday, August 9, Peter Martin had just returned that day from a holiday so he was completely in the dark about the Dolejs case. His boss, Chief Prosecutor Manfred Delong, rang him up and quickly briefed him. The RCMP wanted to talk about the case. What charges would be appropriate? What kind of evidence did they need to shore it up? Would he meet at the Cochrane Detachment tonight?

When Peter arrived, he was met by half a dozen officers including Lyon, Cantafio and Merv Harrower. Everyone's chief concern was the welfare of the children. There was still lingering hope they might be alive and the fear was because of the very dense wilderness in the bush where they found his vehicle, they might be confined and unable to get help.

The officers told Peter about Al calling Danny Lyon to his cell and how his demeanor had changed. They told him the gist of Al's proposal. 'Maybe we can make a deal. If you drop this first degree charge and change it to second degree, I'll show you where the kids' bodies are.'

In Canada, there are two types of murder, first and second degree. In first degree murder, the Crown must prove three elements, that the murder was intentional, planned and deliberate. If it's only intentional and not planned or deliberate, it's second degree murder.

The sentence for first-degree murder is life imprisonment, no parole for 25 years. It's automatic.

The sentence for second degree murder is also life imprisonment, but there is more flexibility in the question of parole ineligibility. The period of parole ineligibility is fixed between ten years, at the low end, and 25 at the high end. It's up to the judge.

The police were in favor of accepting Al's proposal, even though it was implicit the sentence could be life imprisonment with no parole for ten years, the lowest sentence available for second degree murder.

The officers gathered in the boardroom. They were all dog-tired. They'd been searching non-stop since Thursday and it was now Saturday, 48 grueling hours. Everyone was running on empty. They had had very little sleep and they wanted to make this deal.

If the Crown accepted the proposal, Peter would be obliged to live by it. It was a matter of Crown honor and further, if the Crown broke its word, when dealing with the next guy in a similar situation, he'd say, "Well, what about the last guy? You gave him your word and you broke it. How do I know I can trust you?" The idea that they might make the deal and then renege on it was not an option.

Cantafio watched Peter take a deep breath and hold up his hand for quiet. "Guys, just hang on a second here. Suppose he takes us to the bodies and it's apparent it's first degree? We can't later say, 'Tricked you. Now we're going to charge you with first degree anyway.'"

The room was silent as everyone contemplated the problem. They all felt the killing was unlikely an impulsive one, but rather, intentional. That obviously troubled Peter on a number of fronts. Foremost, if they agreed to the deal, Al would be escaping the full consequences of his act. This was about as serious a crime as one can imagine, a parent killing a child. Peter had to make a decision and make it now.

He said, "Okay, here's my call. I won't do this deal and I don't share your views that we can't prove a murder. I think we will be able to prove a murder with or without the bodies, so don't be concerned about that. Leave that to me. We'll prove it. The only issue will be whether it was first or second."

Turning down the deal would be a tough sell, because police training teaches that a body is needed to sustain a murder conviction. Without one, prosecution was a risky, if not impossible, proposition. The traditional view was, "Unless we have the bodies, we're in real trouble here."

Harrower wasn't happy with Peter's advice. Peter was passing up a quick way to wrap this up. If he said yes, they could take Al out that night or next morning first light.

Cantafio felt differently. "Peter was an awesome prosecutor. And I still have high, high regard for him. He's probably one of the best, if not the best prosecutor I've ever worked with. Because it was Peter, I figured, 'Okay, if Pete says we can do it, we can do it.'"

Peter added another thought. Since Al initiated the deal, it was a statement that could become evidence against him. Al hadn't really admitted anything, but had wanted to put it on the table. It was ambiguous. So Peter turned to Harrower and said, "Listen, we can use that evidence. And frankly, I think you should go back and further discuss what he means. Get it air tight."

The men left with the understanding that Peter wanted confirmation Al was willing to take them to the dead bodies of his children and in exchange for that, he would plead guilty to second degree murder. Danny went back in the room and began talking to Al when Harrower walked in, making it clear to Al he was the superior officer.

Harrower said to him, "I understand from talking to my men that you want to make a deal here and the deal is this." The language was carefully chosen. "You want to show us the location of the bodies of your dead children in exchange for us charging you with second degree murder."

The key element in the question was the information that the children were dead and that he wanted to show the police their bodies in exchange for a charge of second degree murder. This would confirm the children were dead, dispelling any lingering doubt they were confined somewhere. Implicit in his wish for a second degree murder charge was that Al caused their death, as opposed to some sort of accident.

Harrower then handed Al a pen and a map of the area marked with an X of where Al's truck was found on Sylvester Trail. He explained to Al that in order to make a deal they needed more information. Perhaps it would help if Al would show good faith by indicating on the map the area where the children's bodies could be found. Al examined the map for a moment, then drew a rough rectangle north of the X. Harrower squinted at his prisoner.

"As I understand it, these bodies were not sexually assaulted and you are willing to take us to where they are located."

Al shook his head. "I can't do nothing like that anyhow."

Lyon and Harrower exchanged glances.

"It's no joke," Al assured them. Then he told them he was unable to get erections any more.

Harrower asked if they would need any equipment to retrieve the bodies.

Al shook his head in the negative.

Sergeant Harrower stood up to leave. "I don't have the authority to make this decision you understand. I have to make a recommendation to the prosecutors."

Al nodded and Harrower left.

Danny Lyon looked at Al. "Is there anything else on your mind at all, Al?"

Al pursed his lips in thought. "How did you find that priest? Who is he?"

Danny explained they'd looked for someone of his faith who could speak Czech.

Al nodded. "I made a decision after he left."

"A decision?" Danny repeated.

Al blinked. "To talk to you."

"He's supposed to see you again."

"Yes," Al said. "Sunday."

"Let's go have a shower, Al, unless you have anything else."

August 10, Morning

The search for Paul and Gabi Dolejs expanded to 42 people today. This includes nine armed forces personnel who are working with three tracking dogs. Searchers broke into groups of eight, each led by an RCMP officer. It was called off at 8:00 PM, but will resume tomorrow. Searchers have so far, covered 110 square kilometers of brush south of the Elbow Ranger station. Civilians are asked not to help lest they interfere with evidence. RCMP have decided not to send in any more team divers as they are satisfied the children will not be found in any nearby bodies of water.

Sergeant Harrower called Peter and talked again on the phone the next morning. He again urged Peter to accept Al's offer.

Peter was not convinced. Al had made the statement confirming the children were dead. Peter had what he needed. At Al's request, the matter was left between John Bascom and Peter Martin.

They couldn't make a deal.

CHAPTER TWENTY-ONE

THE ANGER

The next time Al beat Liba, Gabi was almost a year old. He lost his temper over some insignificant issue. His muscles were hard because he'd been working construction and his anger increased his strength. He pushed her into a corner by their bedroom window, but it was summer and their windows were open. Their next door neighbors, a Chinese family, were out on their patio entertaining a group of friends. They were laughing and chatting non-stop in Cantonese.

Al began punching her in the same spot on her shoulder, over and over. Liba started screaming. Suddenly their neighbors stopped talking. There was a noticeable silence. A light came on in Al's eyes. People could hear! He ceased hitting her and walked away. Her arms were so bruised and sore, she could not lift them over her head for three weeks and had to wear long sleeves to hide the marks.

A few weeks later, he got mad at her again. This time he stormed into the kitchen and grabbed their heavy wooden salad bowl. Liba gasped as he threw it with all his might against the stainless steel sink. The bowl split in two and dented the sink.

Another time, Liba was vacuuming. She tried over and over to pick up a piece of lint on the carpet, but the vacuum's suction wasn't strong enough. Al grabbed the vacuum still running and, hoisting it over his head, heaved it down the stairs. Liba was dumfounded. He'd just spent days painting and sanding the baseboards in the stairwell until they were perfect.

When he was very young, Paul was a poor sleeper. As hard as he tried, he could not get to sleep easily and when he did, he woke at the drop of a pin. Often after Liba put him to bed he'd get up several times for water or to go to the bathroom or to tell her something. He was anxious. There was always an excuse.

One night when he was two, Paul appeared in the hallway as Al was on his way to bed. Al got rough, grabbing Paul and shaking him. Paul started howling. Liba came running. Al glared at her as she pushed past him to get to her son. Paul was standing in the hall, beside himself.

Liba took his hand and led him back to his room saying, "It's okay honey. I'll go to the bedroom with you." She closed the door and tried to calm him down so he would feel safe. "See, I'm here to protect you. Nobody's going to hurt you. Mommy will make sure of that." Liba knew the probable reason for Paul's feelings of insecurity at night was Al's constant angry outbursts.

Suddenly, Al flew into the room yelling at Liba for being an over-protective mother. "He's going to grow up a sissy! He'll never be a man with you babying him like this."

Liba rolled her eyes. "I'm sorry. He is two years old and he is scared. Just leave us alone." She got up off the bed, pushed him out and closed the door and locked it.

Infuriated, Al stood there staring at the door. Suddenly, he began savagely kicking at it. Liba held Paul tightly as the sound of the kicks thundered throughout the house. Finally the door splintered and Al's foot came through. Then he calmly turned around and retreated back to the living room and the comfort of the television.

His anger wasn't always vented on Paul. In 1975, Gabi was fourteen months old and Liba was offered a partnership in a new land survey company. She knew the risk in doing this, but saw it as an excellent opportunity to get out of a salaried position. She decided to take it. Al was against it.

"It's bad idea," he grumbled, but refused to elaborate.

The partnership required a small initial investment to set up an office. They had fifteen hundred saved to build a garage. She insisted they use the money to set up the business instead. Al was furious, but couldn't say much because it was money Liba had put away. The partners were to meet on a Sunday afternoon to finalize everything, so Liba got up early, fed the kids and made their lunches. She did the laundry and laid out Gabi's diapers and a change of clothes and left her cooing happily in a little plastic rocker chair in the living room beside Al, who was watching television.

"Please Al, all you have to do is watch them. Gabi needs out of her chair in ten minutes. Then change her every hour or so. Their food is on the table in the kitchen and if she gets cranky just put her in her crib for a nap." Liba glanced at her watch. "It's after twelve now, I'll be home by five or six."

The meeting went well, but Liba was worried. She left just after four and, though it was usually an hour's drive, she made it home in 45 minutes. As soon as she opened the door the stench of soiled diaper hit her like a brick in the nose and she nearly tripped over the mound of toys scattered in the foyer. Gabi was sitting in exactly the same place Liba had left her and her face was a deep purple from crying. Liba ran to her and quickly unbuckled the safety belt. As she lifted the baby out, she cried in dismay. Gabi had not moved in five hours. She hadn't been fed and was covered in her own excrement, which had leaked out of the diaper.

Al walked past the room. "Al!" Liba yelled at him. "She is in shit up to her armpits!" He ignored her and retreated to their bedroom. Paul came in dragging a blanket full of toys. He hadn't eaten either and looked exhausted.

Liba got the message. "Contradict my wishes, and your kids will pay the price."

The verbal abuse Al hurled at her escalated. He used the most foul construction language imaginable. He began accusing her of seeing other men.

"You fucking bitch, I know you're screwing around with everybody at your office. You don't work late, you're fucking around with Jerry Votypka!"

"I'm not stupid. I've got enough trouble in my life with one man. Why would I want to have another one?" she shot back.

Jerry, a land surveyor, was a newly divorced co-worker of Liba's. A good ten years older than she, he was taller than Al, slim and balding with a beard. Jerry was sharp as a tack and could be quite nice. He did come on to her a little, but Liba never gave him a second thought.

Jerry socialized with both Al and her. On occasion, she would go for lunch with him, but always Dutch treat. She mentioned this once to Al and immediately regretted it because after that he began accusing her of sleeping with him.

Al was fired from one job after another. He couldn't get along with his bosses or their customers. He was far too confrontational, so he decided to start his own contracting company. He called it Roecliffe Homes. Al owned fifty-one percent and Liba forty-nine. He took out a large mortgage on their existing home and began to build another. Liba studied for her realtor's license so she could sell anything he built and save on broker fees. But housing prices were down, so after all their effort, they barely covered expenses.

Nevertheless Al continued to build houses. The family would move into them and sell the old ones. The reason they weren't making any money was the homes he built were too small. Al decided the answer was building a 2,000 square foot home in Woodbine. Liba disagreed. It was ridiculous. Building a house that size could ruin them financially. But Al was adamant and they bought a lot at 39 Woodglen Road in Woodbine, a new subdivision on the southwest edge of Calgary.

By the time the Woodbine house was completed, Calgary's oil industry was in a slump and nothing was selling. They put it and the small home they lived in on the market at the same. The smaller home sold first, so they moved into Al's 2,000 square foot white elephant. He decided to freelance his services, but had problems soliciting work. When people called for an estimate, he'd go over and ridicule their plans. He'd tell them they were stupid to want a patio built this way or that. He landed some small contracts, but that was all.

Soon after, Jerry dropped in to share a glass of wine with the two of them. He brought his son, David, who was exactly Paul's age and they played together nicely.

It was important to Al to maintain a prosperous front. He started talking about his business, boasting of his success. Liba jumped in supporting him and painting a very rosy picture, emphasizing Al's triumph in being his own boss.

The next day at work Jerry took her aside. "You know, I know Al isn't doing that well. I just wasn't buying your story."

Liba looked at him incredulously. "I don't give a damn whether you bought it or not. The main thing is, he did."

———————

Jerry had a friend named Joe Pecenka. Joe was into white water rafting and kayaking. Although he was a little overweight, he was powerfully built, athletic and had a great sense of humor. Everyone liked Joe. He was a fun guy. He worked as a pipe fitter and had a good income. In the spring of 1977, he bought a sporty green Fiat convertible. Wanting to show it off, he drove to Liba and Jerry's office and went upstairs to fetch them. They came down, admired the car and then went back to work.

Ten days later, Al came home excited. "Jerry's friend, Joe, just bought a new sports car and is it nice."

"Yes I know," she interrupted. "I've seen it."

Al's face contorted in anger. "Where?" he demanded.

"At work. He came by to show it to Jerry."

"When?" he screamed.

Liba shrugged. "I don't know, ten days ago?"

"I knew it. I knew it!" he shouted. "You're doing nothing at work but sitting on your fucking cunt. Sit and yak, going out for lunches and going to look at fancy cars. Nobody else has time to do that. You lazy fucking stupid bitch!"

She walked away shaking her head. She should have known to keep her mouth shut. The violent incidents were growing closer together and escalating in intensity. She was afraid for herself and the children. Everything seemed to set him off.

The next day at work, Jerry could see there was something wrong. Liba told Jerry about the yelling and the accusations.

"Why don't you get a divorce?" he asked her.

Liba spoke from the bottom of her heart. "I've thought about it, but I don't want to because I want the kids to have a father. Anyway, it's kind of a funny feeling. He's eight inches taller, seventy pounds heavier and he's screaming at me until his face turns purple. I guess I should be afraid, yet I feel I am looking down at him. I feel like a much bigger and stronger person."

Liba and the kids were enrolled in Altadore Gymnastic Club. They started going when Paul was six and Gabi four. The minimum age was five, but Gabi really wanted to join. One day as Liba was talking with the program head, Rick McCharles, he noticed tears running down Gabi's face as she stood beside her mother. "What's wrong?" he asked.

Liba ran a gentle hand under Gabi's damp chin. "She really wants to start, but she's only four and a half. I don't suppose you could take her in the program?"

Rick bent down and picked Gabi up from under the armpits. "You know, she's a really solid kid. Why not?"

So began Gabi's foray into gymnastics. Liba got bitten by the bug too and signed up for adult recreational gymnastics. After putting the kids to bed, she'd work out twice a week from nine to ten thirty in the evenings. She carefully organized things so she wouldn't require Al's assistance. He'd heard there were a couple of black guys on the team and this seemed to get his goat. Often as she was leaving, he'd confront her on the stairs.

"I know where you're going! You're going to the gym to fuck those Negroes. You can't fool me you bitch, you cunt!"

Liba stopped replying to his ridiculous accusations and that seemed to infuriate him even more. "You don't even deny it! You fucking whore."

She began secretly scanning the classifieds looking for places for her and the kids to rent. On a Thursday just before Mother's Day, she found a small house in Queensland, a family neighborhood about two miles east of their Woodbine home, and made arrangements to view the house with the owner on the following Monday. She had to be careful Al didn't find out.

She woke up early Sunday morning as usual to get the kids dressed, feed them and make Al breakfast. Then there was the laundry and cleaning. As she sat rubbing her eyes, she could hear Al whispering to the kids in their bedroom. Then she heard them padding down the stairs. She cocked her head puzzled at the sound of cupboards opening and closing in the kitchen. What in heck was going on?

The master bedroom door opened and Paul burst in proudly, carrying a tiny flowerpot with a small Hawaiian Bird of Paradise plant. He had a look of pure joy as he held it out to her and exclaimed, "Happy Mother's Day!" Al was right behind him, holding Gabi's hand. He wore the same lopsided grin he always had when he'd done something awful and felt sheepish.

He had argued with her a few days earlier while in their bedroom. Furious, he'd stormed into their little ensuite and started pounding at the new vanity he'd just installed. It was a fairly sturdy unit so his fists made no impact on the thing. Grabbing his keys from the dresser, he'd gone down to his truck. She had watched out the window as opened the door and rifled through his tool kit. Finding a hammer, he closed the tool kit, locked the truck, came back up to their bedroom, entered the ensuite and went berserk. He demolished the vanity with the hammer. Once done, he seemed calm again. The incident had steeled her resolve to move out.

Now, Liba clasped her hands to her breast and sighed, "Oh Paul and Gabi, it's beautiful!" When she opened her arms, both kids tumbled in.

Liba spent the rest of the day completely torn. She'd grown up in a broken home without a father and she swore she would never do that to her own kids. Now here she was, contemplating that very thing.

Al certainly wasn't the best father in the world, but the kids loved him. He could be nice to them when he felt like it, though he wasn't sincere. But the kids seemed to buy it. It wasn't his natural disposition to be pleasant, but he spent the rest of the day trying hard and she appreciated the effort.

She didn't understand where all his fury was coming from. Maybe he was lonely. He had few friends. He seemed to hate his English environment. He saw nothing positive around him. He was always on guard. If anyone was friendly toward him, the first thing he said was, "This is fishy. What does this person want from me?" Or he'd tell Liba they weren't really nice, "Just phony."

Always suspicious, he became convinced he wouldn't be paid for his contracts. "I know they're going to rip me off. I'll never see the money for this job. You go collect it," he would order Liba. "They won't say no to a woman."

This happened a lot with a Czech contractor named Thomas Pesta. He and his wife ran a Czech restaurant in downtown Calgary called Praha (Prague). All of Liba and Al's friends used to go there, but it closed and Thomas got into construction. Al did carpentry work for him on occasion, but always suspected he would get stiffed on his paycheck. He would make an appointment to pick it up and then send Liba in his stead. Thomas lived in Ranchlands, almost an hour north of Liba and Al's.

Pesta had a modern ranch-style bungalow with French doors leading to an office. She'd follow him into the den with its elegant, expensive office furniture. Rather than just writing the cheque and giving it to her, he'd give her the third degree.

"Where's Al? Why doesn't he pick up his own cheque?"

Liba would have to make up some excuse. He had a cold or he forgot he had to go to the dentist. "What difference does it make to him?" she thought. "Why does he always make me feel like a peasant begging for food?" Thomas would eye her suspiciously as he reluctantly handed over the cheque.

Ten years later in the late nineties, Liba found herself at a banquet for a Czech diplomat at The Palliser Hotel, one of Calgary's oldest and finest establishments. It took her only a moment to realize she and Thomas Pesta were seated at the same table. She had a new name and he didn't recognize her. During dinner conversation, one of the fellows sitting to her right said, "Remember Alois Dolejs? Has anyone heard about what happened to him?"

Pesta piped up, "Believe it or not, the guy actually used to work for me. It was always weird because his wife would come to pick up the money. I was never sure what was going on there, why she felt it necessary to take his money?" Pesta shrugged. "She always collected his paycheck."

Liba had a choice. She could keep her mouth closed or defend herself and satisfy his curiosity. She kept her mouth shut.

When Al wasn't watching television he was sleeping. He constantly complained of being tired. One day while cleaning out some boxes in the basement, Liba found out this was nothing new. Two years of army service was mandatory in Czechoslovakia so, after engineering school, Al was forced into the military. He never told Liba much about his experiences there and said he had no pictures or souvenirs.

However, she came across a picture of a whole bunch of the guys who were with him in his unit. They'd been together the entire two years. In the picture, there was a photo of each guy's head cut out and attached to a drawing with captions. Each fellow's caption was an inside joke. Al was portrayed lying on a cot. Underneath was written, "Just let me sleep."

Liba started chuckling. She could relate. "Man, did they ever hit the nail on the head," she whispered to herself.

When she showed it to Al, he became quite annoyed. He referred to the cartoonist as an idiot. "He didn't know anything about me."

Liba slipped the picture back into the box. "Oh, he knew you all right," she thought.

The only time Al seemed relaxed, or a little bit happy, was when he was with Jiri Srom, his only friend. Liba and Al met Jiri during English classes when Liba was married to Stan. Jiri was a carpenter, a nice looking guy with dirty blonde hair and friendly gray eyes. Unlike all their other immigrant friends who were fairly intense because times were so tough, Jiri took everything with a grain of salt, which made him fun to be with. He and Al sat near each other and he'd break up the class with his wisecracks. One time, each student was asked to describe in English their breakfast that morning. When it was Jiri's turn, he stood up and said, "A Pilsner beer and a Rothmans cigarette." Liba chuckled appreciatively. When they got home Stan berated her.

"Why did you laugh at Jiri like that? Do you have a thing for him?" Liba rolled her eyes. "No Stan. Everyone thought it was funny except you."

"I don't think he's funny." Stan grumbled.

One day toward the end of her relationship with Stan, Jiri came up to her with Al in tow.

"What's wrong with that husband of yours?" he asked. "He's always giving me dirty looks."

"Never mind him." Liba sighed.

"No, what is it? Why is he always mad at me? He told Al here," he thumped Al on the chest with the back of his hand, "I am not welcome to your house for a beer."

Liba cleared her throat and blinked, embarrassed. "Aw he…he thinks every man I talk to, is after me."

Jiri flushed. "That guy's a bonehead!" Beside him, Al nodded in agreement.

"I know." Liba waved it away. "Don't worry about it." But she could hear Jiri complaining to Al as they headed out the door ahead of her. "He's got some stupid ideas, that Stan. Such a weird guy!"

After she and Al moved in together and before they had kids, Jiri often joined them cross-country skiing. They'd get up early so Jiri would spend the night on the couch. Sometimes, after Liba went to bed, Al and Jiri would slip out to the bar, usually the York Hotel, a seedy downtown hangout popular with cabbies. If they got there early enough, they'd have twenty beers or so each, enough to get very drunk.

They'd look at the odd hooker or pretty girl who wandered in. Once in a while Jiri would flirt, but Al was never interested. One of Al's favorite observations when talking to Jiri was. "We couldn't do things like that in the army." Usually, Jiri would crack wise and Al would laugh in his quiet way. Al didn't like to open his mouth. He was self conscious about the way his eye teeth stuck out further than his front teeth. He developed a way of laughing through his nose with his lips clamped shut.

Jiri nicknamed Al, Cannon, after the popular television detective played by William Conrad. Cannon always wore a serious expression and never took off his long coat, even inside, like Al. At the bar, Al would unbutton his long felt overcoat, but he'd leave it on. Because of this, people thought he was a taxi driver who had just stopped in for a quick beer. Customers were always asking him for a ride. This amused Al to no end. In the morning Jiri and Al would sleep it off in the back seat, while Liba drove them up to the mountains. She didn't mind. It was good for Al to have friends.

Jiri and Al would occasionally go hunting with another friend, Peter Hruby. Al never bagged anything, even if they went for two or three days. The three would split up and Jiri or Peter would bag a deer, but Al always came back empty handed.

One time, Jiri, Al and Peter took Jiri's two nephews, aged twelve and thirteen, on a fishing trip. Jiri bought a pig he'd purchased from some Yugoslavians. They planned to barbecue it at their campsite. They found a campground near Carsland, a small town east of Calgary. They set up a couple of tents and dug a fire pit filled with charcoal between them. Once the coals were white hot and the pig was settled on top, the men decided to drive back to Carsland for a drink at the bar. They ordered the nephews to watch the pig and away they went. But it was still light out and the boys were bored. There was a river nearby so they grabbed their rods and decided to catch a couple of fish.

"Hmmm…" wondered Jiri, as the Carsland Volunteer Fire Department raced past them on their way home from the bar, "I wonder where they're going?"

The grass around the smoldering pig had caught fire and destroyed their tents, all of their camping equipment and bushes nearby. No one was hurt because they'd pitched their tents a considerable distance from anyone else.

Jiri and Peter thought it all a great joke and later when Al worked at Interior Wood Products, he laughingly told the story to Gerry Bursey, but his English was so rough, Gerry thought Al said they'd burned down someone's garage while roasting a pig.

CHAPTER TWENTY-TWO

WILL HE BREAK?

In 1986, Sandy Harder was a member of the Royal Canadian Mounted Police stationed in Calgary with the General Investigative Services section. This section was split into two units, crimes against persons and crimes against property. Sandy was on crimes against property, but if something major came up, everybody was involved in it in one way or another.

Twelve years earlier, when she was eighteen, Sandy wanted to go to university, but didn't have the funds. Her mother came home one day with a newspaper article reporting that the RCMP was hiring women. Sandy joined in 1976 and moved from Ontario to Regina, Saskatchewan for training.

Her Calgary unit was plain clothes. When homicides occurred, their job was to support all the detachments in Central Alberta, south to as far as Nanton and north to Red Deer. She was the first and only female in GIS so it was she who was asked to speak to the wife of a guy they had in custody for kidnapping and possibly killing his kids.

August 8

It was 8:45 AM when Sandy arrived at Stuart Engineering in downtown Calgary. At court, Sandy often dressed in simple suits with midi-length skirts. Today, pants and a shirt covered her long, lean figure. Her hair was short and brown, blow-dried in a windswept wave across her forehead. She wore little makeup, just a touch of shadow and eyeliner.

The RCMP didn't encourage it and thanks to her natural good looks, she didn't need much.

Liba's look was even more conservative. She had a trim, sport figure, a little on the busty side. She always felt more at ease in a pair of sweat pants and a tee-shirt than a skirt, but for work it was a necessity.

The first word that popped into Sandy's head as Liba strode toward them at the reception desk was 'Baptist.' Liba's sweater was done up to two buttons, with a white blouse buttoned to her neck and a camel hair skirt hemmed well below her knees.

Liba shook hands almost timidly and searched the officers' eyes. When Sandy and her partner, Burt Broster, informed Liba that Al had been arrested, but was remaining tight-lipped about the kids, she was very quiet. There was no outpouring of grief. It was almost as if she was in shock.

"I don't believe he would hurt the kids," was all she said.

It was Sandy's impression that for the past ten days Liba thought he had them tucked away somewhere and now it was only a matter of time until he revealed where they were. "Oh my God," she thought. "If this woman's children are dead she's going to be totally devastated. I don't think the idea has even crossed her mind."

Sandy's gut instinct told her that since Al was picked up without his vehicle after living in the bush for ten days, he had probably killed them.

She told Liba it was best if she avoided talking to the press. "We're still investigating missing kids so, when you're dealing with a fresh case, you don't want people talking to the news media and saying something that might cause the investigation to get off track. Anything could slip out and if the kids are being held hostage somewhere, it might cause them to be moved. You know what I'm saying?"

Liba nodded. She showed Sandy a letter she received from Al's sister after calling her on July 30 to see if the kids were in Czechoslovakia.

Dear Liba,

I am writing the same day as you phoned. At first I thought that Lola went with the children somewhere for a holiday as I mentioned to you. Of course I didn't know that according to the court's decision the children were not allowed to be with their dad overnight. I have never heard of such a thing before. Lola phoned me a couple of days before you called. He reassured me that he continues to lead an orderly life and mainly, he is in contact with the children.

He is sad because of the separation from you. It bothers him how things ended up between you. And as I analyze this from all sides, we must consider all possible motives and actions resulting from those motives. I am beginning to be afraid more and more that something abominable happened to them.

We are so far away. I tried to dial Lola's phone number but no one answers. I pray that everything may end well. It is difficult really, but there is nothing left but to wish that everybody stays alive and healthy, whatever has happened. When I think of you, I try to put myself into your shoes, but feel just terrible I cannot help. Before you receive this letter, the whole affair will probably be cleared up.

To write you the truth, I am afraid of further information, but the uncertainty is also horrible.

In case the children are home already, pass to them many greetings from me.

Elunka (Gabriela)

Liba expressed a strong interest in helping and Sandy was determined to include her. Liba obviously had a good head on her shoulders and it would be so much better for her than staying at home worrying about the kids. Later on that day, Liba and Sandy boarded an Alberta Forest Service helicopter equipped with an infrared scanner and flew all over the Kananaskis. But the rain was so heavy they couldn't use the heat detector.

Liba's task was to lead them to places she and Al had visited in the past. The RCMP wanted to search for structures Al might be familiar with. They told Liba people often returned to places they previously scouted. She knew of one place west of Bragg Creek. There was a group of corrugated sheet metal shacks used for storing oil field equipment. Then the chopper flew Liba and Sandy over to Sheep River. Liba was amazed at how close to the ground they flew. They were contour flying, following the terrain very closely. She was shocked at how much she could see. She even spotted an empty cigarette package on the ground. "Gabi would love this," Liba caught herself thinking.

She directed them to a place known as Old Burns mines, way up in the mountains on a plateau in the upper reaches of Sheep River and Elbow River. She spotted two old log cabins she and Al had once hiked to. They landed the chopper nearby and forded a creek. Liba's heart was pounding when she approached the cabins. They looked deserted. Oh God, what would they find? The doors were unlocked. The cabins were empty.

Next they flew to a place where the family used to go for Sunday picnics, just south of North Fork Bridge, west of Millarville, by the entrance to Ware Creek Game Reserve. There was a little clearing and a small creek running by their special spot. The creek was pretty with a rock wall on one side and shallow enough for the kids to play in when they were little. The pilot put the chopper down and the little group struck out again. This time they encountered hunters, but no one had seen any sign of Paul and Gabi.

August 10

At Liba's suggestion, Sandy Harder contacted Al's only friend, Jiri Srom. Would he come in and talk with Al?

When he first moved out at Easter, Al stayed with Jiri for a couple of weeks. Jiri remembered Al talking incessantly about the kids, how he wanted to see them more and when was he going to see them next? He'd even set up two big framed eight by ten school pictures of Paul and Gabi on a table right beside his bed in the basement. Jiri shook his head. Now the police were saying he killed them! It didn't make sense.

Jiri took Sandy up on her offer. He'd been sitting on pins and needles anyway. His wife was crying all the time. His own kids were upset. What had Cannon done?

He drove out to Cochrane and the police briefed him. They needed to know where the kids were, dead or alive. The more he could find out, the better. He was led into an interview room. Al was sitting in profile by a table. His shoulders were slumped and head was hanging down.

"Cannon!" Jiri barked.

Al's head snapped up. Seeing Jiri, a faint smile passed over his face. The door closed behind them and Jiri strode over and stood in front of his former friend.

"What the hell happened to you, you stupid idiot?" he roared.

Al ducked his head and looked sheepish. "Something…" he began, as Jiri sat down across from him. "I don't know why or how it happened. Something was not in my head. My brains didn't work, you see. I snapped. I didn't know what the hell happened…until it was too late."

"What do you mean?" Jiri demanded.

Al sighed and shrugged. "I can't remember nothing. Nothing 'til it was over, Jiri. Then…what can I do? It's too late."

Jiri cocked his head disbelieving. "I don't believe in such things as that. Tell me where the kids are buried, Cannon."

Al began to say something, then cleared his throat. "I would like to tell you. I really would like to Jirko! But my lawyer tells me not to say anything. To nobody."

"That's stupid not to tell because everybody is looking for them! Don't be so stubborn, Cannon! Don't be stupid! You are listening to lawyers instead of yourself and your friends?" he sneered. "What do lawyers know? Forget about lawyers! My wife is crying, crying, all the time. Everybody will feel better if you just tell where the kids are. And you won't have to talk about it no more. Come on!"

Al gave him a hangdog look. "I was trying to be a good father and take care of whole family. But it don't work out. Whatever happened can't be fixed no more. I just wish it didn't happen. If I ever get out of here I would like to spend my life doing something good for people."

Jiri continued firing questions at Al for the next little while, but got no satisfaction. Al stubbornly refused to admit he was to blame and would not reveal what he had done with the kids. "I don't know why I did it. It just sort of happened. I don't want to say anything about where it happened or what happened."

Jiri shook his head sadly. "Kids should be taken care of and buried properly."

Al nodded. "I would like that." There was silence for a moment, then Al said, "How is Liba?"

Jiri's eyebrows shot up in surprise. Why would he be asking with such concern about his wife after doing this terrible thing to her? "I haven't seen her, but my wife is talking to her on the phone. I am going to see her today."

At this, Al sat quiet, looking depressed.

"I am getting pretty pissed off at you, Cannon," Jiri growled. "I helped you when I could. First, I helped you learn carpentry. I showed you my books and taught you all the basics. When you needed a place to stay, I let you stay with me and then I helped you find a motel and gave you rent because you wanted your own privacy. I helped you get your job! My wife even baby-sat your kids. Now I want a favor and where are you? Pfffft!" He snapped his fingers angrily.

Al bent his head and shuffled his feet.

Jiri had been at it three quarters of an hour. He realized he was getting nowhere. "Okay. So you prefer to look into the gutter than talk to me." Jiri stood up. "Forget it. I don't want to see you anymore. Good-bye."

Danny Lyon and Merv Harrower were disappointed. They'd hoped they would be spending the day wrapping up the case. But when Peter had turned down Al's offer, they had to start all over again. Time with Al was taking its toll on all of the interrogators. Danny girded his loins and entered the interview room.

Al spotted him and smirked. Danny cleared his throat. "The Crown Prosecutor doesn't want to entertain anything you've said. I guess they are looking at it from a legal point of view and you and I are looking at it from a humanitarian point of view. We're trying to do the right thing for the kids. And, like you said yesterday, they don't care about the kids, do they? What do we do now?"

Al's jaw tightened and he mumbled something incoherent.

"We can have this finished very quickly if you want. I'll tell you, looking at this realistically, you said you wanted the charge dropped from first to second degree and that's natural. That's self preservation."

Al folded his arms across his chest. "We are staying as we are staying. First degree." Al was singing a different tune. Bascom must have told him he didn't think the prosecutor could make a first degree charge stick.

"That's what it's probably gonna be. Because the prosecutor says he's not going to entertain anything else. I told you that yesterday, didn't I?" Danny said.

Al scowled.

Danny sighed wearily. "Like I said, I felt there was enough evidence and they probably wouldn't listen to anything. Sure they'd like to see the children found and dealt with. They will be anyhow. We'll find 'em." He paused and looked at Al.

"Hum? You don't think so? You're shaking your head no. Of course we will. You know we will. It just might take a little longer. I think we talked about selfishness before and I think you are being selfish now. Instead of doing one good thing for those children now, you are just trying to look after yourself.

"The best thing for those kids is to have them dealt with properly. Like you said, we could go out there at six in the morning and it can be done with. That's what you wanted to do. And I agree. You said you wanted to do something for the children but you wanted something for yourself. I understand that, okay? But I can't influence the defense lawyer and the Crown Prosecutors. They can't come to any kind of agreement."

Al shook his head. "I'm not asking you to influence to somebody."

Danny continued asking Al to examine his conscience. Then he said, "It's your decision. If you want to go, we'll go. I'll help you accomplish that task. I've been honest with you, haven't I?"

Al shrugged. "Maybe."

Danny frowned. "Maybe what?"

Al narrowed his eyes. "Maybe you did. Maybe you didn't."

"Didn't what?"

Al's head tipped forward and he stared at the floor peevishly. "Lie."

"No, I didn't." Danny assured him. "Why have you changed your mind? Because you can't get something for yourself?"

"No," Al mumbled.

"Is that why you are hanging your head? Because you feel embarrassed about being selfish?"

"No."

"You say you're not selfish, but what the heck am I supposed to believe? I'm saying, 'Look there's no sexual assault here.' They say, 'Well, we can't be sure until we see.' How am I going to convince them? I've talked to you. I believe you. They say they have to see for themselves."

Al sat back and stared at the wall across from him. "You can talk to me for hours."

Danny rubbed his chin. "Um hum."

Al gave him a crafty sidelong glance. "Or you can go back home."

Danny stared at him hard. "Maybe we should get you some running shoes, go for a drive out there and get this resolved."

Al stuck out his chin. "You cannot do that. It's not going to help."

"You don't think so?"

Al rocked back and forth in his chair. "You say this force is best in the world. It's the same tactic as Gestapo. Second War. Czech police don't drag people over their mountains."

Danny shook his head. "I just said we might go for a drive and have a look."

Al snapped at him. "Drag me around the lake and so on! Sure you...you can grab two guys and drag me wherever you want to. Drag me to Hudson Bay, go ahead!"

"I didn't say I was gonna do that. Morally, I think those kids should be dealt with properly."

"It's over." Al said sulking.

The third and last time Father John saw him, he observed Al was feeling a lot better about himself. Their conversation seemed to flow a lot easier and each was more candid.

"Remember Al, should you elect to receive the sacrament of reconciliation, I cannot say anything. I will not say anything to anyone about what you tell me. Are you not concerned for their souls, Alois?"

Al fixed his gaze upon the priest and nodded again. But indicated nothing more.

After a few moments Al told Father John that he had felt shut out of his wife's life and that she hadn't given him any opportunity to try to come back or to reconcile after their separation. From that, Father John gathered Al's reasoning for not returning the children.

"Basically he was saying, 'Well there is only one way that I am going to hurt you because you have hurt me.' And so he took the children away from her."

Father John spent nearly an hour with Al and although Father John described the conversation as rather warm and close, they talked only in general terms. Later Father John would say, "That's what I found the greatest challenge. No matter what I tried to suggest to him, there was no way that he was going to respond. There was no willingness to communicate whatsoever. It just seemed that there was so much bitterness there, so much anger toward his wife that he just wouldn't bring himself to give up any kind of information. It was like he had shut everybody out."

The experience affected Father John deeply. He felt enormous sadness in his heart for Al's wife, Liba, the children and Al. Even though, intellectually, he knew he could not make Alois talk about the children, he had a sense of regret. Maybe if he could have done this or said that, maybe something might have changed. Perhaps Al would have shown some remorse, broken down, cried or done something.

"I think," sighed Father John, "that was my agony."

CHAPTER TWENTY-THREE

DADDY SOMEDAY

Paul always got along well with his sister. Even when they were little, they never fought and loved playing together. Gabi adored Paul and stuck to him like glue. As soon as she learned to walk, she was two steps behind him. And, unlike a lot of big brothers, he never found her irritating. Knowing she was always behind him seemed to give him a certain sense of security. Liba and Al both got a kick out of watching her follow him, especially when she was tiny. They called her his little puppy dog.

One day when Gabi was three and Paul five, Al was watching television with Gabi playing on the floor at his feet. Liba was sitting opposite him on the couch reading a book. Paul was piecing together a puzzle in the dining room area adjoining the living room. Liba had the area cleared of furniture and they used it as a playroom.

Paul decided to go to the kitchen for a glass of juice. As soon as he stood up, Gabi was on her feet following him to kitchen. He took down two glasses and poured one each. They drank it up, put their glasses on the counter and she followed him back into the living room. She made her way over to Al and stood watching Paul. As soon as he sat down to his puzzle, she plopped down on the floor and resumed playing. A few minutes later, Paul got up to get a cracker and Gabi was right behind him. As his parents watched Paul move into the kitchen with Gabi on his tail, Al and Liba's eyes met and in a rare moment of warmth, they both started to laugh.

Al was nicer to everybody when company was around. That autumn his parents came over for a visit from Pardubice. They were supposed to stay for six weeks, but the kids really loved having Grandma and Grandpa there. Especially Grandma. They were all over her, snuggling and hugging. Mother Dolejs was talkative so it was a huge boost for their Czech vocabulary and both parents were well educated so they wanted to know how things worked in Canada. Liba was glad to elaborate. She found herself really enjoying their visit.

Al's mother was a matronly type, five foot two, an inch shorter than Liba, a little chubby, with scrubbed cheeks and cropped gray hair pulled out of pincurls. She made it her business to make sure everybody was fed. She cooked and baked and her house was spotless. Her life centered on the family. In contrast to Liba's tomboy nature, Al's mother was girlish and quite emotional, but, like Liba, she was keenly observant. Al's father also centered on the family, but in a more passive manner. He seemed to have no other interests or pursuits of any kind.

Al was a good boy when his parents were around. He minded his manners, but it was difficult for him. Once in a while, he would slip a little and begin making a rude comment to Liba or start complaining about something and then he would remember and back off. Liba could see his struggle, but his parents seemed oblivious to it.

Al smoked two or three cigarettes a day. He would light up at coffee breaks on construction or at home after supper. But he knew his parents wouldn't approve, so he quit smoking. Mother and son did not talk a whole lot. The atmosphere between them was strained. When she was around, he was careful not to cross her. He worked hard to look like a model father and husband.

Paul and Gabi shared a room so there was an extra bedroom. Everyone was very comfortable. When Al and Liba were lying in bed one night, Al turned to her and, in his sweetest voice, broached the subject of having them stay longer.

"Liba, what if we invite them not to go back after six weeks? They are retired so what difference does it make?"

Liba thought about this a moment. She loved the way Al acted with them there. He was as tame as a kitten. Al's mother was great with the kids. They just loved her and since she'd arrived, the kids had not spent any time in daycare.

"Well, I like your parents, Al. The kids are picking up the Czech language really nicely. I always wanted them to be bilingual. So it sounds fine."

Together, they presented Al's parents with the idea of prolonging their stay. Father Dolejs replied, "We'd be happy to stay an extra week or two or so."

Liba smiled. "What we meant was more like half a year. We have to cancel your return flight and it's fairly expensive to make a change so we'd like you to stay a lot longer to make it worthwhile, not just two weeks or so."

"We'll have to discuss it," Mother Dolejs informed them. "We'll tell you tomorrow."

The next day, Mother Dolejs announced she would stay, but Alois Sr. would go home as originally planned. They had placed an order for someone to fix the garage door at home and he was expected just after their scheduled return. In Czechoslovakia, you wait for a service like that for at least four months and they did not want to miss it. Also, they could defer mail for some time, however if the pension cheques were not personally signed for, the government could cut them off.

"Are you sure?" Liba offered. "We would like you to both to stay."

"No, no, the decision is made," answered Mother Dolejs and that was it.

Al merely shrugged, "It's my mother's decision, not my father's."

Mother Dolejs stayed for half a year. She was very organized and took over the house which didn't bother Liba in the least. She loved coming home to her mother-in-law's wonderful meals and Al was a changed man, except for the little slips. It was okay to be a good boy for six weeks. It was more difficult to be a good boy for half a year. But he managed to put the brakes on, except for one incident.

It was spring and they went for a picnic to a place called Blue Rock, southwest of Calgary. Al and Liba had been there many years before. They remembered the area as being quite nice, sort of wild. But when they arrived, they found an organized campsite with gravel roads, picnic tables and concrete washrooms. As they walked around, Al became really upset.

"You are so stupid!" He stormed at Liba. "Why the hell did we come here? Couldn't you have picked a better place?"

Liba blushed and said quietly, "Well, we haven't been here for five or six years, Al. How was I supposed to know that they fixed it up? I know we like things in a more natural state, but there are still a lot of trees and a little creek. Let's explore."

Al flatly refused. He sat down at one of the picnic tables frowning, with his hands bunched in his jacket pockets. Ignoring his bad mood, Liba and Mother Dolejs took the kids and played in the creek, wading and skipping stones. An hour and a half later, they returned to find Al exactly as they had left him. He pouted all the way home.

When they were alone in bed that night Al complained bitterly about his mother. "When I was a kid any resistance to her will was not tolerated. She made all the decisions. And I will tell you now, I will never listen to another goddamn woman as long as I live."

Unfortunately, when Mother Dolejs went back to Czechoslovakia everything returned to normal. Al was just as nasty as ever, worse even.

His pent up vitriol came spewing out when a letter came from his mother. Without telling Liba of its existence, Al read it and was extremely quiet for awhile. Three days later, when Liba got home from work, he threw it at her as soon as she stepped in the door.

"Fuck you!" He screamed. "Have you written my parents? What did you tell them? What did you say about me, you bitch?"

Liba was stunned. "I said nothing." She hadn't complained to anyone about Al's erratic behavior, not even to her own mother or sister. She still pretended everything was fine. She felt they couldn't help her anyway so what was the sense in involving them in her domestic problems? She picked the letter off the floor and read it.

Dear Lola,

First of all, sincere greetings and I think of you often. You are always on my mind.

I must write to you about something that has now worried me for some time. It is something I have continually put off writing and perhaps should not have for quite so long. Now my age and health condition make me realize that I cannot put it off any longer.

When I returned from my visit with you, I told Dad that several times I witnessed fights between you and Liba. Fights where Liba was hardly ever or not even at all at fault. Your behavior grieved me. I cannot condone such behavior. I told Dad that I am scared that if you continue to treat Liba in this way that she will not want to stay with you.

Since then I've opened all letters from you with trepidation, worrying about what could be in them.

Lola, each of us has faults. But during my stay with you, I could not see why Liba should deserve such mistreatment. I couldn't understand how you could behave like that. I kept thinking about all the letters Liba wrote us praising you so. Dad and I were very pleased to read them. To such praise, I responded that he takes after his father who is such a kind man.

Think of him and try to behave as he would and you used to. Knowing you, I am sure you are worried. Because your character won't allow you to stubbornly behave, especially when you realize that what you were so angry about is not as important as you originally thought. Peace in the family is more important than always getting your own way.

It will be very hard if Liba decides to separate. It's hard on a family, especially the children. I see it in your sister's family.

Dad and I are still trying to compensate for what is missing with her and her children, but it's impossible to do it fully. Once a broken family, always a broken family. It cannot be completed.

I am not very eloquent, but understand how deeply I wish I could help you. How I wish that sometime I will receive another letter from Liba full of praise for you once again.

I pray for all of you. I would also suggest the same to you and that you go to church with the children. Even Protestants are Christians.

Let my letter bring you and your family some peace. Don't throw it away. Read it several times and think about it.

As proof that you are not angry and that you have taken something good from it, write.

Write to me Lola. Please write.

Your Mother

Liba was shocked. Mother Dolejs was a lot more aware than she'd realized. Jeez, and Al had been on his best behavior. If she knew how he really behaved, she'd faint.

"What are you talking about?" Liba defended herself. "Your mother clearly states she's speaking from her own observations. So why are you asking me if I wrote them? I didn't write anything, but why don't you do as your mother says. Read it several times and think about it."

Al made an angry face, but kept his mouth shut. He said nothing more about it after that. Liba could tell something was brewing she just didn't know what.

———————

In the fall of 1981, Gabi was in kindergarten. Paul was entering grade two and needing school supplies. They were walking through Woolco looking for crayons when Gabi gave out a big sigh and said, "I need a change in my life. I need a new blouse." Liba glanced at Gabi's serious expression and burst out laughing. Gabi was such a character.

Cabbage Patch dolls were the craze. Gabi had a few and they were her babies. She'd use them to act out all sorts of things. She would play school with them and, because she was such a wonderful mimic, Liba could hear her kindergarten teacher in Gabi's voice. She made up real life situations and as Liba worked around the kitchen, she'd turn off the radio so she could hear Gabi's entertaining patter in the playroom.

One day when Paul was seven he quietly sauntered in during Gabi's game. He sat down beside her, picked up a doll and began participating in the play. The dolls were having a lovely conversation about what they were going to wear to the grocery store. Liba was within hearing range, sweeping the kitchen floor, and had to bite her lip from laughing. It was so cute.

Al shuffled downstairs to watch television and came upon them playing. He saw Paul with the doll and frowned. "Boys don't play with dolls," he growled. Paul continued dressing the doll.

"Well," Paul reasoned. "It's like a baby."

"You shouldn't be playing with babies," Al grumbled.

Paul remained unruffled. "Well, one day when I grow up, I'm going to have babies of my own."

By this time Liba was standing in the doorway ready to intervene. Al looked at his son like he had two heads. Then he addressed Liba accusingly. "Boys don't think like that!"

Liba winked at Paul as Al shook his head and plunked himself down in front of the TV.

————————

Paul was a gentle boy. He'd played hockey since he was five, at Al's insistence, although Liba thought it was a good idea too. She wanted to hold off registering him until he was a little older. But a neighbor who had a boy Paul's age said that hockey was so popular in Canada that, if they waited until he was ten, all the other kids on the team would be a lot more skilled and experienced. Besides, it wasn't often Al was interested in Paul and he seemed excited at the prospect of going to his games. Ironically, Al could barely stand up on skates himself.

Paul was small, but he was smart and quick. He could read the play. He was one of those players always in the right place at the right time. He didn't like playing offense, because the violence and roughness bothered him. But he was great on defense and had a good sense of right and wrong so he would mediate disputes.

Hockey is a rough sport and when Paul got checked into the boards, which is illegal until kids are thirteen, he wouldn't retaliate. He knew it would draw a penalty on the offending player, delighting his coach, but infuriating Al. On the ride home, Al would yell, "I'm raising a faggot!" and "What the hell did you pass it for when you could have easily skated up and scored yourself? You sissy."

Of course, Paul knew a lot more about the game than Al. His coaches were always praising him for making the smart play. Nevertheless, Al would taunt the boy all the way up the drive and into the house. He shouldn't be doing this. He shouldn't be doing that. Sometimes he'd swat Paul in the head with the flat of his hand.

As soon as they walked in the door, Liba would leap to Paul's defense. "Gee whiz, you know, this is not NHL. Give him a break! Don't you touch him! You keep this up, Al, and…"

Al would turn on her. "Oh I see, you're protecting the faggot again. Congratulations. You've done a great job of making him into a girl!" And then in a low, menacing voice, Al would repeat a statement he'd made many times in the past. "If you think you can do anything about it, like leave, I will make sure you never see Paul again. Ever."

The family was broke when Al wasn't working. In the early eighties the job market was miserable. With the oil boom over, construction had pretty well shut down. On top of which Liba took a salary cut so she and

Al had less income, but their expenses remained the same. They had a builder's mortgage so they paid principal and interest but no monthly taxes. Then in June when their $1,400 tax bill would come due, they would have to scrimp even more.

Being from the old country, Liba knew how to cook from scratch so that saved some. She never seemed to sit down, despite the fact Al was home all day with nothing to do. The kids were in daycare after school until she picked them up and then she did all the cooking and cleaning. After supper she would take the kids to gymnastics where she coached and they participated.

One day, she came home late from work and began peeling potatoes, then sliced and put them in the deep fryer along with some fish she had dredged in flour and pepper. She was in a hurry to get to the gym. She quickly prepared a lemon wedge for each of them and added a dollop of ketchup to each plate. Knowing that wouldn't be enough for Al, she also heated a tin of chicken noodle soup and spooned it into a bowl for him.

Liba took her accustomed place at a chair against the wall with Al across from her. The kids flanked them on either side. Everyone started in on their fish and chips. Al gobbled his up quickly, then lifted a spoonful of soup to his lips. Liba got up and headed to the fridge to get the kids more juice when suddenly, Al picked up his bowl and threw it across the kitchen at her head. A lifelong athlete, her reflexes were fast. She ducked. It missed her, but hit the wall and exploded.

"You expect me to eat this pig slop?" he roared.

Instantly, the kids quit chattering and watched wide-eyed as he stalked out of the kitchen and into the living room to watch television.

Liba gathered the kids in her arms and held them tight. "I know this is really difficult and I don't like the situation either." Gabi was pale and on the verge of tears. "But let's stay calm if we can. I'm not hurt, but there is no excuse for behavior like that. Daddy's very wrong for what he's doing."

CHAPTER TWENTY-FOUR

FIRST COURT APPEARANCE

August 11

The search for two Calgary children in Kananaskis Country again has turned up nothing. RCMP and Forestry Officials decided against downscaling their efforts and have set no deadline for discontinuing. Alois Dolejs, a 42-year-old carpenter, appeared in Court for the first time today.

Escorted by two RCMP guards, Al was led into court. His hands were cuffed in front and he was dressed in a red and blue lumberjack shirt, open at the neck, with the sleeves rolled to his elbows, casual gray pants and blue and white running shoes. His oversized aviator prescription glasses sat a little askew on the bridge of his nose. He was looking straight ahead, ignoring the scrum of journalists jockeying for position.

Justice John Reilly read the two charges of first degree murder and John Bascom entered no plea. Justice Reilly remanded Al back into custody until his next court appearance in two days.

With Sandy Harder and her mother by her side, Liba sadly made her way into the courtroom. She sat quietly in the front row, staring at Al while he was being arraigned. Stretched around his oversized eyeteeth, his mouth was drawn up in a tight, angry frown. She could see little pools of spittle forming in the gaps at the corners. She felt she was looking at something repulsive and slimy, like a snake or a lizard. The idea of touching him or going near him made her shiver.

Later, Sandy was scheduled to take Liba back to the detachment where she had been spending most of her time lately. All other avenues had been exhausted so the RCMP requested Liba confront Al. The three women slipped out into Sandy's car where photographers were staked out. They stole a picture of Liba slumped over in the front seat, her hands covering her face, sobbing. The next day it appeared in The Calgary Herald with a caption that read, 'Overcome with grief.'

Mami's eyes were swollen from unending tears and she walked around with balled up tissue in her fists. She could not bear watching Liba sit alone in the middle of the dining room play area staring at the piles of toys and games, sometimes reaching out to stroke the bangs on a Cabbage Patch doll, or finger a favorite toy car. So Mami spent most of her time in the spare bedroom, except to come out and make meals and clean up a little. At first, Liba could not eat. But Mami wisely started making soups and easy snacks. In ten days, fourteen pounds melted off Liba's tiny frame.

If Sandy came over, Mami would perk up a little, putting on a pot of tea. She was very gracious with Sandy and seemed to like her a lot. Sandy would watch her fuss over Liba, fetching tissue if she cried and trying to do her best. Even though Mami could not understand what was being said in English, sometimes when Liba started to talk, she would breakdown crying. Sandy thought she was a sweetheart.

For Sandy, the scene was especially heartrending because she could relate. "You know, this type of work that we do tears at your heart. I mean there are certain things...if you're dealing with a hooker murder, or a biker, something like that, I mean, there's absolutely no feeling there. You feel nothing. But when it comes to families and kids and abuse and...I was raised with abuse in my own home and so when Liba or her mother started crying, it would tug at my own heart and I would turn away. I would try not to let it hit me because I didn't want it to interfere with my doing a good job."

Sandy's step dad beat her mother. Going out on domestic dispute calls and seeing the kids sent her mind reeling back, remembering what she had witnessed as a child and the terror she'd felt. This case wasn't exactly the same, but that didn't make it different. When she became an RCMP officer, she was called to many cases where the male in the home had beaten the mother, often in front of the kids. Sandy would try to hide her satisfaction as she slapped the cuffs on these guys.

"Been there, done that. Revenge is sweet."

Dr. Arboleda-Florez, M.D., D, PSYCH, FRCP (C) FAPA, DABFP, Chief of the Psychiatric Forensic Division at The Calgary General Hospital, visited Al from 5:40 to 6:40 that evening and was struck by Al's cool and capable manner. Al insisted he had nothing to do with the death of his children, but Dr. Arboleda-Florez later noted, "Even if he had not committed this crime, because the children were missing, any normal parent would be suffering and I saw no sense of that. No remorse, no sense of guilt."

Dr. Arboleda-Florez found that Al had a rigid or obsessive personality.

"These people follow a script and do not panic. They see the world in two colors, black and white. They use this method to tie up the anxiety they feel inside. He wants order in his life, but his family refused to march around military-style, so he sees this as a rebellion by them."

Dr. Arboldea-Florez considered Al to be an inhibited individual who, "keeps his thoughts and feelings to himself and who is authoritarian and unbendable. Rigidity and authoritarian personalities are not infrequently found in individuals who abuse spouses or children.

"He sees others as the problem and this leads to paranoia, suspecting that everybody is trying to thwart him, so he develops a hatred of others. The problem with these types of personalities is, if they go untreated, they become more and more rigid as they get older. They may never agree that there is anything wrong with them.

"Al may never choose to talk about the murders because he feels too brittle inside. Once he did it, he closed the chapter. However, this doesn't mean he is mentally ill." Dr. Arboleda-Florez found Al fit to stand trial.

CHAPTER TWENTY-FIVE

HIS DOMAIN

In addition to a full-time job, Liba took two part-time jobs, cleaning offices and selling real estate. Al was still unemployed. He was becoming more and more slovenly. His life was reduced to three activities. Sleeping, eating and watching TV.

The living room had become his domain. If he fixed himself a sandwich while Liba was at work, he left the plate on the floor beside his chair. Ashtrays overflowed with butts. Empty pop cans littered the floor. It was disgusting, but with three jobs, plus cooking, laundry and taking care of the kids, Liba had no time to remedy the situation. When she walked downstairs towards the kitchen, she refused to even look to her right. It was terrible.

Al was one guy at night and another in the day. He'd been a virgin when they met and was open to her suggestions on how to please her sexually. If he wanted to make love, he'd kiss her gently on the neck or offer soft caresses. If she was too tired or not in the mood, all she had to do was say no and he'd roll over and go to sleep without the tantrum he threw when he couldn't get his way on other issues. Liba preferred to avoid the situation completely so she never went to bed at the same time he did. She'd wait until he was asleep, creep quietly into their room and slip under the sheets. He didn't seem to mind, but she was never sure how he felt because they never discussed sex.

After a while, she bought a second TV, just a little one, for the master bedroom. He moved up there when the family was downstairs doing homework or practicing piano. When she and the kids went upstairs to bed, he would shut that one off, go downstairs to turn the other one on and watch all night. When she left with the kids in the morning, he'd go up to bed and sleep most of the day. It was creepy.

Yet, there were instances when he was surprisingly supportive, like the time Gabi saved Liba's life. It was the winter of 1982 on a Saturday morning. Gabi was six. Al had taken Paul to one of his hockey games and Gabi needed a pair of cross-country ski boots. Liba phoned around and found some across town at a place called Fresh Air Experience.

She loaded Gabi into the Datsun and away they went. As they were driving north on 14th Street, approaching an intersection across from the Rockyview Hospital, she got a flat. Not wanting to stop in the middle of the busy thoroughfare, she forced the car through the lights and pulled over into a merge lane.

The spare tire in the Datsun was under a well in the trunk. Liba clicked on her flashers and unloaded real estate signs and sheaves of paper onto the side of the road. She yanked out the spare and a rusty jack.

It was freezing, but for safety's sake, she ordered Gabi out of the car and onto the berm beside the passenger door. Gabi did as she was told, but after a few minutes of shifting from foot to foot and jumping around to stay warm, she started crying due to the cold. Liba pulled off her toque and gloves and gave them to the child and started jacking up the car. The flat was on the driver's side at the back so she was facing traffic. She shook her head disgusted. The car was only two years old for Heaven's sake.

Liba was struggling to remove the factory-tightened lug nuts when Gabi started yelling, "Mommy, Mommy, a man stopped!" A car had driven past and was backing up to help.

Liba stood up and turned around. The Good Samaritan's car had come to a halt in front of hers and she could see the driver smiling at her. She took two steps toward him, when she heard the most tremendous crash accompanied by Gabi's terrible shriek.

A driver behind them had been changing lanes and didn't notice they were stopped. He ploughed into Liba's car at seventy kilometers per hour. The Datsun went flying up the berm, sideswiping the Good Samaritan's car and barely missing Gabi. The collision occurred at the very spot Liba had been squatting, demolishing the Datsun sedan. If she hadn't moved when Gabi called, she would have been crushed.

Gabi was absolutely frantic. She was screaming hysterically and shaking violently. Liba wasn't sure what had happened, but she dashed up the hill to grab her daughter.

"Our little car, our little car!" Gabi kept crying over and over.

Liba embraced her. "Gabi, it's okay, it's only a car. The main thing is, you're okay and I'm okay."

"What is daddy going to say?" Gabi wailed.

Liba was so grateful Gabi was safe, Al's reaction was the last thing on her mind.

The police dropped them at home. When Al and Paul arrived, Al put his arms around Gabi who was still shaken.

"Oh, it's only a car, we have a good insurance on it. It's okay. It could have been worse type of a thing, right?" He chucked her under the chin, then smiled reassuringly at Liba and patted her arm. "Don't worry about it."

But two years later on Sunday, April 1, 1984, Al just lost it. He was lounging in his usual spot in front of the television in the living room. Directly across the street from their home was a small greenbelt with evergreens and poplar trees where the neighborhood kids often played. He caught a sudden movement out of the corner of his eye and stood to look out the large plate glass window.

There, he saw four children, all around eleven years old, Marie Koli, Kevin and Trevor Morrison and Simon Gidluck. Simon had a hockey stick and was whacking at one of the evergreens to, as he put it, "Knock down some egg corns."

Al watched as branches from the tree snapped off and fell to the ground. He became utterly enraged. He was a taxpayer. He owned those trees. How dare that little bastard destroy his property! His face contorted in anger, he stormed out the front door and made for the child. Too angry to speak, he grabbed Simon by the shoulders and began shaking him, then slapped the terrified child across the face, leaving an angry red welt.

Simon ran home on legs made of rubber. He told his father what happened. Marcus Gidluck kept his cool. He followed Simon to the Dolejs house and confronted Al, telling him it was a serious offence to assault a child and he was going to call the police. Al just stared at his accuser without reply.

Sergeant Gary McAuley investigated the complaint. Al flatly denied slapping Simon, despite the claims of the boy and his three friends.

"I pay taxes!" he told McAuley. The officer issued Al a Promise To Appear notice for a level one assault and advised Simon's parents to keep the boys away from the park area and to play in nearby playgrounds instead.

In court, Al received a one hundred-dollar fine. A slap on the wrist.

CHAPTER TWENTY-SIX

THE PLEA

The police knew there was little more they could do. Al wasn't talking. They decided to turn to his wife for assistance. At first, they'd been reluctant because they were convinced he had killed the kids to spite her, but now what did they have to lose?

Sandy Harder thought Mrs. Novak a lovely woman, but could see immediately she and her daughter didn't get along all that well. Even though Sandy couldn't understand Czech, Mami seemed to be making an effort, speaking to Liba in soothing tones.

After Al's court appearance, they piled into Sandy's car and drove to the Cochrane RCMP Detachment. Liba's mother commented on the appearance of the building as they pulled up. "Such a little jail."

"I know," said Liba. "It's not intended to hold anybody for any length of time." Hope and despair were waging a war in Liba's head and she had a migraine. She felt the importance of this meeting weighing on her. She didn't want to accept that Al might have killed the kids. It was crucial for their survival that she find out where they were. Today.

As they arrived, dark thunder clouds unleashed a torrential downpour. Liba and Mami stepped out of the car and ran into the building on Sandy's heels. When they were safe inside the foyer, Liba held the door open a crack staring outside. "It's so wet and cold. Such a rainy summer." She squinted up at the clouds. "But both kids have warm jackets."

A few moments later, Sandy led her to a small interview room filled with three chairs. Al was sitting in one of them, handcuffed. Sandy introduced herself, told him who she was, full name, her position, and added, "I'm Canadian, I don't speak the Czech language, I don't know what you're saying. I'm just here for security reasons."

Al nodded. He understood.

Liba started right away. She was nervous and talked fast. She knew Father John had been visiting him so she tried to find common ground.

"Mami and I had a discussion with Father John Bastigal and we agreed on a Catholic funeral if it's all right?"

Al looked at her and frowned. "Huh?"

"We are going to give the children a Catholic funeral."

Like a lizard sunning on a rock, Al slowly blinked, then stared past her, disinterested. "Oh, that's what you said."

"Where are they? Are they cold? Are they tired? Are they hungry?"

After each question, Al gave his head a tiny shake.

Liba swallowed hard and continued. She tried phrasing things from his perspective. "We brought the children into this world. We're both responsible for what happened, maybe me to a lesser degree, but I'm still responsible too, we're in this together and we should...we should bury them together."

There was no reply.

Liba's voice began to falter and she struggled to keep her composure. "Did you build any kind of shelter or box for them?"

Al stopped acknowledging her presence and stared at the wall behind her.

Liba was beyond desperate. "Did you at least carve a cross on a tree, or build one, or put a stone by the head of the graves?"

Another slight shake of his head.

"So you just left them there like a scabby dog? Oh Al, if you hated me that much, why didn't you just come and kill me? Why kill the children? I would have traded my life for theirs anytime. Any life...any life they could have, even a hard life is better than… what you've done!

"We were their parents we gave them life! Nobody has the right to take it away from them, not even you. They loved you and trusted you!" Liba closed her eyes and lowered her voice.

"Don't you remember how soft and cute they were when they were babies? Big brown eyes, eyes like yours. And how wonderful they were to touch and smell. Why you used to feed her and bathe her. And oh how fond they were of their daddy. Especially Gabi. Remember how she was always asking you to pick her up? She would say in her little baby talk, 'Pick up the girl!' And ah, you always did.

"And later on, when they got a little older and Paul got his first bike or when we went together and picked out his first hockey equipment. He was so proud of it. That parent evening when Gabi was in kindergarten. I'll never forget…we visited her classroom and she entered the room holding your hand, and she loudly announced to everybody, 'This is my Daddy!'"

At that, a facial muscle on Al's cheek twitched involuntarily.

Liba took note. Perhaps she was getting to him after all.

"Remember her little hands? So sticky. She used to touch our glasses and get them all fogged up and dirty and we would laugh? It didn't matter. Oh, and the time when Paul was just little and they went to dump some garbage in an old construction box and he walked around a mud puddle to get there. Then you called out not to step in the mud and he couldn't hear so he walked straight through the puddle and said, 'What did you say daddy?'

"Those incidents. At the time we were annoyed, but they are beautiful to remember now. He used to call her Unkunka because he couldn't say Elunka. Then Oluku." This made Liba smile. She looked up at Al, her eyes glistening.

"Please, let's give them a Christian funeral so their souls can be freed from their disfigured bodies and we can let them go where they belong, to a better world. The bodies should be put where they belong. They shared a room. They shared their toys. They were always very good to each other. Are they buried together?"

Liba sobbed and suddenly Al met her eye. He couldn't help himself. He loved it when she was wrong. Pleasure swept over his face and she knew they were buried separately.

"Your parents always cared so much for the kids. I know they wanted them christened. But it's not too late. Let's do it now. You know by not giving them a decent burial, you are only piling up the sins on your soul, higher and higher. Why don't you answer me?

"Gabi loved little bunnies so much. She will never see the sweater your sister made for her, poor little darling. They must have been so scared, Al. Are they still scared? And the Cabbage Patch boy you bought her just two weeks ago. She loved him because you gave it to her. My mother just fixed the neck and paws on Paul's favorite stuffed doggy. Let's put the Cabbage patch dolls and the doggy in their coffins so when they are buried they won't be afraid anymore.

"I'm not afraid of you any longer, Al. I know you are a different man now. Whatever you did, it must have been a spur of the moment decision. If you want me to, I will go with you anywhere in that bush, just the two of us together. I will ask the police not to go with us. I trust you, Al. I trust you enough to do that. I don't care how far or how hard it is to get to it."

Again, she received a look. It meant they weren't far.

"We'll go out there alone and we'll go dig out the children with our bare hands. If you don't want to do it, I will. Their hands were so little, I want to hold them again." Tears were running down her cheeks.

"I'm sure the police will do this for me if I request it. And I will ask for it. We are in this together. We have to live with what happened for the rest of our lives. I know you have to live with it, but so do I. You are not alone. I will even visit you in prison. We will get over this together. It's still our responsibility. It's our job. That is the least we can do for the children, give them a decent burial."

Sandy sat holding her breath. She couldn't understand what was being said, but she could see him sitting there leering at Liba. Just an evil, hateful, stare. As she watched this strong, proud woman, begging for the lives of her children all Sandy could do was hope. It was chilling.

Liba thought she could see Al weighing his options. He certainly could inflict more pain on her by dragging her through the bush to the bodies of the children. But legally, it would not be the best thing for him to do.

"Call me," she continued quietly. "Call me anytime, night or day. I will come to see you in your cell. I have nothing but time now. I will listen to anything you have to say. I'll do anything...we must bury the children together. Please, please, tell me where they are."

"I'll think about it. I'll think about it," Al said without expression.

Liba nodded to Sandy. The interview was over. Sandy escorted her out and led Mrs. Novak in.

———————

Al's dislike for his mother-in-law was immediately apparent. It was a very quick two-minute visit. She spoke briefly to him in Czech.

"You wanted to talk to me, but now I want to talk to you. You told me you will never take the children away from Libushka, but you lied to us and we believed you. You claimed the children were always with us, not you, and we bribed them. You said, if you had a chance to be with them for a longer time, they wouldn't want to come back to us. Where are the children? I only have two grandchildren. Do I still have them? Where are they? Are they alive?"

He answered her, "I didn't lie." Then he looked up at Sandy and said, "Take her out."

The ride home was quiet. Sandy felt it may have been the first time Liba had come to grips with the fact that Al had done something to Paul and Gabi and they were gone forever.

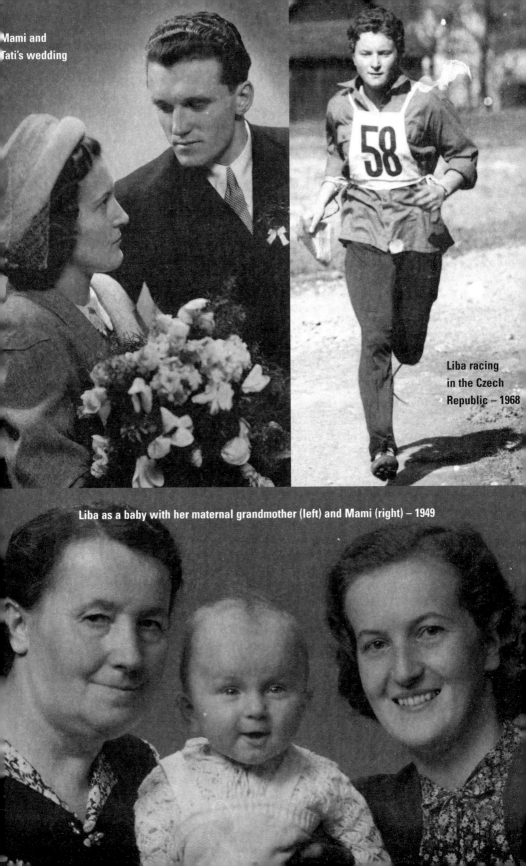

Mami and Tati's wedding

Liba racing in the Czech Republic – 1968

Liba as a baby with her maternal grandmother (left) and Mami (right) – 1949

Paul was a tiny newborn
(5 lbs, 10 oz.) – 1974

Gabi and her babies – 1981

Al in a rare photo of him smiling
with baby Paul and Liba – 1975

Al was often affectionate
with Gabi – 1980

Al took an active
interest in Paul's
hockey – 1981

Al was a 'good boy' when his mother was around. Family portrait in 1980.

Liba and Tati – 1980

Gabi giggling in grade one – 1982

Al and his brother
Josef (Pepa) – 1982

Al's sister Gabriela
(Elunka) Docekalova – 1983

Al only hugged Paul in photos – 1984

Dr. Robin Reesal – 2000
(photographed by Jared Sych)

Sgt. Merv Harrower – 1985

Cst. Burt Broster – 1985

Cst. Wally Purcell – 1985

Cst. Dahl Chambers – 1985

Cst. John Cantafio – 1985

Cst. Sandy Harder – 1985

Mami, Gabi and Paul at Frank Slide on their way home from Expo June 1986

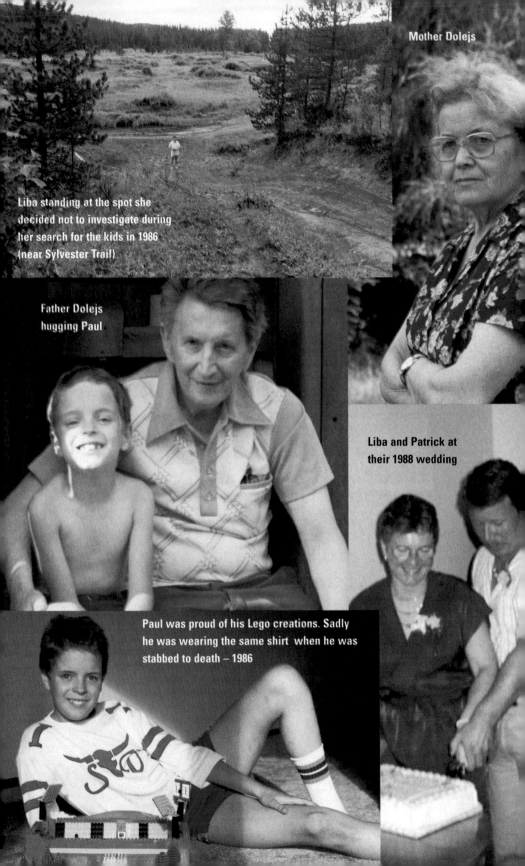

Mother Dolejs

Liba standing at the spot she decided not to investigate during her search for the kids in 1986 (near Sylvester Trail)

Father Dolejs hugging Paul

Liba and Patrick at their 1988 wedding

Paul was proud of his Lego creations. Sadly he was wearing the same shirt when he was stabbed to death – 1986

The family spent many weekends in the mountains

Liba on top of Mt. Nicolas, Banff, Alberta – 2000

Paul loved hockey

Paul winning the Sergeant for a day contest with Sgt. Vic Norman – 1986

ba – 1999

The house Al built on Woodglen Road in Calgary. It was their last home together.

Defense lawyer John Bascom

(Phot Court the A Law Socie

Gabi's overalls and shi with stab wounds

Crown Prosecutor Peter Martin

(Photo Courtesy of the Alberta Law Society)

Paul's shirt back

Paul's shirt with 13 stab wounds (front)

CHAPTER TWENTY-SEVEN

LITTLE CHICKS

Liba loved putting the kids to bed. It was a special time. Gabi would go to sleep easily. Paul was tougher. He couldn't read himself to sleep. It was too stimulating so she worked on relaxing him. Sometimes she'd read fairy tales in either English or Czech. There was one they really liked. It was a Czech variation of Hansel and Gretel.

A game warden meets some children in the woods. They were sent there as a punishment by their wicked stepmother. He hides the kids to keep them safe and comes upon a wicked witch. The witch begins asking the gamekeeper a bunch of questions. He pretends he's hard of hearing and repeats her questions, but gets them all wrong. This drives the wicked witch crazy. Paul and Gabi thought it was hilarious. It also gave Liba a chance to enhance their Czech vocabulary. It was fun.

But all was not well and the kids knew it. They reacted to their domestic situation in different ways. Paul would often get a bleeding nose at night. Gabi was prone to an upset stomach and headaches. On a number of occasions she threw up in the middle of the night due to nerves. Liba could relate. She started having severe headaches at around thirteen.

Al had been lying low watching TV and sleeping a lot, which suited Liba fine. At least he wasn't in her hair. It was March. Liba and the kids were home when Al walked in with a box of twelve little partridge chicks and a bag of feed. The kids jumped up and down with excitement. They had never had animals in the house.

Liba stared at him open mouthed, "What's that?"

Al said, "We'll feed them and when they grow up we'll eat them."

Gabi who'd been holding one of the fuzzy little birds and gently petting it with her index finger stopped and stared at her Dad in horror. "You're not going to kill them, are you Daddy?"

He looked at her. "Yeah."

Gabi burst into tears. "No, Daddy, you can't do that. They're so little and cute."

Liba interrupted crossly. "We don't have any money and you do something stupid like this. How much were those chicks?"

Al flashed her a defiant look. "Forty dollars and I don't see nothing wrong with it. It was a good deal."

Liba tried to remain calm. Forty dollars! They could barely afford groceries. She began ticking off points on her fingers. "First of all, who is going to feed them? Who's going to kill them? Who's going to clean them? Who's going to pluck them?"

He looked at her as if she were daft. "You are."

Liba shook her head. "Oh, no. I'm not touching them. I'm not doing it." She massaged her temples. "Besides where do you intend to keep them?"

"We'll keep them in the garage." He glared at her belligerently. The garage was full of construction materials. It was so crowded they couldn't use it to park their cars. Nevertheless, he did haul the chicks out there. They were in a cardboard box for two days.

On the third day, half of them escaped. They were all over the place and Al had to hunt them down on his hands and knees. Finally, he got them all together and built a makeshift wooden coop. The front panel was made of chicken wire. He moved it to the balcony adjacent to the living room where it was sunny.

Liba came home the next day and a couple of the chicks were dead. There were blood and feathers everywhere in the coop. The kids were very upset and clung to Liba at the sight.

"What the hell happened? " she demanded. Al had been home all day sitting right across from the sliding doors to the balcony.

He didn't even bother to look up from the television. "I dunno. Maybe cats."

Liba sighed. The house was on a sloped lot. There was quite a bit of backfill in the yard. A cat could possibly climb up there, but how would it get through the chicken wire? She didn't know and didn't dare ask.

The kids were crying so loudly, Al reluctantly got out of his chair and removed the dead chicks. The next day they came home and three more were dead. Again, Al shrugged, "Cats." By the end of the week, the wooden crate had disappeared.

The kids were disappointed when they came home from daycare as usual and ran out to see the chicks. "Oh, they're gone. Where are the birdies, Daddy?" Paul asked. Al replied, "I took them all to Fish Creek Park and set them free."

Gabi smiled, relieved they wouldn't end up on her supper plate. "Oh good, now they're happy!"

It was still cold outside and snow lay on the ground in the shaded back yard. It faced north and without the sun the temperature remained below freezing. Then one day a warm Chinook wind blew in and melted everything. Paul and Gabi put on their rubber boots and headed out to the back yard for a play. Liba was in the kitchen when they ran back into the house. They were shrieking.

"Daddy killed the chickies! Daddy didn't let the birdies go! They're all dead in the back yard!" sobbed Paul.

Liba went out to investigate and, sure enough, he'd left the box full of dead chicks sitting in the side yard. Liba was angry over the trauma to the kids, but what puzzled her was why he hadn't made any attempt to hide the box or bury the birds? He blatantly lied and didn't care about being found out.

Mother Dolejs wrote a letter soon after telling Al it would be very good if the kids had a pet. She suggested a puppy. Of course, she was completely ignorant about what had happened to the chicks. Al waited until Liba left to run some errands then called the kids to the living room.

"We are going to get a puppy! Would you kids like that?"

The kids were ecstatic. "A puppy! Yes! Yes! Yes!"

When Liba walked in the door they were all over her, jumping up and down. "We're going to get a puppy!"

Liba sighed. "We can't get a puppy, kids."

Gabi frowned. "Oh yes, Daddy said so."

"Well, I'm afraid this is not a good idea." They followed her into the kitchen, helping her carry the groceries. "It really wouldn't be fair to the puppy because we leave early in the morning and we don't come home until six at night and a puppy cannot just run around a house. A puppy has to be trained. It would be peeing on the carpet and I can't...The only place we could keep it is in the laundry room. Think about it, guys, seven in the morning 'til six at night locked in the laundry room. How would you like that if somebody did that to you?"

Gabi's eyes widened, "Oh no, that wouldn't be very nice for the puppy." Paul nodded in agreement.

"Not only that," Liba continued, "a puppy has to be walked every day and we have a hard time leaving on time every morning as it is. How would you walk the puppy in the morning? And somebody has to come home in the middle of the day and feed it and let it out and walk it at night."

Liba was glad the kids were being so reasonable. She thanked her lucky stars Al hadn't just gone out and purchased the damn dog. Getting rid of it would break their hearts. But why had he promised them one without even discussing it?

"I'm already working three jobs trying to make ends meet. Who is going to walk the puppy? It sure ain't going to be me," she thought.

Al was always doing stuff like this. It was bad enough he didn't contribute, but did he have to try to sabotage her relationship with the kids? A few months before, she'd had a fight with Gabi because Al told her he was going to take her to the hairdresser for a perm. Gabi's hair was stick-straight and when she tried growing it long, it stuck out all over. But Liba knew when she reached puberty that would change. Her hair might even develop some curl. She also felt it was unhealthy to perm preteen hair. The shaft of the hair wasn't developed and it could cause damage. Liba put her foot down.

"No way. If she doesn't like the way her hair looks long, we can keep it short, but she's not getting it doused in chemicals!" Gabi had been crestfallen.

When Al got home, Liba told him of her decision about the dog.

"You mean bitch. Kids deserve a puppy. They're entitled. They should have a puppy! Stop being so selfish and think of them for once."

Paul and Gabi stared round-eyed at their mother, feeling guilty for Al's onslaught.

"Fine. We'll discuss it." Liba said quietly. "Who's going to walk it?"

"You will," he sneered.

"There aren't enough hours in my day," replied Liba. Turning on her heel she walked into the kitchen to finish making supper.

CHAPTER TWENTY-EIGHT

THE SEARCH

The psychics were coming out of the woodwork. They started calling the morning of August 9th and continued into October. First, there was *John Biggar. He got hold of an investigator named Scotland. John said he was a psychic who often helped police with investigations. His voice was nasal and effeminate.

"The father is a very intelligent man who would not harm the kids," he insisted. "This is purely a domestic matter between the father and mother. The children are safe, but far away. Either in the U.S. or Prague."

Sergeant Burt Broster caught the second seer. *Don Stevens was fairly specific. He had a premonition the bodies could be found just past Elbow Falls in a creek on Elbow Falls Road. They were two hundred yards up this creek on the right hand side.

GIS received a call from *Michala Toth. She said she knew nothing about the missing children, yet when she was at the small fishpond five minutes southwest of Canmore, she had a feeling there might be some dead people in the area.

"I am not a witch, but I have had strange feelings before and they have been proven to be correct," she told the investigator.

They also followed up a tip from *Jane Brown. Jane admitted this was her first major case. She said she had a flash of a sign bearing the name of the subdivision, Redwood Meadows, after hearing about the missing children on the radio. Then she had a flash of Bragg Creek and an area behind a golf course. The children, she felt, were behind the golf course along the riverbed, away from some houses, near an area which had been burned. Burt Broster noted she did not appear mentally unstable. Police sent her a map and she pinpointed the area for them.

———————

A card-carrying psychic, *Patsy Greenway, from Stavely, Alberta, a one-horse town south of Calgary, contacted Frank DeHeer, the officer who first arrested Al. Patsy said the bodies of the two children could be located thirty miles from the search area. Both were under water in chains and weights. However, one had come loose and had partially surfaced. She was given a map and circled the area.

———————

Psychic *George Kowalko from Vegreville, a small town founded by Ukrainian settlers east of Edmonton, simply left a message with police stating, "I feel I know where the children are."

———————

*Dasha Adamova wrote the investigators. Her name was Czech and she mentioned meeting Liba and Al years before. She said she had an unusual dream. She was in a forest crawling around on her hands and knees and saw three cardboard boxes containing a dead boy, a dead girl and a live woman. There were pine trees on one side and a body of water on the other.

Liba remembered Dasha as a wonderful cook, who lost a five-month-old daughter to Sudden Infant Death Syndrome. "No wonder she's having nightmares," Liba said sympathetically.

———————

Calgarian *Doris Daniels called up, directing investigators to Spray Lake, west of Canmore. She had a premonition the kids were in the south end of the lake and saw stumps and roots nearby.

---

*Judy Pincher visited Sergeant Phillips and said she had a dream regarding the whereabouts of the bodies. She supplied a map on a piece of foolscap with a rough drawing of a forest area across from a body of water, near a campground.

Legal secretary *Brittany Anderson told Sergeant Pedlar she felt investigators should look for a rundown shack in the Quirk Creek area, near a gas field southwest of Calgary. She envisioned Paul slapping Al's face.

"Was the father's nose bleeding? Was there blood in the back seat of his vehicle? I think the father has arthritis in his right hand. I also think he's been in combat and has a nasty wound on his legs," she added.

*All psychic names are pseudonyms.

August 12

New teams of searchers were brought in today to replace exhausted investigators who, for four days, have been battling mosquitoes and rain looking for two missing Calgary children. A provincial agriculture inspector on horseback and two other riders are now combing the area. No horses have been used previously because, according to Constable Paul Arliss, "It's kind of muskegy out there."

Wardens from Banff and Jasper and a Calgary Police dog team have joined the search along with an Alberta Forestry Service helicopter.

Today, they concentrated on a steep seismic line past the Sylvester Trail. This southern edge of the McLean Creek Recreational Area is leased by the Crown to Bragg Creek ranchers for prime grazing.

Today, Banff RCMP confirmed Paul Dolejs complained to them about an assault by his father last Easter.

The Cochrane Detachment contacted Banff RCMP after Liba related the events of last Easter to them. Banff sent back confirmation that, indeed, Paul sought refuge with them after claiming he was afraid of his father and refusing to stay with him. When they checked with Calgary Police Services, they found Al had a previous charge of assault, stemming from the Simon Gidluk incident.

According to Paul's statement he ran because his dad threatened he was going to take him away from his mother and he would never see her again. It was a threat he'd made before, but Paul felt his dad was serious that day. Banff RCMP said Al acted bewildered at the accusations, but when they advised him to seek counseling in Calgary, he looked unhappy. At the mother's request, they refused to release the boy into his father's custody.

———————

Al called his sister, Gabriela, whom he addressed as Elunka, from jail. Never one to weather crises well, she was semi-hysterical. Al asked her to pray for him. She said she hoped God would give him the strength to tell the truth, whatever it was. He asked to speak to their mother, but Elunka informed him she was at their summer cottage and didn't know anything yet.

"It's going to kill her!" Elunka reported tearfully.

"Do you know everything?" he asked.

"Yes," she sobbed. "I know what you are charged with, but I am afraid to ask you what happened."

Al cleared his throat. "It is better for you not to ask."

"Pepa and I...Pepa..." Elunka swallowed a few times, trying to get the words out. "Pepa and I are praying for you. We are praying for our mother's sake, and in memory of our father, that God will give you the strength to tell the truth, whatever that truth might me."

"I have to go," Al responded curtly. "Bye."

"May God be with you," she replied and hung up.

Al stood grasping the receiver tightly in his fist for a long time.

Wednesday, August 13

Early morning rainstorms plagued the sixth day of the search for two missing Calgary children, Paul and Gabi Dolejs. Forty to fifty searchers scoured an expanded area from 9:00 AM to 7:00 PM.

Their father, Alois Dolejs, appeared in court today for the second time. Justice John Reilly set September 11 and 12 for his preliminary hearing. Dolejs elected trial by judge alone. Reilly also read two new charges in addition to the first degree murder charges he faces. They are that he breached custody orders by not returning the children to their mother on July 27.

RCMP are now handing out pamphlets with the children's pictures to people going into the area.

John Bascom was upset as he hung up the phone. Al was complaining that shortly after his court appearance, the RCMP started interrogating him quite heavily. It was one thing when they questioned him about the whereabouts of the children, hoping they could still save them, but now Al was charged with first degree murder. Anything he said would only incriminate him.

Al told John, not only was he questioned frequently, they wouldn't let him sleep. John thought this violated the Canadian Charter of Rights and

Freedoms, Section 12; "...a person is not to be subjected to cruel and unusual punishment."

John called the detachment back at around 3:00 PM and voiced his objections. The RCMP promised they'd quit questioning Al for the day. John could sense their yearning. More than ever, he was convinced they were going to get the information they wanted one way or another. They would just keep at him until he broke.

John expressed his dissatisfaction to the police, often objurgating them, but they shrugged him off. Finally, he decided to talk to the newspapers.

"I've never seen a situation like this in Canada before," he told The Calgary Sun. "I have a low boiling point. They've been questioning him now for a week. Enough is enough."

RCMP media representative Corporal Barry Hornung said that was boloney.

"He's been treated like a human being, fed, watered, the whole shot. We have a responsibility to feed our prisoners and they are permitted sleep."

John and the RCMP were now duking it out in the papers. John wanted Al transferred to The Calgary Remand Center, a cement block facility adjacent to the Central Police Station in downtown Calgary, but Hornung told the Sun the RCMP was "within the law" keeping him in Cochrane.

Pepa called at 7:30 the next morning. He told investigators he was concerned with only one thing. He wanted his brother Alois to start talking. He said he would like to speak with him personally and, though he would not be asking him anything specific, he thought he could say something to him that would spur him into telling the truth.

Al called him back later that day. Pepa told him that no matter what happened, Al was still blood, thus the family would stand behind him and give their full support.

"If you wish, I will come and talk with you in person," Pepa offered.

"You and Elunka could both come. I have enough money," Al bragged.

"Lean on God, Al, with the help of this priest you have seen. Make a confession and receive absolution. May you have the strength to tell the truth." Then Pepa quoted the sacred family motto. "Truth above all!"

Al was silent.

Again Pepa offered to come. Pepa told Al he knew he wouldn't consciously hurt his children, but it was possible in the time of greatest despair, when everything he laboriously built far from home was collapsing, he might have done something he never thought possible.

"Does our mother know?" Al wondered.

"No, not yet," Pepa replied.

"You have to tell her something." Al pondered a moment. "Tell her it was an unfortunate accident."

Liba called Pepa immediately following his conversation with Al. She had always gotten along well with him. She stayed with him and Al's sister, Elunka, on vacation in Czechoslovakia. In the late '70s, the floundering Communist government had a change of heart and allowed former illegal emigrants like Liba and Al to come back and visit their relatives. It was an excellent way of attracting a large influx of foreign currency.

Liba and kids were in Prague with Al's siblings for four days. Liba found Pepa quite nice. He and Liba talked for hours. He was very much interested in how business ran in Canada. They worked in similar industries. Liba was a draftsman in a land survey company and Pepa was a civil engineer.

Al and his parents had told Liba that Pepa's wife, Anna, was just awful. But after meeting her Liba disagreed. Her family, the Semerads, had been very well off in land and possessions before the Communists took over. They were farmers and very down to earth people. When they lost everything, they managed to keep what was important in perspective.

Pepa became quite attached to the family and the Dolejs clan saw this as a betrayal. When Pepa and Anna married, Mother Dolejs wrote Al and Liba saying, "We've lost a son. He's become one of them now. She and that illiterate family of pigs has taken him away from us." Mother Dolejs was incensed that Pepa would listen to his wife instead of coming to her.

Al's sister was different. Elunka was emotional like her mother. If Mother Dolejs wanted something she would blink back tears. Her daughter used the same tactics. Mother and Father Dolejs meddled constantly in Elunka's life. They took care of her two daughters so she was dependent on them and was forced to listen to them. When she displayed any resentment, Mother Dolejs turned on the waterworks.

When Liba stayed with Al's sister for a couple of days, she was shocked when Elunka broke rank and complained about her mother.

"She means well," Elunka began. "She wants to help but, she always sticks her nose into my business. I'm an adult and I'd like to run my own affairs, but mother won't let me. I can't believe this bind I'm in. She's basically blackmailing me. If I ask her to butt out, she'll stop taking care of the girls for me. She has absolutely no respect for me or my wishes."

Then Liba stayed with Mother Dolejs and she groused about how ungrateful Elunka was and how she refused to take the good advice offered to her.

"All she wants is the babysitting. She uses us."

Secretly Liba took Elunka's side. She'd witnessed Mother Dolejs stepping on Elunka's toes and it was painful to watch. While she was there, Elunka dropped her two daughters, Sara and Lenka (psuedonyms), off for the day. Lenka, a Grade One student, had bitten 9-year-old Sara on the back and drawn blood.

Mother Dolejs was incensed. How could Elunka permit such aggressive behavior? Elunka deeply resented the questioning of her child-rearing skills, but as usual she didn't confront Mother Dolejs on the issue. When faced with her mother's authority, Elunka opposed her indirectly through passive means, pouting, obstinacy and eventually trying to kill herself. Father Dolejs never said a word. Liba was beginning to understand where her husband's behavior was coming from.

Pepa said he was willing to help find the kids, but he believed Al wasn't really to blame. He told Liba he wrote Al and told him he was sorry the wound caused by the loss of his wife and everyday contact with his children didn't have time to heal. He knew Al loved the children above all and lived only for them. He said he remembered Al's words before his departure to Canada after their last visit.

"And again Liba and I will be like a small isle resisting the environment," Al had sighed. Pepa said it was unfortunate Al had such an unapproachable nature, but that Al's thinking was always clear and frank and only people close to him would understand.

Thursday, August 14

Alois Dolejs was moved from his cell at the Cochrane RCMP detachment to a segregated cell at the Calgary Remand Center today at noon. The RCMP have released a statement saying there is no longer any need for him to be held there.

It had been difficult for John Bascom to drop everything to see his client in Cochrane. He lived in the south end of the Calgary and it was a good two hour drive, there and back.

He told reporters, "It's appropriate he's no longer at the beck and call of RCMP investigators. He's now under the authority of the Remand Center authorities and will also be more accessible to me. It comes down to a question of when the interrogation becomes a form of torture."

RCMP Corporal Barry Hornung wasn't quite as pleased.

"There was nothing wrong with what we were doing. I really think the whole thing is Mickey Mouse," he grumbled.

Friday, August 15

It's been one week since the search for 12 year old Paul and 10 year old Gabi Dolejs was instigated in the rugged area of Kananaskis Country, southwest of Bragg Creek. Today searchers stumbled across a number of discarded items including old clothes, tents and disposable lighters, but none connected to the Dolejs children.

Meanwhile, more psychics were coming forward.

In Cochrane, Wally Purcell caught an interesting call. A self-proclaimed psychic named *Ted Wilde had a dream about Paul. He saw him near a decrepit building under a pile of logs. Ted's parents wrote from Quebec to verify Ted's claims. His mother stated that just recently she told Ted that one of their elderly neighbors was in the hospital and he replied he had recently dreamed the man was in a wheelchair.

---

*Janice Standingcrow from the Blackfoot Reservation contacted RCMP. She advised she was psychic and she had some information on the murders. She said one of her neighbor's children was watching TV and saw pictures of the kids and said, "There's Gabi," as if she knew the child. Janice said her powers told her the children might be buried in the Sand Hills region and they would not be coming back. Although the investigators found her strange they drove around the area anyway, but found nothing suspicious.

*Lorne Tasker drove from Calgary to the Cochrane detachment to discuss the case with investigators. He said he didn't know if he was psychic, but he got terrible dreams about the Dolejs children.

"All I do know is they are alive and unharmed." He had nothing else to add, except he'd spent time in the hospital in 1983 after hitting his head in a construction accident.

Again, none of the psychic leads furthered the investigation.

Sunday, August 17

Paul and Gabi Dolejs have now been missing ten days and searchers are becoming frustrated as they tramp the same area over again with no success.

Al's family was completely mystified. Mother Dolejs in particular could not believe Al would kill his own children.

"He was good boy, who never got into trouble. He was an altar boy," she protested. She wrote him in jail.

My Lola,

We are here in Pardubice with Elunka and you must know all we do is think and talk about you.
Elunka and Pepa told me they talked with you.
Lola, I agree fully with what they advised, especially what Pepa said and I feel the same way.
I pray for you all. How else can I help you? I pray ardently

especially for the children, for Paul and Gabi. I beg and
plead with the Virgin Mary all the time. I beseech the Holy
Spirit who is God's love, the highest love, unegotistic and
forgiving, that he may enlighten us all and instruct us how
to act properly and comfort us.
I am begging you, if it is possible to correct anything in
these events, do it! Do it even at the cost of the greatest
sacrifice.
If you can, write me. Write.
I commend you to the protection of God and the Virgin
Mary.
Your Mom and Grandma

Al's sister Elunka added a line: I pray for you all and think of you.

Liba knew it was crucial to have Al's family come and pressure him
into revealing the whereabouts of the children. If anyone could get him
to do it they could. She understood the cost was out of their reach and
hadn't a penny of her own to pay for their trip. Father Dolejs was now
dead, so Mother Dolejs existed on a monthly government pension of 500
koruna or crowns and, despite a prestigious job as a civil engineer, Pepa
made only around 3,500 crowns a month. One crown was equivalent to
five cents so, in Canadian dollars, Pepa made $175 a month, which he
needed to feed and shelter his own two children, David and Matthew
(pseudonyms). A return airline ticket was $2,250 or 45,000 crowns, a
year's salary.

What Liba did not know was the RCMP invited the family to Canada
and offered to pay all of their expenses. They wrote Interpol requesting
help from the Czech Embassy with the family. They informed Interpol the
investigation was stalled without the bodies and that, although Al was a
self-centered and paranoid individual who showed little or no remorse for
his act, he maintained strong ties to his family in Czechoslovakia.

They asked the Czechoslovakian government to find out if the family would assist in the investigation and come to Canada at no expense of their own. The only condition was they would like Al not to be warned. They wanted the family to take him by surprise. They also wanted the Czechoslovakian government to find out if Al had written or called recently and what he said.

Interpol forwarded the letter to Consular Operations at External Affairs in Ottawa. The Embassy of the Czechoslovak Socialist Republic replied that according to their records, Paul and Gabi had not visited their country since 1982 and that none of Al's relatives intended to come and help, yet. The family agreed only to continue to write and call him in Canada.

Pepa wrote the RCMP and asked for Al's address and phone number, explaining he could not get it from Liba because she was a liar. He said he could not come to Canada to help because his youngest son, Matthew, was an epileptic and prone to seizures so he did not want to leave the country.

Pepa said he did not agree with the condition the RCMP imposed that Al not know of their coming in advance. He said that he, his sister and mother were all Al had in the world and they didn't want to lose his trust. It would make Pepa feel guilty. He said he might think about coming if they let him speak with Al about it.

He said there were some things he wanted the RCMP to know about Al's life and marriage, including the content of letters Liba had written their family early in their union praising Al. He said his sister, Elunka, spoke with Al just before the deed and the family considered the whole thing an unfortunate accident. They wanted to clarify the whole matter through the Ministry of Czechoslovakian External Affairs. Their feeling was the problem started when his children were taken away from him by force. Al loved them so much, he just couldn't handle it.

Then Pepa wrote Liba excusing Al's behavior, criticizing the police and chastising her for not communicating enough with Al.

Dear Liba,

The bad luck of our family isn't over yet. Matthew suffers
from epilepsy, complicated by a low white blood cell count.
For that reason, I have to turn down the journey to Canada.
I don't think Al would talk anyway...In my opinion talking
is a long term affair if the right approach is chosen...I mean
slowly bringing him back to God.
I don't believe he did what he did out of bad will, but rather
out of stress. I have a feeling he doesn't even know where
the children are. In critical situations a person starts acting
like a machine without even realizing what they are doing.
What he did happened involuntarily.
It is too bad that in stressful situations he starts smiling and
ignoring people. It isn't his fault he inherited that quality.
Our grandfather, our father and I do it too.
I am sorry the Canadian police don't show any interest in
knowing about his character when we offered to tell them
about what he was really like. They know they can
communicate with us through the embassy and save us
having to travel. When I look at the letters they sent us, and
you sent us and the Embassy sent us, I feel there are so
many discrepancies, I am very suspicious.
The story of your marriage should be a testimony for others
to think about. How to act and what are their priorities in
life. When two people get married a new world can be
created, but they have to have the courage to stay open with
each other until they become one in a spiritual sense. From
the beginning you need honesty and the help of a good
priest and most importantly, a prayer for the Grace of God.

Pepa

Pepa's father-in-law, Cenek Semerad, a man Liba greatly admired, wrote Liba the truth. He told her Pepa and Anna were having a terrible time with their sons, David and Matthew. Matthew was very aggressive. He would throw terrible tantrums, breaking anything he fancied. Pepa's family lived with the Semerads in a house in Prague. Pepa and Anna had secured a high rise apartment, but couldn't move in because they were afraid Matthew would jump off the balcony or set a fire. David was a little easier to handle, but also terribly disobedient and constantly at war with his father.

It was clear the Dolejs family had retreated to their pattern of banding together, blaming others and protecting their own, at any cost.

CHAPTER TWENTY-NINE

TWO FACES OF EVIL

Since 1975, when Gordie Johnson had spent his weekends helping Al build the Parkland house, he and his wife, Dorothy, were the only Canadian couple Liba and Al and the kids visited regularly. They'd often spend special occasions with the Johnsons who were a generation older than Liba and Al.

Gordie was one of the few people Al respected. He had a nice home and a good job. He was well educated and prosperous, but Gordie's tolerance and benevolent nature mystified Al. Liba and the kids thought it was funny that Gordie preferred peanut butter and jam sandwiches to leftover turkey, but Al was incensed. A man should demand full course meals, served hot and fresh. His laundry should be washed and pressed properly. How could Gordie, a seemingly sensible man, have a peanut butter sandwich for supper and be happy about it?

Dorothy's mother, Grandma Peterson, and Gordie's mother, Grandma Johnson, would often join them. Both ladies were in their early eighties and quite refined. Paul and Gabi adored them. They had so little exposure to older people, they adopted Dorothy and Gordie as auntie and uncle and their mothers as grandparents.

But the big surprise was the way Al acted around them. He would cater to the ladies' every whim.

"Oh, Mrs. Peterson," he'd smile, "would you like more tea? More sugar? Can I bring you a cookie, Mrs. Johnson?"

If one of them attempted to stand, Al would leap to his feet and gallantly hold out his arm. Liba would watch dumfounded. Mrs. Johnson was always remarking what a wonderful person Al was.

"Oh you married such a nice man." She'd pat Liba's cheek fondly. "I'm so happy for you dear."

But the moment they got into the car to leave, Al would make disparaging remarks about them. "Why do we have to go there and talk with those old raisins? I hate it."

There was a huge incongruence between the appearance of what others saw and the behavior that occurred at home. Gordie was a perceptive man and one day took Liba aside. "What's wrong?" he asked gently.

Used to covering for Al, Liba tried to keep her face a mask of blank indifference. "Oh, nothing, why do you ask?"

Gordie looked her straight in the eye. "I haven't seen you smile for about three days. Your lips are so tight I can't even see them."

Liba blushed and cleared her throat. She didn't know whether to be relieved or mortified that somebody finally noticed. She made a snap decision. She could trust Gordie.

"I'm under a lot of stress and I'm just…being treated lousy at home."

Although she avoided specifics, Gordie was very understanding. He told her she could turn to him and Dorothy any time she needed help. Liba felt terribly relieved. The door to getting support had opened a little.

Soon after, she confided to Dorothy about Al's two-faced behavior toward the elderly Johnson relatives and Dorothy's jaw dropped. She'd known Al for seven years and said she would never have guessed he acted that way.

"Don't worry," Liba reassured her. "It's taken me over a decade to realize this is what he's really like."

CHAPTER THIRTY

LIBA'S DREAMS

Monday, August 18

Searchers for Paul and Gabi Dolejs found an axe and shovel in separate locations today. RCMP are investigating whether they were used in murdering the two children.

Last night was bad. Liba dragged herself up to bed at midnight and finally drifted off to sleep at around 1:00. But instead of waking at 3:00 as usual, she woke up at 4:00 and realized she was sitting on the edge of her bed. She dreamed she was in the kitchen and Gabi was at the table in the nook drawing pictures and making her own books like she always did. Her little stapler was there and all of her crayons. Liba saw Peter Martin sitting next to Gabi.

Gabi was showing Peter her picture. She said, "This is my Mommy and this is my Daddy and this is my brother, Paul." Liba felt overwhelmed with pity for her little girl. She noted that Gabi had said, "This is my brother, Paul," not "this was my brother, Paul." The poor little thing didn't know her brother was dead.

Liba thought, "I must go and hug her and explain to her that Paul is no longer alive." She was about to do that when she woke up and realized Gabi wasn't there either. There was nobody to hug.

Liba sat at the kitchen table, gripping a small white registration form. She turned it over and over in her hands wondering what to do with it. Today, Paul was to start hockey school at Southland Leisure Center. Should she call and tell them he wouldn't be there?

Wednesday, August 20

The search for two Calgary children was scaled down yesterday, from 35 to fewer than ten searchers. But the RCMP says they are determined they will continue for at least three more days.

"Maybe this is what it's like to lose your mind." Liba thought. Try as she might, all she could do was wait by the phone. Her inability to help her children paralyzed her with guilt and grief.

She knew they were dead. They'd been gone almost a month. Someone had made an offer on the house and she'd spent last Sunday cleaning out the garage. She came across Paul's hockey bag, all packed and ready for the rink. It broke her heart. She held up his favorite red hockey jersey. It was so small. He was just a little boy, but always so responsible and wise. She thought of him as older and bigger. She closed her eyes trying to summon up his face.

Sandy suggested maybe she should have a garage sale.

Another psychic, *Talia Whittaker from Maryland, phoned RCMP investigators. She was well spoken and claimed a female outside the family would break the case. She saw the kids on the left side of a stream. The ground was soft and had been bulldozed. The father had dug graves up to his waist and there were rocks over the graves. Within thirty minutes of the site, they would find a river named after an animal.

Friday, August 22

After two solid weeks of full-fledged searching, police have called off the hunt for two missing Calgary children in the McLean Creek area. A search master and three investigators will remain in the area to follow any new leads.

*Jean Watts called Wally Purcell and said her friend *Tina Langois told her she saw flashes of Mr. Dolejs hitting the boy with a board. Jean said she agonized whether to report this to the police, but felt it was the right thing to do.

The last psychic to call, *Eva Castlegaard, told Wally she dreamed the bodies were buried in a large open field near evergreens.

The police treated each and every caller politely and appreciatively. They followed up every lead, but none panned out.

CHAPTER THIRTY-ONE

THE ACCIDENT

On July 4th, 1985 Liba had a very close call. She was working for Stuart Engineering at the time. They owned a fleet of trucks for field crews and their mechanic worked out of his own garage across from Henry Wise Wood School on Elbow Drive. Her Datsun needed a new clutch so she dropped it there first thing in the morning, and strolled over toward the bus stop.

A few cars came to a halt and Liba began crossing the street on the pedestrian crosswalk. She squinted at the bright sunshine through the tops of the huge poplar trees. She was across the first lane when she caught a flash of something hurtling towards her. Then she heard the squeal of brakes.

Twenty years of gymnastics gave her the reflexes to dive and roll. She was already airborne when the car hit her in the hip. The only thought that flashed through her mind was, "So far so good."

She hit the road in a break fall she had practiced in judo. When she opened her eyes, she was staring close up at the pavement and saw all the little pockmarks in the asphalt. The smell of dust filled her nostrils. Then everything went black.

When she opened her eyes again, she heard voices. "Oh my God, she's not moving. Should we turn her over?"

"No, wait for the ambulance."

Liba processed this. "I'm thinking, so I'm not dead," she thought. "But if my back is broken and I'm paralyzed, I'd rather be dead." A heavy feeling settled upon her and again she drifted out of consciousness.

The next time she woke up, she summoned up everything she had and tried to move her left big toe. Success! She allowed her mind to surface. "I'm not paralyzed. I can move. I can deal with everything else."

Paramedics were asking her questions. "How are you feeling? Do you hurt anywhere? Do you want us to take you to the hospital?"

She turned herself over. "I don't know, I guess I'm fine." They helped her stand up.

By the time she made it to the police car, she was having problems. Small muscle control was gone. She couldn't even pull her driver's license out of her purse. An officer did it for her. After all the forms were filled out and the driver of the car that hit her was issued a $40 ticket for not yielding to a pedestrian, the officer asked her what she wanted to do. She said she'd been on her way to work, so he drove her there. She made it to her desk and slumped down.

"Where have you been?" demanded the surveyor in charge and he proceeded to give her hell for being late.

A terrible bruise started forming up her left hip and by the afternoon, she couldn't move. She caught a ride home and stumbled in the door. Startled by her early arrival, Al looked up from the television.

"I was hit by a car," she gasped in pain. "You'll have to pick up the kids. I've got to lie down."

He rolled his eyes and turned back to the TV.

"Lazy bitch," he muttered.

CHAPTER THIRTY-TWO

THE SALE

Saturday, August 23

Sandy and her husband Jeff, a city cop, got up early Saturday morning and headed all the way from the north side of the city to Liba's southwest home in Woodbine. They were going to help her price out items for the garage sale. On the way over, Sandy told Jeff she thought they should try to be as light-hearted as possible for Liba's sake.

"You know, this'll take her away from the sadness and the memories. Putting his tools and stuff out to sell, you know how hard that would be. Let's make it a fun thing."

Jeff agreed. He was a good-hearted person with the cynical sense of humor and pessimistic view of life many policemen have. Jeff had a tough exterior, but his insides were made of marshmallow. He had grown very fond of Liba and her mother whom he and Sandy both called Mom. They had even invited them to their home for spaghetti suppers.

As they pulled up, they saw a guy in a battered pickup loading armfuls of tools and camping gear into his truck. He walked back to Liba, shoved his hand in his pocket and gave her some money, but it didn't look like much. Liba didn't even count it. She just stuffed it into the old cookie tin she was using as a bank.

Sandy turned to Liba. "What, are you nuts? Didn't you see what he took?"

Liba shook her head and shrugged. "No. It was all junk. His junk."

Jeff came running over towards them. "There's a guy leaving with a super duper power saw that you sold him for twenty bucks!"

Liba grinned. "Yeah, I know."

Sandy understood. She folded her arms and grinned back. "Oh, that would piss Al off now, wouldn't it?"

Liba smiled. "Yeah, it would."

Jeff started making jokes. When cars pulled up, he'd give the driver the once over and whisper comments like, "Oh, oh. We got us a professional garage saler here. He's serious. Watch him, watch him. All right now, what have we here? Hmmm, the baseball cap says Old Fart. Okay, now the wife is getting out of the truck and her hat says...Old Fart's Wife. Well, I guess we know who wears the pants in that family." It made the whole day much easier.

Liba continued to sell Al's tools and possessions dirt cheap, knowing it would rot his socks if he knew. She included a few things that had belonged to the kids, games and toys they'd outgrown, and by the end of the day everything was gone.

CHAPTER THIRTY-THREE

SUCH GOOD KIDS

The kids took care of her. On days when she had horrendous low back pains and wasn't able to roll over in bed, they'd massage her spine. Eventually, her whole right leg went numb and she couldn't walk without dragging it. To get into the car, she'd open the driver's door, lift her arms up, grab the roof of the car, lower herself down to the seat, pick up her right leg with both hands, put it inside the car, then repeat the same action with her left leg. If he noticed, Al would roll his eyes or make a snide remark. Paul and Gabi, on the other hand, would rush to her side.

Was it truly beneficial for the kids if she stayed so they could grow up in an intact family? Or should she leave their father and live in fear of retribution? He was still reasonably nice to Gabi. He tolerated anything she said or did without rebuke. But lately he'd not only physically isolated himself, he began to drift off mentally too and Gabi found that frustrating.

At the supper table, Gabi liked to hold forth about her day. A perfectionist, she loved rules, was good at school and was becoming an aggressive sports competitor. One night, she talked about a picture she drew and how it didn't come out the way she wanted, so she'd ripped it up and started all over again. And when that hadn't worked, she'd drawn it five more times before it suited her.

Then Paul and Liba exchanged amused glances as she critically recounted how some girl at soccer left her zone and missed a pass. After that, she sighed and launched into a tale about a classmate who tried to initiate a conversation and how unfair it was that she, Gabi, got caught talking again. In the middle of her story she realized her daddy wasn't listening. Affronted, she leaned close to his ear and called his name repeatedly.

"Daddy? Daddy? Daddy?" Turning up the volume each time. Finally she yelled, "Daddy!" and he snapped to.

"Oh." He blinked at her like a man waking from a coma. "Yeah?"

Exasperated, Gabi shook her head and tsked. "Daddy, I'm trying to tell you something."

"Okay." He nodded and listened, but a short while later, it was apparent his mind was gone again.

Early in the winter of 1984, the phone rang at three thirty in the morning. As Liba swam to consciousness, she realized Al was already out of bed and on his way into the spare bedroom she used as an office to answer it. He would wake her if it were important. She drifted back to sleep and forgot all about it.

A week later, she reminded Al they would be dining with Gordie and Dorothy Johnson on Christmas Day, as usual. Al glared at her.

"What the hell are you talking about? Do you think I'm going to go to some kind of a Christmas party after my father just died?"

Liba frowned. "What?"

Al folded his arms in front of his chest and stuck his chin out belligerently. "He died a week ago."

Suddenly she remembered the phone call. "But you never told me, Al." She didn't understand his reasoning for keeping it to himself. She knew his family was secretive, but this was ridiculous. There was something mentally wrong with him. But how do you tell a crazy, temperamental guy he needs to see a psychiatrist? She tried.

"Al, things are not right with you. You treat me and the kids like the lumber you hammer on at work. We are human beings. What if...you looked into some counseling?"

Al blew up at the suggestion. "You are the one who is fucked up and crazy. They put ideas in your head and before you know it, you believe these ideas. You need a psychiatrist because there's nothing wrong with me! If I'm going nuts it's because you are driving me nuts!" Then he stormed off.

His angry outbursts were now everyday occurrences and Gabi and Paul were intimidated. The drive to day care gave Liba twenty five uninterrupted minutes every morning and night with the kids. Liba used the time to talk and teach them Czech nursery rhymes or songs. One morning, after the kids witnessed Liba endure a particularly vicious tongue lashing from Al, Paul and Gabi climbed quietly into the car and when they were safely on their way, Paul gave Liba a shy sidelong glance.

"Can I ask you something?"

Liba smiled reassuringly at him. "You can ask me anything anytime."

Paul swallowed. "Do we have to live with Daddy?"

Liba's breath caught in her throat. "No, no we don't have to."

Paul's shoulders dropped in relief. "Could we move away?"

Liba watched the road and tried to appear matter of fact, so as not to upset him. "Yes, we could. I just don't know exactly how to go about it."

Paul fiddled uncomfortably with the strap on his lunch box. "I just hate seeing how he treats you."

Liba knew he was right. She couldn't pretend there was a marriage or a family anymore. She tapped the steering wheel with the flat of her hand.

"Good, Paul. I'm glad you let me know how you feel. We have to have that kind of understanding between all of us, because if I'm making a decision, I have to make it for both of you as well. I need to know how you feel about it."

Liba caught Gabi in the rear view mirror. The little girl was choking back tears. Liba continued softly, "What Daddy's doing is all wrong. It's wrong to treat a person the way he treats me. You don't do things like that. And I don't want you to see it for much longer. We won't have quite as nice a place as we have now because we'll have to rent. But we'll be okay. We won't be poor, but we'll have to watch our money. It may be little difficult, but it's only temporary. Things will get better."

She glanced at Gabi again. Gabi was nodding and seemed to have regained her composure. Paul met his mother's eyes.

"I think that's a good plan, Mommy," he said gravely.

CHAPTER THIRTY-FOUR

LIBA'S QUEST

Liba was numb. Cold. She lost sensory feeling. She could not even tell whether the tea she sipped was hot or cold. She spent most of her time puzzling out different case scenarios. The kids had spent enough time in the mountains to know they should follow any moving body of water downstream. They knew if it flowed into a bigger creek, to follow it down. She'd assured them eventually the river would come out of the mountains and go to some town or civilization.

They could drink from the rivers. They had good jackets, they had clothing, but no food. They knew what berries were safe to eat, and they could always munch on grass, but she fretted about how hungry they'd be. And if they were wet, they might develop hypothermia. When she tried to close her eyes at night, it wasn't the thought of them scared and huddled together that gripped her heart so hard she could hardly breathe, it was the knowledge that they would be very brave to reassure the other.

Sometimes she'd accept the idea they were dead, but that always lead to the horrifying possibility that one had watched the other die. Paul would have died first. Because that's what Al always had threatened. He never, ever, threatened Gabi. But it would be worse to die second, because you'd see what was coming. Liba was sure Al's hatred of Paul would be needed to fuel the first killing. He probably killed Gabi because she was a witness and he was a coward and would protect himself at any cost.

Perhaps, she tried to console herself, he told them they were going to go play hide and seek. It was something they'd done with the kids before. That way he could have killed one without the other knowing.

She remembered how Al was always watching TV looking for perfect cases, perfect murders. He watched lots of court proceedings. She knew he figured if the police had no bodies and he came up with a lie or stayed silent, they couldn't pin it on him. He considered himself smarter than everybody else. He was always commenting on how stupid the rest of the world was.

She didn't go near the kids' bedroom. It was too rough. Instead, she spent a lot of time sitting in the playroom trying to reach out to them. If she concentrated hard enough, maybe they'd be able to connect with her somehow. But there was never any response. All she got was a void.

She had to do something, so she approached Sandy Harder. Could she join the search for her kids? Sandy consulted with the team and they flatly refused. Liba pestered Sandy daily, but to no avail. Liba knew they were trying to protect her, knowing that if she came across her kids' bodies she might contaminate the crime scene or never recover from the sight.

Finally, Liba gave up trying to convince them she could handle it. She'd go on her own. Liba was not an average hiker. Her bushwhacking experience as an orienteer and the fact she worked as a land survey draftsman made her more qualified to search the area than most of the people out there.

She had her own topographical maps and picked up an additional map from the Park Information Center. It was the same map Al had used to navigate Sylvester Trail. She cut aerial photographs and maps from The Calgary Herald and compiled all information made public. She knew the RCMP thought the bodies would be close to the truck so they were doing a grid search north of a major cut line, then heading south towards the truck. One thing Liba's orienteering taught her was trust your gut. Her gut wanted her to go further north of the cut line, past the search area.

She got up early and dressed carefully. Running shoes and running tights. There was no need to pack provisions. She had a plan. Today, she would find her children. They would most likely be dead. She could picture it. She would gather them in her arms and never leave.

She sped along the highway west and turned into the McLean Creek camping area. Following the signs, she found Sylvester Trail and floored the pedal on the Datsun up and through huge mud banks. She managed to steer around the low spots which were completely flooded. She wanted to go to where Al's truck was found. Maybe he put the bodies back in the truck to drive them further into the bush. Then he got stuck. He would have had to carry them and bury them within walking distance. Granted, there was little blood in the truck, but maybe he poisoned them. He had the whole day to do it. The possibilities were endless.

Unwanted thoughts kept creeping into her head. He was a hunter. He could have bled them first. If he cut their throats while they were alive, it would be gushing and in twenty minutes their bodies would be drained. Once she'd seen a dead salmon on the shore. At first she thought it was alive because it was moving around so much, but on closer inspection, she realized it was full of maggots and now her babies…

"No, no, not here!" she screamed at herself. "You can play these mind games when you're lying awake at home, but not when you're out in the bush like this. You can't afford to break down here!"

She gripped the wheel tight and forced it all out of her mind. She needed to concentrate on the task at hand. She couldn't get emotional. Her primary problem was not to get lost because nobody knew where she was. She was north and east of where the truck was found, in front of a huge pool of water banked by five-foot walls of mud. She pulled over and parked by the side of the road.

She knew this area had been searched thoroughly and the kids weren't here. She started running. Thankfully it wasn't raining, just a drizzle here and there and it was cold, so there were no mosquitoes. But she couldn't avoid the mud, which was so deep, she sometimes sank up to her knees.

Logic suggested Al wouldn't attempt a dead end trail in muskeg because his truck would get stuck and he'd be caught for sure. But her gut told her that's exactly where he'd head. An area like that wouldn't be traveled due to its limited access. He'd have to turn off this main trail, which was difficult, but it would afford him privacy. Privacy was what he needed.

She ran south, straight past a second cut line. She knew she should have eaten something, but didn't feel hungry, thirsty or tired. She didn't feel anything except anger. She was angry because the police wouldn't bring her here and she had to do it on her own. She was angry because Al, the stupid bastard, was arrogant enough to believe the kids were his possessions and like garbage, he felt he had the right to throw them away. She was angry with herself for not being killed when that car had hit her on Elbow Drive. If she were dead, maybe her babies would be alive today.

About four and a half kilometers south from where she parked her trusty little Datsun, she came to where he'd abandoned the truck. She continued south another kilometer and a half until somehow it started feeling wrong. She turned around and came back. There was a ravine on her left. She slowed down. It was a possibility. It got quite deep and the grass was tall. A good place for dumping bodies perhaps. She slid down the wall, picked up some branches and started beating the grass near the bottom. She looked up toward the trail. She was too visible from the road. Any clothing with color would stand out. She thought of Gabi's red parka. They weren't here.

She made her way back up to the trail, running north. She was now five and a half kilometers from the Datsun, a kilometer north of the search area. She studied the ground. It was clay, covered with big rocks, heavily rutted.

She stopped in front of a grassy slope. It looked like it had once been an ATV trail. She looked at her map. It was, but it dead-ended into muskeg. She took a few steps up. It was so narrow and steep there would be no place to turn around. There were huge slabs of slate at the top of the rise. His truck could never make it, especially in this mud.

She changed her mind and joined the main trail again, not realizing her kids were just three hundred feet away.

CHAPTER THIRTY-FIVE

SPEED FREAK

Like her mother, Gabi was a speed freak. Paul preferred caution, but Gabi loved the adrenaline rush of going really, really fast. Liba had to watch her carefully when she took the kids for bike rides in the country. Calgary is surrounded by foothills and during one foray, after an arduous push to the top of a steep hill, Gabi grinned with pleasure at the sight of a long road down. Liba could see what Gabi had in mind.

"Gabi," she warned, "take it easy here. There is a corner, then another corner, then a narrow bridge at the bottom." But before her last words were uttered, Gabi was flying down the hill.

"Brake, Gabi! Brake!" yelled Liba.

"No, I'm okay! I'm fine." Gabi laughed. She had absolutely no fear.

Liba realized she would have to channel Gabi's need for speed. She signed up both Paul and Gabi in a luge club. It was fall so they began dry land training, which involved sleds on wheels. Burnco road is a long truck road on top of a mini-mountain that now houses Canada Olympic Park, a small ski resort on the west edge of Calgary. The sight would be used for ski jumping, bobsled and luge during the 1988 Winter Olympics.

It was a steep road with sharp corners, unused on weekends. The coach set up pylons on the road for slalom practice. The children learned to steer with their ankles. Paul followed the course and did what he was supposed to do. Then it was Gabi's turn. She completed the first four turns, came flying out of the pylons and swooshed straight down the road at more than fifty kilometers an hour. The coach started screaming at her.

"Make the turns! Make the turns!"

But Gabi refused, yelling back, "I don't want to, they slow me down!"

CHAPTER THIRTY-SIX

THE FINAL MEETING

Father Vladimir Redgjka, a Franciscan Monk from Czechoslovakia now living in British Columbia, happened to be visiting Calgary on September 9th. He called the RCMP offering his services. They took him up on his offer and arranged for him to meet with Al the next day. He arrived at 5:30 PM for an hour and a half visit. But it proved fruitless. He came out of the meeting shaking his head and informed them Al refused to discuss the children or their fate. He told them he had promised Al he would return with a Czech Bible.

That evening at 9:30, Al was told he had a visitor. It was late, past visiting hours. It must be the priest with his Bible. He yawned and stretched. Good. He could read himself to sleep. He shuffled toward the visitor's room, a guard at his side.

Sandy picked up Liba and drove downtown through a lightening storm to the Remand Center. It was raining torrentially and the thunder was deafening. Liba was in jeans and a sweatshirt because she had been asked to wear baggy clothing. The RCMP intended to have her wear a wire.

A huge black prison guard, built like a linebacker, escorted her down a long and narrow concrete corridor. The lighting was harsh and bleak and except for their echoing footsteps, there was no sound. He was half a step in front and she had to hurry to keep up with him.

Suddenly, a loud, sharp click bounced off the walls around her and her knees almost buckled. The guard turned and gave her an understanding smile.

"Don't worry about it. That click gets to lot of people. It's behind you, in the wall. There is this hidden bullet-proof glass door and as you walk through it, it slides closed so you can't turn around and escape."

They proceeded through a set of steel bar doors into a square room where all the radio transmitters were set up. Sandy was there and they retired to a bathroom so Liba could remove her shirt and have the wire taped to her chest. Hands pressed up against the cold bathroom tile, Liba felt her lungs constrict. She tried to talk, but like in a bad dream, could not raise her voice above a whisper.

Mother Dolejs used to send them stacks of Czech magazines. These parcels would take two to three months by boat to reach them. The RCMP suggested Liba bring the latest unopened package as an offering. And because Al smoked they thought she might throw in a package of Rothmans.

She was taken to the visitor's cell, which was a six by eight room lined with unpainted concrete. It was barren with only a desk and a steel chair on either side. The visitor's chair faced the door. Liba was shown a panic button on the inside of the desk by her right knee.

"If he tries anything violent, if he reaches toward you, punches anything, all you have to do is press it and the guard outside the door will be here in seconds," Sandy said. The button was red.

Liba found herself wishing he would attack her, then she would be justified in going for his throat. But she knew he was far too cowardly to start anything here. He preferred to pick on the helpless. Anyway, it wasn't the thought he could hurt her physically that scared her. It was the knowledge that if he chose to, he could really go after her emotionally and get her at her core.

She pictured the incredibly huge black guard outside the door. He was young, maybe in his late twenties, six three or four, 240 or 250 pounds of solid muscle. He was so friendly, she wondered what the heck he was doing in a place like this? Knowing he was there did make her feel safe. But she was like a cat on slippery roof, especially when Sandy said, "They're going to get him," and left her there alone.

She mentally prepared herself. Her feeling for Al was one of pure revulsion. Dealing with him was filthy business.

When Al walked in, the big guard was just behind his left shoulder. Al spotted Liba and it was as if he were spring-loaded. He literally jumped straight up in the air, at least a foot. He twisted 180 degrees and slammed into the big guard's chest. It was a huge reaction.

"I don't want to see her!" Al whined.

The guard grabbed him by the shoulders, spun him back around and plunked him in the chair.

"She's here, might as well talk to her," he said and closed the door behind him.

The scene gave Liba a little bit of satisfaction. "Surprised you, eh?" she thought.

Her posture was tense, hands clasped in front of her on the desk. The package of magazines and smokes lay between them. She tried to relax a little. The best she could manage was a loud whisper. She studied the creature in front of her. He was posed like a big rat, head and shoulders frozen together and eyes darting back and forth. When he looked at her, she saw fear.

"These came in the mail. They're addressed to you. It's from your mother so I figured you should have it." She pointed at the package.

He swept it to one side as if he couldn't stand to look at this disturbing reminder of reality and his family, but she knew he would open it later. Then he leaned back a little. His expression was stone again.

"I don't care," he said.

"I came here for another reason. I feel that the kids should be given some kind of a memorial, some kind of a good-bye or something. I would like to have a mass said for them. I just wanted to know if it was okay with you."

He shrugged his shoulders. "I don't care what you do."

"You must care. They were your children. I was thinking of a Catholic mass."

He stared straight through her.

"I was thinking of asking Father Bastigal," she continued.

He still refused to answer. She could see it was futile. She got up, making sure not to turn her back to him and made her way to the door. She let the guard know they were finished.

He took Al by the arm and as soon as they were out of sight she slumped against the wall completely drained.

Mami stayed home by herself that evening. All she could think about was her daughter at the jail with such an evil man. She sat by the kitchen window watching the storm rage outside. Suddenly, the house lit up with a flash of lightening followed by booming thunder so loud, some of the cupboard doors swung open and the glasses on the shelves danced and toasted each other. It was like a scene in a horror movie. Mami buried her face in her hands and began to cry.

Soon after seeing Al, Liba had another dream. This time, Liba was walking down a country road. It was a beautiful warm evening near dusk. On her right was a meadow gently sloping down into a small valley. In the distance, she could see a simple farm building. She thought maybe it was a barn. A light shone within.

As she watched, Paul walked out of the light and came to her. She sat down on a stump and he sat on her lap. She could smell his sweet scent as she wrapped her arms around him, cuddling. He was relaxed and happy. She murmured in his ear.

"How are you doing sweetheart? Do you hurt anywhere or feel any pain?"

He gave her a beautiful smile and assured her everything was fine. "No, Mommy, I feel good."

Liba held him tight and in a quiet voice said, "Honey, I know where you were that day up until one o'clock in the afternoon. Can you tell me where you went after that?"

Paul looked at her, eyes full of love and concern and said gently, "Mommy, you know I can't tell you that." Then he said, "I have to go," and he got up and walked back into the building leaving her completely empty.

CHAPTER THIRTY-EIGHT

EASTER SUNDAY

On their way back from Banff after Al came close to drowning Paul that Easter Sunday, Liba asked the truck driver to take her to Dorothy and Gordie Johnson's house. She called and arranged for the social worker, Twila Harding, to meet her there.

She and Paul talked the whole situation over with Gordie and Dorothy and Twila. Paul told them his gymnastic coach, Jesse Anderson, was at the Hot Springs that day. Al had never met him and didn't know he was paying attention to what was happening. Paul gave Jesse a couple of panicky looks, but Al played it right on the edge. He was laughing and made it look like it was a game. Later, Jesse said had the game gotten any rougher, he was prepared to intervene.

Liba understood his reluctance to butt in. "It was sort of like, at what point is it your business? If somebody is spanking their kid does he deserve it or is the kid being beaten and you should stop it?" Jesse didn't know what to think. But he was catching Paul's looks. Paul said it gave him a little bit of a security, knowing somebody was watching.

Twila seemed like a reasonable person. She understood how worried Liba was for the safety of her kids and herself and wasn't the least bit patronizing.

"What is the priority here? What do we need to do?" she asked Liba.

Liba answered, "We have to get my daughter. We just have to get my daughter." She didn't think Al would hurt Gabi, but she knew he wouldn't take care of her either. She wanted her little girl safe in her arms.

Twila considered this. "Is it safe to go there? Are there guns in the house?"

Liba blinked. She hadn't thought of Al shooting anyone, but now she realized she had to consider the possibility.

"Yes, there are guns in the house, hunting guns. And he's pretty volatile. I don't know if it's safe to go there or not." When there were strangers present, he didn't blow up, but she felt she couldn't count on anything anymore.

Twila requested Calgary City Police assistance. It was nearly midnight when they all met at the house and silently trooped up the stairs to the front door. Liba used her key. Al was sitting in the darkened living room staring at the TV. The policeman informed him Gabi was being removed from the home with her mother and the best thing for him to do was stay calm. He needn't have bothered. Al was like a statue and didn't move from in front of the set.

Liba crept upstairs into Gabi's room. She was sleeping in the clothing she had worn that day. Liba had to get out of there fast. Using a bunch of plastic grocery bags, she started packing them full of the children's clothes. Knowing how tough this would be on the kids, she also grabbed Vorisek, Little Pink Elephant, brown bunny, Winnie the Pooh and stuffed tiger.

Gabi opened her eyes groggily. She started to mew. "What's going on Mommy?"

Liba didn't want her to cry, so she wrapped her in a comforter. "It's okay, Elunka," she whispered, "we're going away tonight, that's all."

"No." Gabi was frightened. "Where's Paul?"

"Shhh. I'll tell you all about it in the car. Don't be alarmed. Mommy's here. Paul is waiting. We'll all be together."

Gabi calmed down, but didn't want to get out of bed. Pumped full of fear-induced adrenaline, Liba hoisted her up, blanket, plastic bags and all, and made her way down the stairs.

Liba knew it wouldn't be safe to go back to Johnson's, so Twila arranged for them to spend the night at the Sheriff King Home, an emergency shelter for battered women. She didn't give a damn about any of her possessions, but she needed her car. So she grabbed her keys and left a note to Al, telling him about the busted truck at Chiniki Station.

That night she couldn't sleep. Many times Al had threatened to burn the house down and she was sure he would do it this time.

Liba called a lawyer, Robert Densmore, and secured a restraining order. Al was forced to leave their home and not contact her or the kids. He moved in with Jiri Srom and got a lawyer of his own. He said he wanted custody of the kids. It was suggested he seek counseling and join a father's group first.

Al started going to a group called Fathers of Alberta. The group consisted of fathers separated from their children due to divorce situations or restraining orders. They'd meet and share stories and advice. Al attended a couple of gatherings and Ian Clark, the group organizer, told him frankly he'd have to straighten his life around before he'd ever get custody of his kids.

By the time Al had moved into the Capri Motel, he was desperate to come home. He tried calling Liba, but she wouldn't talk to him. One night he pulled up in front of the house and begged her to come out. Reluctantly, she joined him on the front seat of the truck. He told her how sorry he was and how stupidly he'd behaved. Would she take him back?

"No, Al. Life has been hell for the last twelve years. I've done everything in my power to keep the family together and you haven't lifted a damn finger. You've been abusive to Paul and me, treating us like sub-humans. Who's going to make up for that?"

Al held up his hands. "You are right, absolutely right. I was a fool. But let's not think of the past. Let's concentrate on our future, together. Give me another chance."

Liba looked at him incredulously. "You've had twelve years of chances. We have no future together, Al."

He smiled, as was his habit when in trouble, then quickly covered it with his hand. "I know. I know what to do. You see, I'm going to get counseling."

"Good," Liba nodded. "That's good. You need counseling." She opened the door and slid off the seat. "Please leave me alone, Al, or I'll...I'll have to call the police."

"You'll see," he said. "You'll see." And he pulled away. As he drove off, she stared at the dirty license plate on the Ram Charger. FGH-084.

"FGH," she said out loud. "Fight."

Peter Day was a marriage counselor with an office in the northwest quadrant of Calgary. Al went there on his own and poured his heart out. He had a wonderful close relationship with his wife and children, but was experiencing some minor problems at the moment. Would Mr. Day speak with his wife and try to help them iron things out? Peter agreed. Certainly he would.

Al showed up at her door a couple of days later. Noting her displeasure, he quickly assured her, "I won't stay long. I just want to tell you. I went to a counselor. He was a nice guy and maybe he can help us."

Liba sighed. She knew they would never get back together, but maybe this Peter Day could help Al be a better father. "Okay, Al."

She met with Peter that week. Their one-hour appointment stretched into three. Each one of her answers seemed to douse him with cold water. His face grew in consternation, as he kept looking up at her while taking notes.

Finally, he said, "This is a completely different picture than the one your husband painted. I wouldn't have believed it." He threw up is hands. "I'm at a loss."

Liba wasn't surprised. She knew what a convincing liar Al could be. Peter interrupted her thoughts. "I'd like to get him here one more time." Liba said she thought that was a good idea.

A few days later the phone rang. It was Al. He was hot. "I just talked with that counselor, Peter Day." He spit out the name. "That guy's an idiot. I forbid you to talk to him again!"

"I'm not the one who needs counseling, Al." Liba said and hung up. "I guess Peter didn't tell him what he wanted to hear this time," she thought.

Al tried again. He went to Calgary Family Services and talked with a fellow named Gary Sarginia. Gary called Liba, "In all fairness, I need to talk to you. Would you be willing to come in and speak with me?"

Liba didn't see what harm it could do. "Sure," she said and made an appointment. She took the kids, who played in the waiting room while they talked.

The conversation was a repeat of the one she'd had with Peter Day. Again, Al had lied and Gary was under the impression their problems were really no big deal, just a temporary hiccup in an otherwise ideal relationship.

Al had told him he was having a little trouble with his pre-teen son, Paul. Al had said when he took the kids to Banff swimming, Paul took off inexplicably and it created a really embarrassing situation. Then, Al had smiled shame-facedly. "Well maybe is partly my fault. Paul thought I was trying to program or say bad things about his mother and he get mad."

When Gary heard Liba's side of the story, he said, "You know, I'm supposed to be a mediator. I'm supposed to bring couples back together, but there have been a number of occasions in my career when I have encouraged women to leave. I strongly recommend you do that."

Liba was grateful for the support. "The guy's a born loser," Gary continued, "and I'm afraid it will not change."

"It's not a problem," Liba said. "We already split up. I can support the kids. I don't need money from him. I'm not going back."

"Good. Now, he needs help," Gary looked at her soberly, "and I'd like to help him. So what I'd like to do...I'd like to call him back here. I won't make the same mistake the last guy did and confront him on things because he'll run away again. I'll have to soften it up, but I'll see if I can talk to him because he does need help."

Liba agreed. "Yes, I know I've felt that way for a long time. Whatever you can do for him, fine. I'm glad for his sake. I wonder," Liba blushed a little, "do you think you could talk to my kids. They're torn and distressed over this whole situation."

Gary smiled, "Of course."

Liba called the kids into the office, then retreated into the waiting room while he spoke with them for fifteen minutes. They both seemed to step a little lighter when he was finished.

A week later, Al showed up on her doorstep with a sheepish grin. This usually meant he'd done something wrong.

"I went and I talked to this second fellow again and he said there is no reason you and I could not get together again."

Liba stared at him and thought, "I know bloody well that's not what he said." But she had to admit Al seemed so sincere, that if she hadn't talked with Gary personally, she would have believed him.

———————

The restraining order stipulated Al could not be anywhere near where the kids would be, the day care, the school, soccer fields, the gym club or the house. Paul and Gabi understood safety was a big issue.

Liba carefully explained the rules and said, "If you ever see Daddy hanging around school or anything, you have to tell me. Don't go to him. You go and report this to the principal."

She met with the principal of Southwood Elementary, Nestor Yaremko, and told him about it. She also spoke to the daycare supervisor, Mrs. Spaude, and informed all the people who associated with the kids, coaches, parents of their friends, everyone. She tried hard not to disrupt the children's everyday activities.

In return for gymnastics memberships, Liba was coaching five groups of ten kids and had report cards due. Usually, she worked out twice a week in the evenings after nine, after she put the kids to bed. Now that Paul was twelve, she left them for short periods of time. She changed the locks when Al moved out, so she felt the house was secure.

It was a Thursday night and she slipped over to the gym to hand in the report cards. While she was there, she began to warm up for a quick workout, but she couldn't stay focused. She suddenly felt nauseated, then started shaking and feeling cold. Something was wrong at home. She raced to her car and floored it through the city streets.

Her hands shook as she worked the key into the front door and flung it open.

"Hello!" she called out. She heard quick footsteps on the stairs running toward her.

"Mommy, Mommy!" Paul screamed from the upstairs level. "Daddy's in the house!"

Everything was completely dark with just a slash of light shining through the front room window from the street lamps. She glanced around her, waiting for her eyes to adjust. "What do you mean Daddy's in the house?"

"He's still here. Daddy's in the house. Daddy's in the house," he insisted anxiously.

She peered down the stairs to the basement landing and her heart stopped. A dark figure loomed in the opening. He began advancing toward her and she flew at him. Grabbing him by the lapels of his jean jacket, she demanded, "What are you doing here? Just get out of here!" She pushed him toward the open front door.

"No, let's talk, let's talk, I'll explain," he protested.

"Bull shit!" she screamed. "You're not explaining anything. You're not supposed to be here."

"Don't call cops! Don't call cops!" he sniveled.

The idea of being arrested frightened him. She could see the uncertainty in his face. She seized the moment to shove him out the door with all her might. She then slammed it and locked it. She ran to the kids.

Their faces were white and they were shaking so hard, they were vibrating. She hated seeing them so scared. Gently herding them up to her bedroom, she soothed them and finally got the whole story.

Shortly after she left, they saw his truck driving back and forth through the back alley. They didn't know what to do. Paul tried to phone the gym club, but nobody answered. Liba had been standing near the phone just in case and knew it hadn't rung. The poor kid must have misdialed. And he didn't call 9-1-1 as they practiced. Paul knew the number, but he was confused. If it was his own father, was it still an emergency? Instead they panicked and hid under the bed.

Al broke in through a small basement window. The house was on a back fill and there was a two by six nailed across the casement. He pried the window open and kept banging on the board until he pulled it out of the nails. The loud pounding reverberated through the house terrifying the kids. When Liba walked in, he had just broken in and was making his way up the stairs.

"It's okay, it's okay," she kept repeating. "I'm here. I'm not going anywhere. Daddy's gone. He's not coming back. The house is locked. I'm staying here with you and I'm going to make sure it doesn't happen again."

But she really didn't know what to do because, although she had the right to call the police, it might provoke Al even more and she didn't want the violence to escalate. She called Gordie Johnson and explained the situation.

Gordie said, "You've got to decide who you are going to protect. You're either going to protect yourself and your kids or you're going to protect him."

"Okay, thank you Gordie, I'll call the police."

———————————

Al was holed up at the Capri Motel watching television when the cruiser pulled up. He was hauled in for breaching a restraining order. It was April 17.

He was detained overnight and appeared in court the next afternoon. Liba appeared with her lawyer, Robert Densmore. She was unaware of Al's previous assault on Simon Gidluk and unfortunately, so was the court.

Al stood before the judge looking disheveled. The judge questioned him and Al answered in his most obsequious manner, peppering his speech with lots of Your Honors. He had picked this up from his crime shows, which were all American-based programs. In Canada, the judge is referred to as My Lord.

"Your wife claims you beat her," the judge asked.

"Your Honor, my wife has the same temper as me and, from time to time, assaulted me."

"Your wife says you favor your daughter."

"No, Your Honor, this is not true. When bringing up the children, I have never taken into consideration whether it is a boy or a girl."

"She says you have repeatedly threatened to take Paul away and she will never see him again." The judge looked down gravely at Al.

"No, your Honor, Sir, my wife came up with this thought based on religious belief. In the case of divorce, the boy will go with me and the girl will go with her."

"On Easter Sunday, Paul ran away to the local Banff RCMP because he said you tried to drown him."

"At the swimming pool, Your Honor, with a friend of my wife, we all played together for three hours. It is improbable that in a crowded swimming pool there could have occurred such a misunderstanding." Al acted perplexed.

"Tell me what happened then?" the judge instructed.

"We could not find Paul, Your Honor, after I got dressed and met up with my daughter, Gabi. We went to the local RCMP office and asked for help to find him, Sir."

"Your wife feels you were there to make good on your promise to take Paul away."

"Your Honor, I have never wanted to take one or both of the children away from home and I did not want to bring them any harm."

"Then why were you there tonight? "

"I believe at the present time, Your Honor, the children are not well taken care of and are subjected to undesirable stress." Al put on a sincere look of concern. "The reason, Your Honor, is because they are left alone at home three times a week."

"Can you give me an example?"

"On the ninth of April, she took Gabi to emergency at the hospital, went to the drugstore, then took her home. Once she was home, she gave Gabi medicine then went to gymnastics, leaving Gabi all alone. In the upbringing of the children, she uses abusive and cruel methods, which make my children angry."

The judge continued his interrogation calmly. "Why do you think the children would be better off with you?"

"I know about that here there is a law about the fact she used the children for her personal sexual enjoyment and this danger probably still continues."

"Have you done anything about it?"

"I ask the court to appoint me as legal guardian and give a respective order to that effect, as the children continue to be in danger of sexual abuse. My son, Paul, told my daughter, Gabi, he wants to leave and go somewhere no one will be able to find him. And about two weeks ago he ran away from my wife while she was shopping at the grocery store and did not return home until four hours later."

Al stepped down and the judge asked Liba to take the stand. Although she was disgusted with Al's outrageous testimony, especially fabricating sexual abuse between her and the kids. It was so absolutely ridiculous she didn't even bother to dignify it with a response.

Instead, in her most professional manner, she told the judge Al was a capable carpenter, but unemployable because he could not get along with anyone. He didn't trust anyone. He hated people in general. He was abusive with her and Paul and the children were afraid of him.

The judge eyed Al up and down, then issued his ruling.

"Sir, I've seen many cases here and I've heard many women responding to these allegations. And their language is usually much stronger than the language your wife is using. She seems very reasonable and fair. You should get your life together. Although I could give you thirty days in jail for breaching the restraining order, you have no previous record so I will chalk this up to a simple situation of a father missing his children. Don't let me see you here again, Mr. Dolejs."

Al smirked at Liba. He was out with another slap on the wrist.

———————

Near the end of April he called and asked to see the kids. Liba knew if she didn't allow some contact, he might kidnap them. He was not going to take no for an answer. She told him to have his lawyer call her lawyer and maybe they could work something out, but she had to talk with the kids first. She sat them both down.

Like most children, they had a remarkable ability to forgive and forget. They were still frightened of Al, but Gabi piped up. "I feel so sorry for Daddy. He's all alone and he doesn't see us anyone."

Even Paul, despite the years of pain and abuse he had endured, nodded. "I kind of feel sorry for him too, Mommy."

Liba presented them with a choice. "It is your decision. You don't have to see him if you don't want to."

The kids were silent.

"Don't tell me what you think I want to hear. Tell me what you really feel."

"I know Mommy," Gabi sighed. "But I think we should."

"Just for a few hours," Paul added carefully.

———————

Before Easter, Liba had wanted to invite Mami for a visit, but Al had refused. Over his dead body, he said. He absolutely hated Mami. Liba felt they were too much alike.

The problem Al had with her mother began when he went back to Czechoslovakia for a visit in 1982. Liba had been there the year before and it was his turn. He took the kids and, as was customary, spent time with both her family and his. When he was staying with Mami and Alana, they tried to be sociable. There is lots to do in a small mountain town, hikes and picnics. But Mami wasn't used to entertaining and was at a loss for ideas. She felt obliged to drag Al through the whole town and introduce him to everyone. He didn't do well meeting all these different people. Since they were both so socially inept, they had trouble initiating conversations. Instead, they spent their time stewing over what bad company the other was.

Now Liba was free to do what she liked. She sent her mother a ticket, but Al got wind of this and wrote Mami.

Mrs. Novak,

Mrs. Novak, the first time I wrote you I was marrying Liba and it was a joyful event for me. Now I am writing because she is leaving me and I don't know how to continue, so I will begin from the middle. A man realizes what he has or had only after he lost it or is losing it. I think I haven't quite lost her yet and that is why I am writing to you and requesting your help.

In the past we lived very well but, also we experienced hard times. I think I created a great share of the hard times. Most of the disagreements originated from petty things and grew out of proportion. Sometimes I was pretty bad to Liba. The last misunderstanding happened with Paul and was probably the last straw. Our problems were petty, not alcoholism or anything like that.

Liba has the right to leave me, but there are children involved. As I was thinking of our life, I found out that Liba is a very good wife and I didn't treat her well. Even though she is conscientious and looks after the children well, she will find they are a lot of work if she stays alone and I am not sure she can manage in this country. I know you managed, but it was a different world and different conditions. I also thought about myself and recognized my faults. I talked to Liba and wrote her a letter. She says it isn't all decided yet. There is still hope we can live together. If it happened, she would be in the best hands for the rest of her life. I know she is your daughter and you wish for her the best. Maybe you will say that if you managed, she can manage too. The best of course would be to unite our ties together and help us.

I would be glad if you could arrive sooner and talk to us. I am now a really different man. Maybe you have heard the same about many other people and later they slipped back into their same old ways. This will never happen in my case. Really most of the problems arose from little things. That's why I ask you once more to help us. Will you advise and help us to live together? At least write to Liba, telling her to wait with everything until you come and then we can discuss everything together. I am looking forward to your arrival and hope you come soon.

Al

Al then wrote his sister and told her nothing of their separation. Instead he said his children were behaving badly toward him with much disrespect. He said he suspected Liba put them up to it.

Liba's mother arrived just before summer holidays. Liba had thawed enough to allow the lawyers to start negotiating short visits between Al and the kids. She was happy Mami was here. Rather than having the kids in day care, Mami could look after them. And she only spoke Czech so they'd sharpen their language skills.

Paul and Gabi knew how to take a bus or Calgary's Light Rail Transit, so they could guide her around the city. It was important to Liba for the children to have a relationship with her. Paul and Gabi didn't have the same history with Mami that Liba did. They treated her in the same loving, casual way they treated Liba. It was okay to interact, okay to talk to your own grandmother, okay to say to your own grandmother that you didn't like something or discuss it. The kids bombarded Mami with questions and demands and she had to respond.

Mami tried to be strict, but the kids teased her constantly. She was still a meticulous cleaner. Everything had to be utterly spotless and shining and in its place. When she was young, Liba was forever scolded for spilling something on the tablecloth or leaving a fork mark. Liba was the opposite with her kids. So they spilled and left their place mats a little messy, who cared?

When Mami arrived, she started right in on the kids at meal times. "Paul, you've got breadcrumbs by your plate," or "Gabi, you spilled the sugar."

Liba would intervene. "Let it be. It's okay, we'll wipe it afterwards."

Then one day at supper, Liba noticed Paul's face all lit up, just beaming. She shot him a questioning look. He got up and walked over to Mami. Pointing at her place mat and smiling sweetly, "Grandma, you've got three breadcrumbs here."

Liba held her breath as she waited for the explosion. But when Mami looked at Paul, she couldn't hide her smile. After that, she seemed to relax a little.

Emily Novak was a tough old bird and not easily fooled by anyone, least of all, Al. Liba told her all about the years of abuse and how he treated the children. Mami saw him for the first time during her visit near the end of June after his legal visits began. He came to pick up the children. As they were getting ready, he asked to have a word with her. Mami thought he might want to talk about why the kids often declined his invitations. She led the way into the living room.

Al put on his most earnest expression and sat across from her. "Mrs. Novak," he began, "would you speak to Liba on my behalf? You can see how beautifully we could live together as a complete family. I think you should stay for a year here. Maybe even two. Then you will see it."

She looked at him coolly. "I have spoken with Liba on this subject, but the decision is hers alone. It is her life and the life of her children and I would not dream of trying to influence her in either direction. I do know there are many divorced couples, where children visit and spend time with their father and are able to develop a good relationship with him."

"Yes, but," Al hung his head low and affected a look of concern, "is she capable of bringing children up by herself? In this country it's much harder than at home."

Mami wasn't buying it. "Certainly, she is." Mami couldn't resist a little dig. "Since she has supported you and the children for the past six years. She is saving for Paul to attend university and Gabi wants to be a nursery school teacher."

Al puffed out his chest importantly. "When this house is sold, I will give Liba my portion of the money to set her up in business. Mind you, I have to furnish a three-bedroom apartment that will cost me around ten thousand. But wherever they move, I will always be close by. Like a shadow."

"Um?" Mami hemmed.

"I love Liba more and more all the time and do not feel any hatred toward her." He brought a sheen of tears to his eyes.

Mami shrugged. "Obviously she doesn't feel any hatred toward you either. If she did, she wouldn't let the kids visit you. The fact that they don't always want to see you is something she lets them decide."

Al's anger started getting the better of him. "That's not true. You and she put the children up to that. If I had them for a longer period of time, they would not want to leave me to come here!"

Mami dismissed his complaint with a toss of her head. "We don't put them up to anything. On the contrary, Liba encourages them. She says, 'He is your father and he wants to see you.' But it doesn't always work out." She wagged a finger at him. "It is sad your own children don't care for you and it's your own fault. You are to blame!"

Al swallowed hard. Why waste any more time? He could see he wasn't getting anywhere with the old lady.

A couple of days later, Jiri brought Al his mail. There was an unexpected letter from his sister. Liba must have informed them of their separation. What right had she? He was seething as he opened the envelope.

June 18, 1986

My Dear Little Brother,

Many greetings. I think of you very, very much. I received
word from Liba that you two are separating. It came as a
shock to me. I telephoned her and she called me back. So I
do have some information, but nothing about you. She
refused to find out anything about you, including your new
address. In the end, she promised to send my letter to you
through someone named Jiri. I hope you'll get this. Mother
and I are very sad about the separation and very afraid for
you. We cannot imagine what you must be going through
and how you manage to cope with it all.
We don't want to make judgements about whom is to blame
and for what, I just wanted to write to tell you how badly
we'd like to help you. It's difficult, but hopefully our letters

will give you comfort and support.

It's important you send us your current address.

It's distressing to hear reports about your children who you say don't behave toward you as they should. I care for them deeply but this does not sit well with me. I was so upset by what you said in your letter, I couldn't even work on knitting a sweater I was making for Gabi. Now it is finished, but it does not give me any pleasure to send it to her. Maybe someday I'll be able to forgive them.

You know children don't allow themselves to be brainwashed forever. Sooner or later they figure out the truth. My girls have finally caught on to the fact that their father loves only money, so much so, that he is capable of talking them out of going to school. Yet, I have always tried to be careful to never say anything bad about him, because I don't want to pass judgement on him in front of them. Without any influence, they reached my point of view.

Please hold on, try, try to get on, even though now you are all alone. Do it for the children, there will come a time when they need you very much.

Take care, hold on, don't do anything foolish that would ruin everything.

Elunka

Al called his sister back and gave her his new address. It was true Liba and her mother were programming the kids against him. Her mother was especially abrasive and cruel. But he had been patient and now the kids were visiting with him and loving their time together. Some day they would see what was really going on and want to live with him. The biggest change in his life since his separation from Liba was his return to the church. He had found God again and was leading an orderly life.

Mother Dolejs was overjoyed to see him firmly back in the bosom of the Catholic Church. She wrote him immediately.

Dear Lola,

Elunka called this morning all excited that you telephoned!
I was very worried about you when I found out what
happened with your family. I know it was a severe blow for
you. I worried about how you would handle such pain,
hoping you wouldn't give up in resignation.
It was a difficult time for me with all the thinking, worrying
and many conjectures. Worst of all I was alone. I didn't want
to burden Elunka and add to her problems. But now I feel
much better. It's like being reborn. The fact that you
contacted us is great. And that, as you told your sister, now
the children are visiting you and like being with you. This
makes me so happy. I surmise from this, you didn't give in
and are leading a proper life, fighting and trying to make it.
You lost your family, but you found God. You returned to
God.
I'm glad you are attending Church and I pray for you every
day.
Secretly in my soul, I hoped perhaps Liba's mother would
step in and with wise words and affect a solution. I am so
disappointed in her. Very disappointed.
We didn't say anything about your separation to Pepa. Not
because of him, but because of Anna. She is so snoopy and
this is our business. She is not one of us. She would keep
pestering me and wouldn't extend the same courtesy to me
that I have to her. I know her brother Frank did something
bad and I never bother her about it. I didn't write about it

before, because I didn't want Liba to know about Pepa's problems. Especially since I always suspected that before Pepa married Anna, the Novaks wanted Alana to marry him. Remember how Anna's parents bought two houses, so they transferred title to Frank with the understanding it would continue to belong to them. Well, he won't give it back, and they've invested over eighty thousand in it.

Give Paul and Gabi my greetings. Tell them I think of them and try to imagine how they've grown and how good looking they must be.

Thinking of you,

Mother

Liba had a surprise for her mother and the kids. Expo '86 was in Vancouver. She had saved up enough money and drove them all there for a week. It was wonderful to get away from Al. They had a great time. It took two days to get there, but the scenery was so spectacular nobody minded. They kids were fascinated with Frank Slide, a town on the way in Alberta near the British Columbia border that was buried under ninety million tons of limestone in a landslide on April 29, 1903. They then spent four days at Expo where they all delighted in the food, especially the offerings at the Thai pavilion. The Czech display was a bit of a disappointment. The restaurant never seemed to be open. Mami liked the jewelry- making at the Sri Lanka Pavilion and they all loved the Egyptian exhibition. Stepping into it, they felt they were traveling three thousand years back in time. There was even a sarcophagus of Ramses III on display.

Al was overcome with jealousy. They arrived home on July 12th and he greeted them with a bitter phone call to Liba.

"You're buying their love because I can't afford to take them for a week to Vancouver and you can. You're buying their love!"

CHAPTER THIRTY-NINE

MISSING

Sunday, July 27

It was 6:17 PM, fifty-five minutes since Al's last call and two hours and seventeen minutes past the time the kids were due home from fishing. Liba called the police.

"I have a problem. I've split with my husband and he had the kids for today just for a visit. Previously, I had a restraining order. He wasn't supposed to call us or contact them, but we made an exception that he could have the kids. The reason was that he had threatened before that he would take the kids away and I'd never see them again." Liba prayed she was making sense.

"Anyhow, he phoned me about forty five minutes ago and he said he's taking the kids and he's not bringing them back. I'd like a patrol, somebody to go to his house and see if the kids are there and bring them home."

The Police operator tried to size up the situation. "What did you say? He wasn't bringing them back at all or...?"

"Well that's what he said," Liba interrupted. "That he won't bring them back. On the other hand, he said he'd be here to sign some documents."

"Oh."

"But it only takes twenty minutes to drive from his place to here and he phoned forty five minutes ago and there is no sign of him or the kids. I just want to make sure that he hasn't taken them somewhere. And I do have the court order."

"Okay," the operator said, then explained, "The only thing is, that court order is pretty well broken now, if you've let him…"

"Yeah," Liba sighed.

The operator continued. "…have them. But I guess I can send a car over to your place and then you can tell them exactly what's going on in person."

"Can't they go directly there?" Liba asked.

"Not really."

"And then they can come to my…"

The operator could sense Liba's panic. "They should come and see you first, have a look at the document and…"

"Oh." Liba understood. They had to have proof there was a restraining order. They couldn't just take her word for it over the phone.

"…try to figure out what to do. I mean if he's got the kids now, I'm sure he'll have them in another hour anyway. Or half an hour. We'll send a car over to your place first. If he won't bring them back, it's a form of abduction. I guess we'd be able to arrest him for that." The operator took her name and address and dispatched a car immediately.

A patrol car showed up right away. Liba recognized the officer, Perkins. He'd helped her the night of April 16 when Al defied the restraining order and broke into the basement. She told him about the two phone calls.

Perkins smiled reassuringly and told Liba to stay calm. "There's a chance he's bluffing so let's not panic. We'll give it a few hours, okay?"

Liba felt a little foolish. Was she overreacting?

"If he doesn't show up with the kids, call us again."

Liba nodded and Perkins left.

Liba called the police again at nine that night.

"Hello, I have a problem. My husband took the kids for a visit for the whole day and he phoned me at 5:30 this afternoon saying he's taking them and I'll never see them again. And there was a restraining order placed and I have custody of the kids."

The operator was reassuring. He took her name and address and added, "Okay, we'll send a car crew out to take a full report and see if we can't get this straightened out, okay?"

Liba felt a little better. "Okay, thank you very much."

They arrived at 9:45. This time Liba dealt with Constable Murray Straight and Constable Fraser Dow. Straight did most of the talking. Liba's hands were shaking as she showed him the restraining order and then the agreement by the lawyers. She told them how Al had picked the kids up in the morning. She told how he said over the phone that she would never see the kids again, but mentioned he would be over that night to sign the papers for the property.

Straight looked at the court papers. He advised Liba it was a civil matter and the police couldn't do anything about it.

"You have to," Liba implored. "How else am I going to find them?"

Straight shrugged and told her the lawyers had superceded the judge's restraining order when in fact, the lawyers had no right to do that. He said it was stupid on both lawyers' part, but now she had violated the restraining order. Therefore, it was no longer in effect.

Liba knew it was important not to become hysterical. She would lose all credibility, but she was on the edge. She slapped the restraining order with the back of her hand.

"This order still specifies I have sole custody of my children and he is not to have them overnight!"

Straight sighed and told her there was nothing he could do to help.

She looked to Dow. He agreed, saying in instances like these, it was a civil matter and the Calgary City Police had a policy not to interfere.

Liba was defiant. "That does not sound right to me. Look, restraining order or no restraining order, there are still two kids missing."

Straight looked at her. "Since they are with their father, they are not really missing."

Liba wanted to wring his neck, but instead she said, "May I phone my lawyer?"

The two officers said it was fine by them.

Liba called Robert Densmore at his home in High River. The conversation was brief. He told Liba the officers were wrong. The order was valid and she should not take no for an answer.

She relayed this to Officer Straight, but he was adamant. The lawyers shouldn't have superceded the judge's order. They didn't know what they were doing. There was nothing he could do. Goodnight.

Now she was really upset. Her mind raced. She could not just sit and wait. If the police would do nothing, she would. She grabbed her car keys and headed for Al's apartment.

Back in the car, Straight advised dispatch and was later told they sent a car by her residence and tried calling up to 10:30, but no one was home.

Meanwhile at Al's apartment, his elderly Swiss landlady opened the door. Liba introduced herself and explained the situation. The landlady agreed to call if Al showed up. Liba went home and sat by the phone for the rest of the night.

Monday, July 28

Liba woke with a start. It took her a second to realize she was sitting on the couch in the living room. She staggered to her feet and lurched to the shower. She might as well go to work. What else could she do?

She called her lawyer again from the office. What were her options? He said he would have a letter drawn up by the next day and delivered to the Chief of Police complaining about the lack of action by the officers.

She called the RCMP. Could they help? The dispatcher said she was sorry, but the last time the kids were seen was in Calgary. There was no proof he had taken them out of that jurisdiction. Could she prove they were outside the city limits?

"If I knew where they were, I wouldn't be calling you!" Liba snapped.

The RCMP operator said she was sorry, but she couldn't help.

Liba called her lawyer again. He told her to not give up and to keep calling the police. She was completely within her rights to do so and it might motivate them to help. She called them several times that day, but one operator went so far as to tell her the children weren't missing because they were with their father.

Liba thought she had a fairly clear picture of what Al was doing. He was jealous because she had taken the kids to Vancouver. He felt it was his turn to take them somewhere too, probably British Columbia. It was close, but had a different area code, which would deter them from calling. He probably told the kids she'd given her permission to take them camping, maybe even to a motel.

But what if he was on his way to the Czech Republic? She would call his sister, Elunka.

Tuesday, July 29

Another sleepless night. She hoped the bastard was enjoying his time with the kids, because it was the last time he'd ever get them alone. When they got back she would pull out all the stops. She would make sure to reactivate the order and he could hire Perry Mason, but he would never have unsupervised access to the kids again. On the positive side, Paul and Gabi must be having a good time or they would call.

She called her lawyer again. The letter was done, but he was waiting for confirmation on some facts from Al's lawyer.

Later that night, she stopped by Al's apartment again. Noting her distress, the landlady let her in. All his suitcases were there. His uncashed pay cheque was lying on the kitchen table. It didn't look as if he had planned a trip. It didn't make any sense. Maybe he had just made a spur of the moment decision. She found his diary and read it.

AL'S DIARY-June 14, 1986, 2 to 4 o'clock

First official visit with the children. It was very nice.

"Very nice, indeed," Liba snorted, recalling the day. As soon as he had permission to see the kids, Al started with the games. He knew he was supposed to have them for two hours, but he phoned at noon. Paul answered. Al asked him if he'd like to go to a movie.

"A movie? Sure." Paul answered enthusiastically. "I'll ask Mommy."

Liba was working in the kitchen and heard Paul's side of the conversation. She smiled and nodded.

Paul let his dad know that would be fine, but as he listened further, Liba could see Paul looking more and more confused and a little panicked.

"Wait a minute, what's going on?" she asked, taking the phone and covering the receiver. No sense asking Al, he'd just lie to her.

Paul's face was the color of beets. "He asked us to go to a movie, but he wants to pick us up at 1:30."

Liba got on the phone. She tried to sound reasonable, friendly. Why start off on the wrong foot? "What time does the movie start?"

"I thought they would like to see it. It's a Disney movie called The Great Mouse Detective," Al replied pleasantly.

"Sounds great. Gabi would love it. But what time does it start?"

"Hmm, let's see..." He stalled for a moment and rattled some newspaper. "Five o'clock."

"Oh the movie starts at five o'clock?" She tried to sound disappointed. "Well, that's not going to work. You only have them for two hours, starting at two."

"Oh, right," he replied, as if it had slipped his mind.

"See you soon."

Liba hung up annoyed. He loved backing Paul into a corner and watching him squirm, but he didn't do it to Gabi and he didn't dare try it with her anymore.

"Jerk," she muttered.

AL'S DIARY-June 18, 6:15-8:15

I went to see the boy play soccer. He played very well. The
girl did not want to go with me because she was playing
with a friend. After the soccer game, I went with Paul to
Fish Creek for a while.

When Peter Day and Gary Sarginia hadn't bought Al's story about being lonely, he'd taken his family's advice and gone in search of a priest. This was the week he started going to mass early mornings at a downtown Catholic Church, Sacred Heart. She could picture him kneeling in the front pew appearing to pray.

AL'S DIARY-June 21, 8:00-8:30

In the morning I took the children shopping. I showed them
where I live and introduced them to the people I live with.
At noon I took Gabi home because she was going to a party.
Then I drove with Paul to Fish Creek. We had a barbecue
and went for a walk. It was a very nice day.

Ah yes. She remembered the day well. Gabi had been invited to a birthday party, so she wanted her dad to take her home early. Al was furious over the disruption in his plans.

"You are trying to brainwash her to not be with me!" he accused.

"Give me a break," Liba replied. "She's a big girl. She can make her own decisions. I think it's perfectly reasonable for her to want to go to a birthday party. Besides she's spending the whole morning with you." But there was no talking to him. He saw it as a betrayal. Yet he hadn't touched on the incident in his diary. And he didn't note the meeting he had on the 23rd with a father he had talked to at Sacred Heart. He had bragged to Liba he had talked to a monsignor, who ranked above a priest. Al swore to the man he lived only for his kids.

AL'S DIARY-June 25, 6:30- 8:30

I went with Gabi to Fish Creek. It was a very nice evening.
Paul remained at home.

She knew Al returned to see the monsignor at Sacred Heart again that day. But again, there was no mention of it.

AL'S DIARY-June 26, 6:30

I went to see Gabi's soccer game.

Liba had been out on errands that morning, but when she returned home, Paul approached her tearfully. "I...I lied to Daddy today. I told him I wanted to be his friend."

Earlier, Al got Paul on the phone and told him he wanted to spend time more with him and be his friend.

"How does that feel? Good, right?" Al demanded.

"I want to be friends with you too, Daddy," Paul stammered.

"Good. Good. You should be telling your mother that. Maybe you tell her you miss me and want your father to come home!" Al ordered.

Liba understood immediately. She put her arms around Paul. "It was a grown up thing you did. Sometimes it's necessary to do that and don't feel bad about it. It's just a different situation. It's not like lying and saying you didn't steal something when you did. That's a bad thing. But sometimes when you are dealing with a person like your dad, sometimes you have to say things to protect yourself."

"Okay," Paul sniffed.

Liba told Mami about the incident. "He was crying, not about losing his father, but about having to lie to him."

AL'S DIARY-June 29

In the morning, we went with Gabi to see one soccer game.
Then we went to my place. At noon, we went with Gabi to
see a second soccer game. Then we went for lunch. After
lunch, we went to Southland to swim. It was a very nice day,
even if it did rain.

It had been raining that day, but both Gabi's soccer team and their opponents still wanted to play so the officials gave them the go ahead. Some of the spectators, including Al and Paul, got so wet they decided to watch from their vehicles. Paul came home shaking, not from the afternoon cold, but from their conversation. Once in the truck, his dad had started pumping him for information.

"How are things at home?"

"Fine." Paul answered, pretending to concentrate on the game.

"Perhaps there is something you need. I could buy it for you."

"Nah, that's okay." Paul tried to change the subject. "Hey look, Gabi has the ball!"

Al moved a little closer to Paul. "Does your Mommy talk about me?"

Paul shook his head no. The truck was muggy and his back was sticking to the seat. He shifted uncomfortably.

Al lit a cigarette. "I think it's a good idea if you tell your mother what fun we are having. A boy needs his father around all the time. Not just some of the time."

Paul's heart was pounding so loud he could no longer hear the rain outside. Under no circumstances did he want his father to move home again! But he was afraid of making him mad.

"Uh, it's good to watch Gabi play soccer. She's a great player."

Al tried a different tack. "Girls grow up wild without a father to take care of them. You don't want to see your sister like that do you?"

Paul shook his head. "No."

"No. Just like I thought. Now you are using your head. Is best you tell your mother that when you get home. But first, we buy an ice cream or candy, right after game. That's what you want. Right?"

"Sure." Paul tried to sound agreeable. "Sure Daddy."

AL'S DIARY-July 3

We went to Glenmore Reservoir. At first the children played by the water and then we went for a short walk along the bank of the river. Gabi picked herself a small bouquet of flowers.

Liba felt confused. The whole damn diary was completely censored!

Then it struck her. He intended to use it to build a case for custody. She could hear him now.

"See what a wonderful father I am?" He was so conniving. It would have been less frightening if it had been rambling and incoherent.

The landlady said Al told her he was one hundred percent positive by the time the kids were sixteen they would be fed up with all of Liba's bullshit and move in with him. She said she had laughed and told him that when kids are sixteen they start dating and don't want to live with either parent. She remembered Al had mentioned seeing a psychiatrist and asked Liba if Al were on some kind of strong prescription because of the way he acted and spoke.

Wednesday, July 30

Mami made breakfast, but Liba couldn't eat. She managed to get a little tea down, but that was it. Neither woman said much. After breakfast, Mami retreated to her room.

That Wednesday afternoon her lawyer called to say the letter had been hand delivered to the Chief of Police. She would probably be contacted very quickly.

The landlady's son, Jim, called. He said he spent quite a bit of time talking with Al and admitted he was a strange dude.

"He's a loner," Jim admitted, "but definitely intelligent. He's very cynical and pessimistic. I feel sorry for people like that because they never enjoy anything they do. I think he is extremely depressed and disturbed and somewhat disorganized in his thoughts."

Liba agreed with Jim's assessment. She rubbed the back of her aching neck. If a perfect stranger could see all of this in a couple of conversations, why had it taken her so long?

Thursday, July 31

The kids should be home in four days. She had them in Vancouver a week and that's how Al was. Tit for tat.

Her phone rang at work. It was a police superintendent. He said he received a letter from her lawyer and she had been right, the police officers wrong. The lawyers' agreement did not supercede the restraining order. It was still in effect. A patrol car would be dispatched to her home to take down her complaint. When would be most convenient?

"Right now!" She gave him the address of her office.

The Superintendent hesitated. "Uh, that's downtown and your house is in the southwest. So it presents us with a bit of an administrative problem."

"Oh for Pete's sake," Liba thought, "My kids are missing and he's worried about filling out forms."

"Fine!" she blurted out. "I can be home in an hour. How about eleven?"

Liba hung up and immediately dialed her mother telling her to watch for the patrol car. She was on her way home.

At 12:15, Officer Vanderemalen arrived in uniform. He spoke with Mami. She told him how Al had tried persuading her to help get Liba back. Then a plainclothes detective named Pitcher came to the house and questioned Liba. For the next hour and a half, they asked for the kids' descriptions and took down the details of their abduction.

The police issued a warrant and the next morning the story was in the papers.

CHAPTER FORTY

AL'S PLAN

Al had been toying with the idea for some time now. Batting it around the way a cat fools with a rubber mouse. If it were a real mouse, the cat would tear it to pieces. But this was just a pretend mouse. Something to chew on, for fun. He felt elated every time he envisioned her reaction. Her life would be ruined. She would finally understand how he felt when she destroyed his life by taking his family away from him.

He was prepared. For years he studied every crime show on television and he was far smarter than any of the TV detectives, Columbo, Ironside, Cannon, Rockford, Steve McGarret, Mannix, Stone. They were always lucky. And all of the criminals were stupid. Sometimes they'd almost get away with it, but then they'd trip up and confess.

Confession seemed to be the key. Why didn't they keep their mouths shut? They'd blab about the bodies. Bodies! No bodies, no crime. He had it all figured out. At first he thought he would kill her. But then what? She would be dead. How could she understand his pain if she were dead?

The kids were his wife's life. They were all she thought about, all she cared about. She didn't care about him. She'd made that clear. Heartless bitch. She ignored his calls and his letters. He poured his soul out to her in his letters. He told her everything he'd been thinking. If she paid any attention at all, she would know. It would be her fault if he carried through with things. After all, she had been warned. He dropped the first letter on the windshield of her car, then picked it up and looked it over one last time.

Hi Liba,

Yesterday was one of the best days of my life. When I was
waiting at your place with Gabi, I was spying on you the
same way Gabi used to at the Parkland house when you
were sweeping under the stairs and it was even nicer when
you walked up the stairs and gave me such a nice smile. I
know this smile and I know that things will be good
between us again.

Al made a face. He had to admit his past mistakes. This was difficult
for him to do, but necessary. He was sure it was the thing she most
wanted to hear from him. The letter continued.

It might take awhile, but I know it will happen.
I can't force it to happen right away and I don't want to. But
I think the door is open again. You said you wanted me to
speak nicely, and I would like to. I'd like you to talk to me
on the phone or even better, let's go for a walk in the nice
weather and talk about nice things.
I know there are things between us that are nice and not
nice. I've made a lot of mistakes in the past, but it doesn't
mean I want to continue making them. After frank
discussions with many people, I am sure that these mistakes
can be corrected. I'd like you to be part of this process. I
know that I will need your help with the stipulation we only
talk nicely.
I don't have any reason to hurt you or the children or cause
you harm.

Al licked his lips. Killing the children was all he could think of lately. He'd run the scenario through his mind a thousand times. He would hide the bodies and she would have to beg him on her hands and knees to tell her where they were. And then he would tell her. He would tell her how he killed them, and how they cried for her. He could barely contain his excitement as he read on.

I know how you must feel seeing the kids leave with me.

Al sneered. He knew how she suffered when they were not with her. He needed to reassure her that nothing terrible would happen to the children. She mustn't know what he was planning or she would never let the children near him.

I want to solve this in a reasonable way.
Since we've been apart I love you more and more.
It's difficult to write today. I've so much to say but I'm
worried about how you'll receive this letter. I better stop for
today and await your answer. You don't have to write, but I'd
like some answer.

Al

He waited for her response. A week went by. Nothing. She ignored his letter. Didn't even mention it. He was incredulous. She wanted him to eat more dirt. What he'd written wasn't enough. She needed to see him crawl through the mud. Okay. He could play that game. He would give her what she wanted. He sat down and wrote again.

Hi Liba,

It is quite difficult for me to begin writing this letter. I have
so much to say, but on the other hand, it could be
condensed into one sentence and if there was a chance to
meet with you, it could all be expressed by silence.
I don't want to dig up and shed light on the bad things that
happened between us, but on the other hand I don't deny
them.

Women! He did not want to dwell on his mistakes, but he knew she
wanted him to talk about them.

It is such a pity that for a certain time it dominated the
good things. Without a serious and honest dialogue and an
analysis of our situation, it was inevitable. Maybe in the past
when the mistakes weren't piled so high this would have
been easier to resolve.

Al was angry. If only she had agreed to talk things out, if only she had
paid attention to their problems earlier, they would still be together. He
had no control over any of it. He was just a pawn in her game. He
struggled to control himself.

I don't feel any hate or anger towards you for what
happened in the recent past. You have your reasons for
taking these steps. I feel a lot toward you and toward the
children.

He bared his teeth. Of course he was entitled to feel hate toward the person who rejected him and caused him to not have the family he worked so hard to create. But he was a better man than that.

My feelings for you are becoming more profound and have grown into the best it can be. I know that even you feel we had some special times when you evaluate and analyze our life together. You have to admit there were a lot of nice times, which can't be erased.
We have two very nice children. We can't ignore they are mutually ours. They'll connect us forever. I would like to devote myself to them and you forever. I can offer you a lot. I want to show them it is possible to live in a content family and give them a good foundation for their future. They need us and will need us more and more. When they grow up they will judge us, and I want them to say our parents never walked away from a problem, no matter how big.

He chuckled. She was always going on about a two parent family. She was a sucker for guilt. This was too easy.

You ask, who is going to make up for twelve years of your life. I think it's more proper to ask, can we compensate each other for the bad things that happened in the last twelve years.

He was the real victim. She could not ignore his hurt forever.

I know you and I know that up until now you were the one
offering the helping hand and now it is me offering the
helping hand. I am convinced that together we can
overcome one part of our life and bring forward all the good,
and there was a lot of it, and build on that foundation.

He looked at the letter, satisfied. He had fulfilled his duty. This letter
would show her how much his family meant to him. This was her chance
to stop anything bad from happening. It was up to her.

Again she ignored his writing. He called her. She didn't want to
discuss the letters. She said she wanted nothing to do with him. Now,
when the cat lay in bed at night, he no longer played with a pretend
mouse. He felt the crunch of the rodent's neck between his fangs and
tasted its warm blood as it ran down his throat.

He would give her one more chance. Then he would wash his hands
of all responsibility. He sent her a final letter outlining his plans.

Hi Liba,

Today I became a real man. The sadness and worries are
gone and I am able to judge and think soberly. I won't cry to
you or senselessly beg you. Again I started thinking about
our life. There were many nice things between us, but also
many bad things and of the bad things, I had an
overwhelming share. I don't know what I was thinking of
and I don't avoid my responsibilities in any way. Whatever
happened, I probably won't be able to fix.

It was too late, he knew that. She would never forgive him.

You were getting ready for it for a long time and I practically pushed you into taking that step.

Al ground his teeth. That bitch! She had planned to leave him for a long time and as a result of her plans, he walked into her trap.

Only today I fully understand your position.

He had been such a stupid fool. Believing in her. But now his eyes were wide open. He could see everything clearly. She had planned to leave him all along.

I was a dirt of a man.

She thought she was so smart, always bragging about her salary, rubbing his nose in it. She thought he was dirt.

But when you left, something broke in me. It was probably my vanity, short temper and all the other things which make man's life bitter. Today, I also looked at you closely and I thought people have the right to a nice orderly life. You are still a nice woman and I like you more and more.

He knew she had such conceit that she would swallow this. She had destroyed his life, taken everything away from him and yet she would still believe he cared.

> I know you will laugh, but I was serious when I was talking about what we would do in the future. I would like to go to a dance with you. I never cared much for it before, but with you I would like to experience it again. We could go together to dance lessons.
> I know I will miss the children in everyday life, but that will pass as time goes by. You, I will miss for the rest of my life. I know you'll disagree, but it is so. You know I never cared much about women and probably never will.
> You can think what you want, but you will never escape from me. I know there is the law and bitterness standing between us now, but it will end one day.

By killing the kids, he would make sure she would never get away from him. They would be tied together forever. This would put an end to all those nosy social workers and judges.

The law soon and the bitterness later.

He might be caught and put in jail, but she would be the one who lived with a bitterness she could never escape.

> That won't stop me from courting you again when this is all over. Neither you nor any judge can stop me. I don't want to

say I will bug you, but I will be standing in your life in such a way that you will have to pay attention to me.
I am strongly convinced that I will lead an orderly life and nothing can break me. It seems like I am bragging, but I'm not. A man has to establish proper goals in life and achieve them.

Nothing she could do now would deter him.

I know you have set goals and will strive to achieve them. It's a pity we can't achieve them together. I know you won't write me and maybe you won't even read this letter. I received a letter from my mother. I read it several times, but learned nothing from it. I thought, why is she giving advice to a 45 year old man?

Al thought about his aging mother. What did she know of his life? She had never understood him. He laughed at her conceit.

Maybe it was a mistake to address it, 'For Lola only.' It should have been meant for both of us.
Think what you want, but in the future, even if we get a divorce and each of us goes our own way, you can always turn to me and I will help you. I don't and cannot feel any hate towards you.

In truth Al felt nothing but hate toward her.

To call you and deny it in court makes no sense. I am
prepared to take responsibility for my offences.

He was determined in his course of action and prepared to go to jail
if necessary.

Then if this letter ends up in forbidden hands, experienced
people will judge what offence I committed.
I am going to correct my mistakes, but it's a pity you won't
be there. I wish you would. Notice I don't mention the
children, it's because you are my partner for life.

He would control her for life. Her thoughts would center on him and
what he had done to the children. She belonged to him.

I hope you give this a lot of thought and let me know
through the lawyer if some change is possible. Should this
good change happen, you'll be in good hands for the rest of
your life.

Yours, Al
Capri Motel

He would need food. Something easy to cook. Steak. Why not? He had money, over $1,800 in the bank. He could eat as much steak as he liked. And it would give him strength, like that boxer in the movies, Rocky.

He started packing the truck. He slid the large kitchen knife wrapped in brown paper towels into the glove box. Suddenly checking himself. What was he doing? Did he really intend to stab the children? Was it possible?

He slammed the truck door shut. No, of course not. This was just a game he was playing in his mind. He needed the knife for the steaks.

Pulling into the drive he could see the boy watching television through the living room curtains. Soon the boy would be under his control and not able to go running to his mommy. It made him sick the way she looked at the boy. He was unable to stop himself from goading the sissy.

"Bring your swimsuit, we're going to the Hot Springs," he said.

He saw the look they exchanged on the stairs and an overwhelming sense of satisfaction enveloped him. Soon, they would never be able conspire against him again. He could not help but smile.

The girl skipped past him. He wondered if Liba would miss the girl as much as she would miss the boy. But when she fetched a jacket so the child would not catch cold, then insisted on a long goodbye kiss, he decided she would. He turned to his wife.

"When I come home, I'll have a surprise for you," he grinned.

Catching the puzzled look on her face, he bit the inside of his cheeks to stop from laughing.

Back in the truck he frowned and gripped the steering wheel trying to sort out the details of what he would have to do that day. He looked over at the girl. She gave him a small smile, then yawning like a kitten, nestled her head against the door and closed her eyes. She was already showing signs of disrespect. Sometimes she rolled her eyes at him and raised her voice. Stubborn, like all women, she'd recently insisted on going to a birthday party instead of spending the whole day with him. Soon she would be grown and have no time for him at all. Just like her mother.

"We're going to Canmore Esso for breakfast," he muttered. Glancing in the rear view mirror, he caught the boy looking at him. "Then Hot Springs," he added.

The boy looked away and Al chuckled to himself. He would enjoy killing the little faggot.

Gabi was confused. Daddy was acting stranger than usual. She caught him staring at her all day and he was so grumpy. She had tried to take his hand after breakfast and he'd pulled it away as if he had touched a snake or something. He kept talking about how he had a surprise for them later, after fishing. He said they were going to go into the woods to play hide and seek. She sighed. All she really wanted was to go home. She missed Mommy and her dolls.

Paul decided he liked fishing. His dad bought him a rod and a jar of Red Salmon eggs because they were the best bait for catching fish. They found a secluded spot at Allen Bill Pond and he and Gabi began casting their lines. Paul expected his dad to join them, but instead he sat at a picnic table behind them and watched. A kid named Neil joined them for a while. Paul decided not to get overly friendly because he could tell his dad didn't like the kid being there.

After Neil left, Al loaded the kids into the truck. Paul objected because they hadn't caught anything, but Al said they would try again later. It was around one thirty. Al still had to find a secluded area before nightfall.

"We're going to do some exploration in woods," he said.

The girl lit up. "Where?" she asked eagerly.

"You'll see," Al promised.

The boy climbed in the back of the truck and the girl took her accustomed seat beside Al in the front. He headed back onto Highway 66 and drove toward Bragg Creek, to the McLean Creek turn off. They passed the log-faced Visitors Center and veered onto a small road beyond the campsites.

He knew this was Elbow River Trail and it hooked up with Sylvester Trail. These ATV Trails were usually pretty deserted, especially this summer with the rains so heavy. He gunned it down the road over the ruts and as the truck rose up and down over the mud banks like a small boat bobbing in a big sea, the girl shrieked with delight. The boy, on the other hand, was apprehensive.

"Where are we going?" he shouted over the roar of the engine.

"Exploration," Al responded. As his plans were unfolding so easily, a sense of power began building inside him. For the first time in a long time, he felt in control.

"Hey look!" yelled the girl and she pointed to a group of four riders on ATV bikes, just ahead. Al continued barreling forward. It was up to them to move out of the way.

"Daddy!" The girl's eyes were wide. "Slow down!"

But it was his road, his show. He wasn't going to roll over for anyone ever again. He watched the vehicles shuttle to the side of the road and ignored their friendly waves as he zoomed past.

He looked at his watch. It was after three. He had to call his wife before she notified the cops. The other thing he needed was a map. He turned around and headed back to the Information Center on Highway 66. Standing at the phone booth, he impatiently fished in his pocket for a dime. She expected them home in a few of minutes. He would stall her.

"Where are you?" she challenged.

"On the way. I'll be there shortly. Get the offer ready."

"How are the kids?"

Al could see the boy emerging from the Information Center with a map, spotting Al on the phone. He trotted over hoping to speak to his mother.

"Fine," Al replied curtly and hung up.

He forced a smile and shrugged. The boy was getting suspicious. He had to distract him.

"She is busy. She has a good offer on the house and is too busy to talk to you. She says don't come now. Come little later. She wants me to call again in one hour."

The girl followed the boy out of the building and was holding her stomach with a pained expression.

"I'm hungry," she complained.

Al looked around. The parking lot was deserted. He needed time to study the map, but he didn't want the boy near a public place or anywhere he could ask for help.

"Get buns from truck," he ordered. They would eat at a picnic table nearby.

After careful study, he found a dead-end ATV trail on the map. Perfect. It was 5:22. He dialed his wife.

"Where are you? Where are the kids?" she demanded.

Let her yell, let her scream. What could she do? Nothing.

"I'm keeping the kids. You will never see them again."

"You can't do that."

Al felt anger rise in his throat. Stupid, goddamn bitch. She thinks she can order him now? Well, no police, no judge, nobody controls me anymore!

"Oh yes I can."

"But why?"

Why? Why? He was so furious he could barely find the words.

"It's no good seeing the children like this, under all of these conditions. It's better... nothing!" he spat at her.

"If it's all the same to you, then you don't have to see them at all."

She was purposely twisting his words as usual, but what did that matter? Now he would have to kill the children. She would tell her lawyer he was late and then blow the whole conversation out of proportion, saying he phoned threatening her and them. Why argue with her?

"That's not what I meant. And anyway," he continued, "I have to do it now, because you won't let me see them again after me telling you this." He glanced over at the truck, his breath coming fast. She would call the police as soon as they hung up. Maybe they would trace the call and find him before he had time to carry out his plan. He needed more time.

"I'm still coming over to sign the offer," he quickly assured her.

"Will the kids be with you?" She sounded confused.

"No!" he answered quickly, then laughed at his own indiscretion. He was tempted to tell her everything right now. Oh God, how she would feel knowing they were about to die. He smiled. Never mind, she would know later on tonight. He would tell her in person, just before he slit her throat. He decided he better get off the phone, the shorter the call the harder it would be for the police to trace it.

"I better stop talking. Your phone is probably bugged."

"Why should it be bugged? Is yours?"

He rolled his eyes. She was so stupid. "No," he replied and hung up.

He got back in the truck and opened the glove box, checking for the tenth time that day, to see if the knife was still there. He pinched the brown paper towels and felt the hard edge of the blade.

The girl was tired. She ignored him and retreated into her own world, staring dreamily out the window. But the boy was anxious. "Can we go home now?"

"No, Mommy is still working and wants us not there yet. She has buyers."

"Well, what are we going to do?" the boy wanted to know.

"She said to take you for a drive, then call again later." Al started the truck.

"Are you sure?" The boy sounded like he might cry. Al had to keep the boy's suspicions at bay. He needed his cooperation to make everything run smoothly. If the boy panicked now, the girl would panic too. He closed his eyes and remembered chasing baby chicks all over the garage. He did not want to run all over the woods with a knife, pursuing the kids like some maniac. He wanted the hit to be professional.

"I phoned Mommy. Mommy told me what to do. I am just following her orders."

He turned his head and gave the boy a helpless look. "You know women," he chuckled awkwardly. "She told me, 'Make sure those kids are fed, properly! Not just buns!' Look in Safeway bag back there. Steaks!"

The boy did as he was told and found five thick T-bones. "Great." He smiled weakly.

"Tell you what!" Al boomed enthusiastically, tapping the girl on the knee. "Let's find place in woods. Build campfire and cook these steaks! Good huh?"

The girl looked at him wearily. "Okay."

The boy sighed and nodded. "Then can we go home?" he added hopefully.

Al drove out of the parking lot nodding. "Then home."

CHAPTER FORTY-ONE

THE MURDERS

Paul tried hard to muster up some enthusiasm to please his dad, but he was dead tired. It had been such a long day and now instead of going home to Mommy and a nice hot bath, they were going out into the woods for a barbecue. Why did Mommy have to work so late? Why couldn't they just go home? He gulped back tears. Oh well, at least his dad was in a good mood.

His dad suddenly let out a whoop and stopped the truck before a steep embankment. At the top of the small hill above them there appeared to be a slate ledge.

"Watch your Daddy now!" he cried. "He can do anything!" He floored the gas, making straight for the ledge. Paul held tight to the armrest in the back seat and squeezed his eyes shut. This was weird.

The truck made it part way up the embankment, then slid back. Undeterred, Al tried again. This time loudly cheering the truck to go all the way, they almost made it. Perhaps he should start from farther back. He glanced at the girl. She was silent and her eyes were round with concern. Al refused to let it dampen his euphoria.

"Don't worry!" he giggled. "Next time we make it!"

He backed down the path and stepped on the pedal charging at the incline like an enraged bull. Near the top, he felt the wheels spinning underneath him in the mud. Finally, the tires caught and the truck flew up and over the slate onto the overgrown grassy road leading further up a slope.

As soon as the main path disappeared from his rear view mirror he stopped the truck. Three story birch trees ranged through the forest, interspersed with scruffy pine every color and shape. The trees were spaced only far enough apart to let a man through.

He opened his door and stepped onto the spongy forest floor. It was so quiet he could hear his heart pounding. He slipped the key back into the ignition and turned on the radio to CKXL, the girl's favorite station. Pop music blared from the tinny speakers. Going around to the other side, he opened the glove compartment and removed the paper towels concealing the knife.

"Stay here." He forced a smile at her. Still smiling, he said to the boy, "This is good spot for barbecue. Let's gather wood and start fire."

"I want to come too," the girl chirped.

Al had to use all his will to stay calm. "No, is cold. Listen to music. We'll be right back." Al opened the back door for Paul.

The boy hesitated. "Uh, I'm kinda tired, Daddy. Could I stay here too?"

Al swallowed his anger and took the boy's arm. "But I need a big strong boy like you to help your old Daddy."

Al stepped behind the boy shaking the paper-toweling off the knife and letting it flutter to the ground. Ahead he spotted a fallen log. "There to left."

Paul veered toward it. The woods were dead still. Twigs snapping beneath his hiking boots sounded like gunshots. About a hundred yards from the truck when Al judged Gabi could no longer see them, he grabbed the boy around the neck with his left forearm. Raising the knife, Al aimed for the boy's left chest, assuming that was where the heart was. He stabbed Paul in the top of his chest. Paul was shocked and struggled to get free.

"Please Daddy! I'll be a good boy. I'll be good! I'll be good! I'll be good!" he pleaded. His right arm was immobile, held in the tight vise of the carpenter's strong fingers, but he got his left arm free. Forcing it out from his father's grip, he brought it up and tried to protect himself.

"Stop it, Daddy!" the boy begged. But Al slashed at Paul's forearm, striking him directly above the elbow. Paul twisted his arm around, wrist up in a futile attempt to ward off the blows. Al stabbed him near the elbow again, twice in rapid succession.

"I promise Daddy. I promise! I'll be good, please, please, please! No!" Weak from exertion and pain, Paul dropped his arm, shouting and crying for his mother.

"Mommy! Mom…Mommy, help!" His cries only fueled Al's anger.

"Sissy!" he snarled. "Where is she now?"

He held the boy's frail body harder, tighter, lining him up for a better shot. Six times he plunged the knife directly into the center area of Paul's chest, finally hitting the heart and killing him. Blood spurted out and Al pushed Paul forward so as not to ruin his clothes. He stood over the boy, toeing the lifeless body in the shoulder. Nothing. But just in case, he plunged the knife into the child's back two more times.

He stood up feeling disoriented. It took longer than he'd anticipated. He had to hide the body. If the girl saw it she would go hysterical. Yanking on the arms, he dragged the boy up and over and behind the heavy log. He wiped the knife on the back of the boy's jacket, then slid it up his sleeve, point up. Marching back to the truck, he clenched his jaw in resolve. He had no choice now. The girl was a witness.

When he jerked open the door, she was startled. She'd been half asleep, listening to the music.

"What's wrong?" Her eyes widened with terror at the dark stain on his jacket sleeve.

Al froze. He'd forgotten to check for blood. "Paul. Paul had accident. We need to help." The girl scrambled down from the truck and started to run for the woods.

"Wait!" He gripped her collarbone with his left hand. "Be careful."

"What happened?" she cried in alarm.

"Don't worry." He tried to calm her. "Just a little fall. He skinned his knee. That's all." He kept her close in front of him as they picked their way toward the log.

About thirty feet from the boy's body, Al slipped his forearm around her neck and squeezed, lifting her off the ground. He pulled the knife from his left sleeve and brought it down into her with such force, it sliced right through her left shoulder. She began flinging her head back and forth, trying to escape his grasp.

"Daddy, Daddy, no! You're hurting me. You're hurting me, Daddy!"

Her strength surprised him. Aiming for her heart on the left side of her torso, he stabbed her in the same area twice more. She was screaming in pain and terror as the knife came down a fourth time, lacerating the left shoulder strap of her overalls and nicking her lung.

"Oh that hurts! Stop, Daddy!" She kicked, shrieked and gasped at the pain. Working her left arm free, she grabbed at his forearm around her neck. He slashed at her arm, catching her twice above the elbow and once behind her shoulder. But he hit only muscle and bone. Still she wouldn't let go.

"No! No Daddy! No!" Then he cut into the back of her arm at the tricep, severing the nerves and her arm went limp.

"Mommy," she sobbed. "Mommy."

Al growled, making an unearthly sound. Why wouldn't she die? With her left arm out of the way, her chest became a clear target. He forced her shoulders back and stabbed her in the center of the bib of her overalls, but the knife would not penetrate as it struck on a rib. He tried again, over to the right a little. This time the knife went though cartilage, but failed to pierce her heart. Instead it went low and ripped at her inferior vena cava.

He brought it down three more times in succession with more force. One of the blows hit a large vessel and blood began to gush out. The girl sagged forward, passing out. He let go of her body and it dropped to the ground. No one could survive that. But though she was unconscious, it can still take fifteen minutes to bleed to death.

He stood up feeling dizzy. He could hear the blood rushing through his ears. He was alone now. The task was done.

He stared at the girl's little lifeless body. She was the only person in the world who had truly loved him. Dropping the knife he sank to his knees clutching his head. Squeezing the thoughts from his mind.

A healthy shrub stood a couple of feet from where the girl lay. Al knelt before the bush and, using the knife, frantically began piercing the roots and clay below the surface. He couldn't just leave her lying on the ground like that. He would dig a grave for her.

By the time he was through, it was almost dark. The ground was so tough he had only managed to dig down a foot or so. He lifted the small figure and folded it into the shallow pit, then covered it up. He staggered back toward the truck exhausted. Tonight he would head back to McLean Creek campground and wash up. Tomorrow, he would deliver the news to his wife.

He slept in his truck. In the morning, he dug out a roll of toilet paper from a Safeway bag stashed beneath the driver's seat of the truck and headed into the cement washroom to clean up. Someone knocked on the door, but it was only one of the employees. He tried to hide his face from her as he emerged and returned to the truck. Chances were the police would be looking for him. He remembered how light-headed he'd been after killing the kids. He'd thrown the knife out the window of the truck into a bush. Would the police find it? Could they blood type it? Had he left anything behind? Any clues?

These thoughts plagued him. Maybe he should drive past and take one last look before heading into town to see his wife. He couldn't see her in the daytime anyway. The place would be swarming with cops. He would wait until night, then break in through the basement window as he did before.

He turned the truck back onto Sylvester Trail and headed south toward his destination. This time he put the truck in bull low gear and made his way up the knoll slowly and much more calmly. He parked in the same spot and walked a few feet into the forest toward the bodies. He studied the ground for any telltale signs. He looked up satisfied that nothing had changed.

Back in the truck, he stared at the map. He could make it to the city undetected if he continued heading south and came out past Calgary, west of Millarville ending up on Highway 549, then double back. The police would be looking for him north of the campground. They'd never expect him to head into the city from the south.

He passed the spot where he'd almost run into the family with the Quadrunners. The front tires slipped into some deep mud and got stuck. He tried to rock the vehicle out, putting it into drive, then reverse and back to drive again, but to no avail. The tires spun themselves deeper and deeper into the muck.

Cussing the mud and his truck, he jumped out to take a look. The Ram Charger was stuck fast. Nothing short of a tow truck could get it out. He hammered on the roof with his fist cursing vigorously. Blinded by anger, he flung the useless keys to the ground in front of the vehicle.

"Shit! Fuck!" Maybe God was punishing him for what he'd done. Well, he better find the goddamn keys and try to get a tow. Locating the spot he thought the keys landed, he reached down and sifted through the wet clay with his fingers, but failed to find them.

"Son-of-a-bitch! Fucking keys!" he kicked at the mud. Locking the doors, he decided to hitch a ride to town.

Al thought he'd better stay off the beaten track. By now, the police would definitely be looking for him and he might be recognized. He started to worry about the blood on his clothes. The police would be able to trace it to the children. He wandered north through the bush and found a stream. He took off his jacket and rinsed it out. He tried to dry it on a rock, but it was too cold and cloudy, so he tied it around his waist and continued walking.

He found some wild raspberries to quiet his rumbling stomach and cursed himself for not thinking to bring the steaks along. He had considered it, but at the time, the idea of eating bloody meat made his stomach queasy.

He shook his head in bewilderment. Where did the day go? It was getting dark again already. He found a spot under a thick spruce and cleared it away with his boot. This would do. He curled up on the ground shivering in the cold night and slept fitfully.

The next day he woke up hungry and thirsty. He found a small stream and cupped his hands in the water. Which way? South he supposed. Checking the moss on the north side of nearby tree trunks he headed in the opposite direction, keeping an eye out for berries. Soon, he happened upon Saskatoon bushes near another creek. He grabbed at the sweet purple berries and shoved them into his mouth by the handful. Maybe he should stay here for a while. There were plenty of berries, shelter in the trees and water nearby. He sat down to consider his options.

For the next eight days, Al vacillated between trying to find a road and hitching out and scrambling deeper into the woods to avoid detection, becoming more lost. Then on the ninth day, he found a fairly well traveled road. He tried to hitch a ride, but he looked so grubby, no one would stop. Later that night he climbed a fence into a farmer's field and slept under a tree. His skin burned with hundreds of tiny scratches from the bush. Each threatened to become infected. His head and chin itched from his dirty hair and beard.

He still hadn't given up on his plan to make his way to his wife's place and the idea of getting caught didn't frighten him anymore. At least he'd sleep in clean sheets again.

CHAPTER FORTY-TWO

THE WAIT

Liba started to feel hunted. The media was after her, especially The Calgary Sun newspaper. The three local TV stations, CFAC, CFCN and CBC kept a respectable distance as did the city's other major paper, The Calgary Herald, but The Sun showed no mercy.

On August 9th, one of their reporters, Linda Slobodian, found out Liba's house was for sale and called up thinking she was speaking to Liba's realtor when she was actually speaking to Liba. She introduced herself and said, "I understand that you are the realtor for the Dolejs family. Can you tell me what those people were like?"

Liba caught the disdain in the columnist's voice. "What exactly do you mean by, 'those people?"

Linda sounded a little exasperated. "Well, what was he like and what was she like?"

"You're talking to her." Liba's voice was hard.

"What do you mean?" The reporter sounded surprised.

"You are talking to her. We are one and the same," Liba reiterated.

There was silence as Slobodian put two and two together. Then her voice went up an octave and dripped with concern. "Oh my God, I didn't realize it was you. How are you holding up? Are you okay?"

"How do you expect me to be?" Liba answered abruptly.

Linda realized she wasn't getting anywhere. She signed off with, "We are thinking of you." Then sat down and squeezed a column out of it.

September 11

As the trial date loomed, Liba made a difficult call to Elunka.

"He is still refusing to talk. And he's been charged with two counts of murder," she stammered to her sister-in-law. "Please let Pepa and Mother Dolejs know."

Elunka was nearly hysterical. "We will have to plan how we tell Mother very carefully, because the news will kill her. We'll call the ambulance and have it standing outside her apartment when we tell her, because she may have a heart attack and need to be rushed to the hospital. We'll do it Sunday afternoon when Pepa and I can both go to Pardubice and protect her. How is your mother?"

Liba tried to reach through the fog surrounding her to answer Elunka's question. What was she asking? Something about her mother. Her mother who had been so looking forward to spending time with the kids. "Well, naturally her holiday is ruined. But she is holding up. She is cooking for me and helping…"

As soon as she hung up, Elunka called Pepa. The children were missing and presumed dead, and all Liba could say was that her mother's holiday was ruined. Poor Al, having to live with such a callous woman. Perhaps this was why he was driven to the point of losing his reason.

Liba was hanging on by her fingernails. It was November and the trial had just been set for March 23rd. She sat down and wrote the District RCMP office thanking them for their 'professional approach and the way they treated me from an emotional point of view.' It was a heart-felt note, thanking, 'especially Sandy Harder who saw me through the worst time of my life.'

Superintendent J. Sebastian wrote back thanking her for the letter and offering his sympathy. "The tragedy of this summer's events is difficult to comprehend let alone personally experience." His letter meant a lot to Liba.

Unfortunately, her relationship with Mami was rapidly deteriorating. They never did magically establish any kind of a communication, more like an uneasy truce. Mostly they were silent, both hanging on to hope. But after the first week came and went, hope began to diminish and eventually vanished all together.

While waiting for the trial, Mami served as a bit of a distraction because she couldn't do anything on her own. Even basics like picking up groceries in a store were impossible for her. It helped Liba to think of something other than the children for a few minutes. It also helped that there was somebody else in an otherwise totally empty house.

Her mother liked traveling. She liked history. She liked things with educational value, so she was quite happy to be taken to the Tyrrell Dinosaur Museum in Drumheller, or to go to Banff and visit the Indian Museum. She loved Calgary's Glenbow Museum and art galleries. She was even interested in seeing the inside of a western shop.

Mami was somehow more at home in Canada with Liba's gymnastics friends and Sandy Harder than she was in Teplice. She said she wanted to participate more in conversation, so Liba registered her for English classes three mornings a week and she began picking it up quite quickly.

Liba knew she was a lot more like her father than her mother and that became the basis for renewed trouble. When Mami divorced, life ended for her. She refused any male suitors and she maintained few friends. Liba described it as, "Basically wearing, if not black, sort of gray or navy blue, for the rest of your life." It was as if losing her mate took away her right to enjoy anything.

Now that Liba's kids were gone, Mami presumed Liba would do the same. But Liba couldn't live like that. She had a choice. Kill herself, or do the best she could with what was left of her life.

Liba knew her testimony was needed at the trial, so she would wait until it was over to make her decision. For the time being she would take refuge in her new career as a massage therapist. She'd almost completed the course when the kids went missing and because she couldn't face going back to work in an office environment, she thought she'd try it.

It was late December. A professional massage table was out of the question. The prices were out of her reach and as a former mechanical engineer, she had her own ideas on how it should be constructed. She decided she needed hardwood for the legs so she headed to the local lumber store. A sales guy in his late twenties with sun-streaked blonde hair, an athletic build and gray eyes came up and offered to help. They had a poor selection so she refused everything he showed her.

"No, that won't do. Nope. Not the right shape. Uh-uh not the right size." She shook her head looking up into those gray eyes when he questioned her. "Well, what are you building?"

"A massage table," she answered innocently.

He thought a moment. Massage was a relatively rare field in North America at the time. He thought she meant she worked at an x-rated massage parlor. He looked her up and down. She certainly didn't look the type. But you never knew. They searched some more, but she couldn't find what she wanted so she thanked him and left. As the automatic doors opened into the parking lot, Liba found herself thinking, "Hmm, he was cute."

Two days later, she needed some hinges. This time she kept her eyes peeled for her salesman. Her heart skipped a little when he approached her smiling. They started talking a little more. He introduced himself as Patrick Nelson (pseudonym). He found out she cross country skied.

"Oh, I always wanted to try that," he said, "but I'm a swimmer myself."

"Really," she said. "I'm on my way to Lindsay Park Sports Centre to inquire about stroke improvement classes. Why don't we swap lessons?"

Liba pulled out her card and handed it to him. "Call me and we'll set it up." Then she walked out.

The store manager had been watching the exchange with interest. He knew Pat was a fairly shy guy and had never come on to a customer in his life. "Did that lady just give you her home phone number?" he asked.

"Yeah," Patrick replied.

The store manager looked at him. "How did you do that?"

Patrick scratched his head. "I don't know."

He called her and eventually taught her to swim. They met at a nearby swimming pool at 6:00 AM all winter.

Mami was okay with the lessons until one day at the end of January when they went to swim, got into the pool and found the heater had broken. It was freezing. They got changed and went to Tim Hortons for a hot chocolate.

"Do you like movies?" Patrick asked.

After three or four trips to the movies, Liba noticed Mami's mouth getting tighter and tighter. Although Liba and Patrick were just friends, Mami was furious. She refused to speak to Liba for days if Patrick came to the door. Gradually, she stopped talking to Liba all together.

Neither Liba nor Patrick had much money so they met on morning runs. She'd never had a workout partner other than in gymnastics and found him a joy to be with. His company was a lifesaver for her. But at home, she was getting the silent treatment only half a year since she had lost her kids.

Liba didn't feel she could confront her mother so she reverted to the way she handled the silence as a teenager. She went about her business and accepted it. Mami was scheduled to testify at the trial and Liba asked Sandy Harder if it would be okay if Mami just wrote down a copy of her dealings with Al. Sandy's superiors said an affidavit would be fine.

One Monday toward the end of January, after Mami had not spoken to Liba for more than three weeks, Liba walked in the door and Mami said, "How is your time tomorrow morning? Do you have to be in the office?"

Liba's massage business was in its infancy so she had plenty of time. "I've got time 'til eleven or so," Liba offered.

Mami said, "Could you take me to a travel agent?" Mami told the agent she wanted to leave the country as soon as possible. The next flight to Prague was in a week and she arranged to be on it.

The following Tuesday morning, Mami had not said a word since asking for a ride to the travel agent. Liba loaded up the suitcases and drove her to the airport. A long, very silent drive. Liba told herself, "Just hang in there. It will be over soon."

About a mile from the airport Mami spoke. "Well," she huffed, "you managed to prepare quite a holiday for me here."

Liba slammed on the brakes. Her gut reaction was to kick Mami out in the ditch, shove the suitcases after her, turn around and drive home. But as she began to pull over, she cautioned herself. "You do this, she'll miss her flight and you'll be stuck with her longer."

So Liba pulled back into the lane and continued on to the airport. "I prepared a holiday," Liba repeated quietly. "I prepared this?" It was the only thing she was capable of saying. She was incredulous.

"I arranged the murder of my children to ruin her vacation?" she thought. "It blows me away. It just blows me away." She bit her tongue, took Mami to the airport and loaded her on a plane.

After Mami's remark, Liba came home and ran hard to blow off steam. Then she called Patrick. It was time for their relationship to reach a deeper level.

CHAPTER FORTY-THREE

THE TRIAL

Al still hadn't divulged the location of the children's bodies. He intended to hold that card until he needed it. Peter Martin and John Bascom prepared their cases. It would be a battle of the minds. Brilliant minds.

Peter's ace in the hole was Liba. She would make a fantastic witness. Bright, composed, though obviously grief stricken, and blessed with almost perfect recall. Her retelling of the telephone conversations Al had with her on the day the kids disappeared made it clear they were of a menacing nature. You could sense the evil in them. Basically Al had said, "I have the kids. I now have some of your attention. I can hurt you, Liba."

Then there were Al's lies, especially the one he told Danny Lyon about dropping the kids off at their Woodbine home on July 27. This would have a significant impact on the judge. Peter could also use Al's attempt to trade the location of his kids' bodies for a lesser charge. And Al was the last to see them alive.

Clearly Peter's main problem was proving the children were dead. It was crucial the judge agree to that point. If there was reasonable doubt they were alive, Al would be acquitted.

John Bascom felt he also had a good case. His strategy for the defense was, "You can't prove it. You may have all the suspicions, you may have theories, but you cannot prove the charges as laid." He knew it was a perfectly valid defense.

Rather than saying, "That person did it or somebody else did it," or using some form of technical defense, John's position was, "At the end of the day, if we keep out certain aspects of the evidence, how can you possibly say this is murder, an intentional killing? How do you know they didn't just have an accident?

"If we take our children to the bush and they fall off a cliff, we're not guilty of anything, unless we say to them, 'Go play on the cliff.' Then we would be guilty of criminal negligence.

"There's no way, on this evidence, you can find it planned and deliberate. It's just that simple." He also intended to make the argument that the RCMP had been oppressive, subjecting the defendant to undue pressure during interrogations.

John's other major concern was that first degree murder is automatically assigned a trial by jury. That's the way the Canadian Criminal Code works. Only with the consent of the prosecution can you eliminate the jury. Peter could hold him to a jury trial. In this case, a jury was very likely to be sympathetic to a grieving mother and unsympathetic, to say the least, to a father accused of killing his own children.

John approached Peter. He knew the prosecutor was a very ethical lawyer. Peter would not say, "I'm going to take a jury because that's going to give me a better chance of getting this guy convicted." But because it was such an emotional case, John felt a jury would give Peter a huge advantage.

"I want judge alone," John told him. The appointed judge, Mr. Justice Sulatycky, was a fair-minded judge. John thought of him as "a very polite man."

After Al was charged and after it was known that the police didn't have the bodies of the children, many Calgarians, unable to believe such an evil could live in their midst, voiced the opinion that Al must have sent the children back to his family in Czechoslovakia.

The Crown felt this wasn't true, but Peter still had to consider which was the best way to proceed. The key questions were straightforward: "Are the children dead?" and "Did he murder them?" They would be ones best handled by a judge alone. There was always the possibility of somebody sitting on the jury and saying, "Not without the bodies. I'm not prepared to accept the Crown proved beyond a reasonable doubt that they're even dead and I'm not going to convict the guy."

Whereas a judge would say, "This is reasonably straightforward. He was the last person with the children. He came out of the bush without the children. He said he would plead guilty to second degree murder rather than first and show us where the bodies are. Implicit in that is, 'I killed the children.' John knew Peter had never refused a request to re-elect and, it turned out, Peter never would. The request was granted.

Usually lawyers only make opening addresses when there is a jury. Peter's practice was to always do it. It gave the judge a snapshot of the case. What happened? What would the evidence be like? What should he pay attention to?

Peter's first task would be to establish the children were in fact deceased. He relied on six Canadian precedents where a murder trial had proceeded to conviction without the bodies. But the judge knew of a case in England where the defendants had been convicted and the deceased later turned up alive. The case was a hundred years old and with modern technology, including phones, it wasn't as likely to occur today.

If there was reasonable doubt that the children were alive, it would be fatal to the Crown's case. A large part of Peter's argument would focus on what Al said to Liba during his last phone calls, especially the words, "It's no good seeing the children like this, under all of these conditions. It's better... nothing!"

If the judge accepted that Al said these things, then he hadn't done it yet, the children were still alive at that time. What Al was saying was, "The visiting arrangements are unacceptable to me so I'm going to kill the children." Legally, a plan to kill them didn't have to be sophisticated or long time. Even deciding to kill them at the phone booth during that call made the act planned and deliberate, murder in the first degree.

A year before Peter had prosecuted a man who killed a young boy with a hammer, arguing the interval required to get the hammer, which may have been a minute or less was sufficient to establish planning and deliberation. His argument was accepted and the man was convicted.

The other detail in Al's case that showed planning and deliberation was the meat in the vehicle. Peter would say the food indicated it wasn't Al's intention to bring the children back that day. Al's plan was that he would have some sustenance in the woods, but his vehicle got stuck and he had to change his plan.

The first day of trial John Bascom looked around at the audience. The first two rows included about ten senior citizens, all nicely dressed. John leaned over and whispered to David Stilwell, his co-counsel, "Death Groupies."

The court adjourned for lunch and as John headed for the elevator, he held the door for a lady, one of the Death Groupies. She got in and looked at him. "I know where the bodies are and I'm going to tell you." John slipped out through the closing door and started taking the stairs from then on.

John and Peter were close friends, but winning a case takes psychology as well as legal knowledge and aptitude. Every small victory was important to both men. When a remark or ruling came John's way, the dynamic of their relationship changed.

"I could see when Peter was pissed off. He plays these games. When things are going really well, he's your good friend, but if things turn on him, watch out. That's what was happening. There were a lot of people there and he was under a lot of pressure. I could understand that."

They crossed swords on the second day when Peter was interviewing Nick Kyska, the first officer to question Al. Peter asked Nick why he chose John Bascom when Al requested he find him a lawyer.

"I don't know why I chose Mr. Bascom," Nick replied, "other than I've had favorable dealings with Mr. Bascom in the past and he just came to my mind."

"You understood Mr. Bascom was a criminal lawyer?" Peter asked.

Nick didn't hear him. "I beg your pardon?"

"Did you understand Mr. Bascom to be a criminal lawyer or someone who holds himself out as a criminal lawyer?"

"Yes sir," Nick answered.

"I see. Go ahead."

Justice Sulatycky interrupted and chastised. "You're not being kind, Mr. Martin. Mr. Bascom is very senior…"

Peter shook his head. "I meant only that that was the understanding, My Lord."

Justice Sulatycky continued. "He is one of the leading criminal lawyers in Calgary and there is no doubt about that."

"My friend understands the nature of the comment. I meant him no unkindness or disrespect."

"No," the judge replied firmly.

"Fine. I'm sorry," Peter apologized crisply.

Peter called all the police officers that had been in contact with Al and reviewed every piece of communication between them and their prisoner. They all attested to what a cold fish Al had been and how he refused to co-operate in helping locate his children.

Peter established that Gabi's blood was found on one of the paper towels in the truck and Paul's rare blood type was found on a paper towel and cardboard sheath which could have been used to house a knife. He also pointed out that the quantity of steaks, ham and vegetables found in the truck suggested Al did not plan to return home that day as he had promised his wife. Using witnesses, young fisherman Neil White, Al's co-worker Gerry Bursey, and ATV riders Ruth Lindmark and her family, he proved Al was the last to be seen with the children.

When cross-examining the officers, John Bascom pointed out that once the officers felt they were working on a homicide and not worried any more about the physical welfare of the children, they were violating Al's rights by questioning him so intensely and for such long periods of time.

The death-threats and hate-calls started up at John's office again and his wife, Tannis, was very concerned. She thought of changing their daughter's last name to protect her. Her co-workers, other doctors, accosted her at work demanding, "How can your husband do this?" She would respond, "I don't tell him what to do and it's none of my business." But they had already decided Al was not entitled to a defense.

Peter Martin next carefully laid out how Al proposed the reduction of charges from first to second degree murder in exchange for revealing the whereabouts of his children's bodies. The judge questioned whether Sergeant Lyon telling Al that a call had been placed to the prosecutor about listening to his proposal could be construed as inducement.

Peter cited similar cases and said, "This statement... is an inducement or an advantage or a benefit to no one, not to the accused and not to anyone else. It is no more than a simple statement of fact." He reminded the judge that the idea was Al's. Al had initiated talk of a deal.

John disagreed. He said Lyon broached the subject of wanting to talk about reducing the charges in exchange for Al's cooperating in locating the bodies and that's when Al answered, "Basically."

"The inducement I would submit comes here," Bascom argued, "Sergeant Lyon should have said to the accused, 'No, we're not here to talk about any deals or anything of that nature.'" John then submitted cases that supported his point of view.

Most of the conversations between Al and the police were not taped. Instead, notes were taken. John attacked the reliability of the records, pointing out discrepancies in the police testimony between what was said at the preliminary inquiry and what was being said now, especially in quoting Al. In other words, were the police reading anything into his responses?

John also kept hammering home the point that Al was often tired and hungry during questioning. The first morning when he'd asked for breakfast he wasn't fed until Cantafio and Lyon dropped by Wendy's on the way out of town. And the first night he was allowed to rest, some noisy inmates in the drunk tank kept him up past midnight.

Father Bastigal took the stand and said Al and he had talked about the sacrament of Last Rights for the children and discussed their spiritual welfare. He also testified that Al told him he was being well treated by the police.

John argued that because the police had decided who Al could and couldn't talk to, Al would have considered Father Bastigal an authority figure and therefore his words were not given freely.

But the court decided to admit Father Basitgal's testimony and everything Al had said to the police, including his offer of a reduced charge in exchange for the location of his children's bodies. Justice Sulatycky saw no inducement.

Then Liba was called. Because she was a witness, she was not privy to what had been going on: like all other witnesses she had been obliged to wait outside the courtroom until she was called to testify. Her shoulders square and chin up, she carried the death of her children with her to the stand. Her quiet strength filled the air. She was offered a seat, but she demurred.

Peter began his questioning. He asked her to identify her husband. Al sat slumped, his head slightly tilted forward, as if he were still at home staring at the television. He barely moved and did not meet her eyes.

"Do you see him here now?" Peter asked.

"Uh, yes," she replied. "He's sitting in the box behind you." Then, remembering the advice one of the RCMP officers had given her, not to look at anyone other than the lawyers questioning her, she focused on Peter.

He asked her about emigrating to Canada, meeting Al and the birth of Paul. "He never felt close to Paul, right from the time he was born," Liba testified.

"He preferred Gabi very much."

Peter asked her about the Easter Sunday she'd left her husband, but when she started to talk about how Paul had run away from Al, John objected. "I believe we're getting into hearsay."

The court agreed.

Liba still managed to talk about going to the Emergency Shelter with the kids and getting the restraining order. She told how Al had broken into the house when the kids were alone and frightened them so much. She cited his threats to take Paul away forever if she left him. She talked about the crime shows he watched on TV and how he called and wrote, promising everything under the sun if she would just take him back, and threatening her if she didn't.

"One of the letters also said that I will never be free of him. He will follow me wherever I go. He'll be my shadow."

She told the court about how she eventually agreed to restricted visiting rights through her lawyer, how bitter he had been when she took the kids and her mother to Expo and how he gave her no money for child support.

She described what the kids wore the day he took them fishing, right down to the patterns on their towels. She mentioned how he was in a better mood than usual that morning, smiling and saying, "When I come back, I'll have another surprise for you." But when she tried to describe his phone calls to her later that day, her mind blanked and her voice caught. Peter requested a short break.

She retreated to a washroom and splashed cold water on her face while trying to fight off nausea. Staring at her reflection, she commanded herself to be strong for her children. A few minutes later she returned composed and ready to resume telling her story.

She recounted the strange phone call and his ominous declaration, "It's no good seeing the children like this. It's better...nothing." She spoke of his sarcastic little laugh after he assured her that he'd still be coming over to sign the offer. She had asked, "Will the children be with you?" and he had coldly replied, "No!" Then he ended the conversation suspecting her phone was bugged.

Peter gently prodded her. "Could you just think back? Take your time. There's no hurry and it's very important if you can, please tell us the exact words he said at that point."

"Am I allowed to refer to my diary? Because I wrote the phone call down afterwards," Liba said.

"While the conversation was still fresh in your mind?" Peter asked.

"Yes," she nodded.

Peter looked to the judge. "May she have your leave, My Lord?"

Justice Sulatycky turned to Liba. "How soon after?"

"Part of it I wrote the same evening and part of it I wrote on the following Thursday for the city police. But most of it was written the same evening."

The judge looked at John. "Mr. Bascom?"

"I would have no problem with her referring to the notes she made the same evening," he replied. "I have some concern about the notes that were made the following Thursday. I take it they would be in a language that I cannot read in any event?"

Liba said only one quarter of the notes were in Czech. Most of what she had taken down was in English.

John frowned. "The problem I have, My Lord, is the witness hasn't indicated before now that she needs to refer to these notes."

"She hasn't used that phrase, that's right. She's asked you, 'Can I refer to my notes.'" Peter gave an exasperated little smile. "So that surely isn't a problem."

John pondered this a moment. "No, what I'm interested in knowing is whether there's something in these notes that has not been told to the court, and if that is the case, does the witness recall making the statement in her notes or has she referred to everything in her notes? Rather than Mr. Martin's question, which is, 'Have you told us everything about this?' Now perhaps you could look in your notes to make sure that that has occurred."

Peter's tone was short. "First of all, that wasn't my question. Secondly, my friend places the witness in a Catch 22. If you can't remember what's in your notes, you're not allowed to refresh your memory from them. My question to her was to think carefully about this part of the conversation and has she now repeated his exact words? She has said to me in reply, 'Could I look at my diary where I made notes of this conversation?'"

After this prolonged exchange between the contesting lawyers, Justice Sulatycky told her to go ahead and look at the notes she made on Easter Sunday.

Peter then asked her if she had formed an emergency plan with the kids. Liba replied, indeed she had.

"Right from the beginning, when he started threatening with kidnapping Paul, I instructed the children what to do in case that happened. Both children memorized our phone number. I made up little scenarios for them. Like, sooner or later he has to stop for gas…different situations that might come up to give them an idea of how they could break away if they were taken. I also told Paul that if he is taken away and he has to go to school somewhere, no matter where they are, pretend he is agreeable to what his father is doing. Don't fight or don't argue with him."

Al reacted involuntarily. His head jerked up in surprise, as if to say, "You had a plan? And they were in on it?"

Liba continued, "Just pretend it's fine and then contact the teacher and ask them to contact the police for him. And I told him that if he is taken away, it may be some time before I find him, but just be patient and maybe a few days, or it may be a couple of weeks or maybe two months, but I love him and I will never stop looking for him." Liba's obvious pain held the entire courtroom in its grip.

Peter then led her to her conversation with Al in the Cochrane jailhouse. She repeated her plea almost verbatim ending with, "I…I asked him if the children are afraid, if they're cold, if they're hungry, if they need anything and again, there was a bit of a nod in the negative. It was like, 'No they don't need anything anymore."

In cross-examination, John Bascom headed straight for Al's comment, "When I come back, I'll have another surprise for you." John wanted to establish it was an ambiguous statement, not necessarily denoting premeditation. His tone with Liba was respectful, but firm. "And you understood that to refer to signing the offer for the sale of the house?"

Liba nodded. "That's what I presumed at the time."

"Thank you. I have nothing further." John sat down satisfied. A seed of doubt had been planted.

Peter had one more witness, Kenneth Hendry, a meat manager at Canada Safeway. Reading the dates on the meat packaging found in the truck, Kenneth testified that four of the steaks had been purchased in June and only one had been purchased the day before the fishing trip. In other words, Al had frozen the steaks and taken them out specifically for the trip.

After Peter concluded, John stood up. "The defense will be calling no evidence."

The next morning Peter made his closing argument. Although he began with, "I propose to be uncharacteristically brief as I submit that, notwithstanding the length of this trial, the issues before you are clear and few in number," his argument was 26 pages long.

He went through his points systematically, beginning with, "The issue of whether or not the children are dead." He reviewed Al's conduct that lead to the restraining order and how unhappy the separation from his family made him. He said it was proved by the Banff National Park sticker found in the truck that Al had taken the kids there. This was corroborated by young Neil White who spoke to them while they were fishing.

"So Al is then seen on the afternoon of the 27th of July on this Sylvester Trail in the middle of the bush, in the middle of nowhere, in my respectful submission. That is so according to the Lindmarks' evidence. The Lindmarks say that the time as I recall was approximately 3 to 3:30."

Peter went over Al's phone calls. "At four o'clock that afternoon according to Mrs. Dolejs, the accused phoned her to say that he was coming over. At 5:22 he phoned to say that she would never see the children again. When the accused is seen ten days later emerging from the bush, he is alone. There is no trace of the children other than pieces of their clothing found in the vehicle and, I submit, some of their blood found in the vehicle."

Peter then cited examples of trials where the Crown had proceeded with murder charges without the victims bodies having been found.

"I turn then to the next issue, My Lord. Is he responsible for their death? It is clear he must be." Peter contended if they had died accidentally, Al would have immediately gone for help.

"My Lord," Peter continued, "I come to the final question which must be determined, whether or not these killings by the accused of his children is first degree or second degree murder." Peter repeated Al's threats to Liba, "that if you leave me I will take Paul away and you will never see him again."

"It is apparent that Mrs. Dolejs thought he meant he would take Paul away, and that is really peculiar since Gabi was the one close to him and Paul is the one he didn't care for. Peculiar that he would take Paul away and, pregnant in that suggestion, raise Paul himself and his wife would not see him again, but leave Gabi with his wife. But we know with the benefit of hindsight, because he has killed his children, that what he meant on those occasions was, in my respectful submission, he will take Paul and he will kill Paul.

"At the time he took the children that morning at eight o'clock, he knew he could not regain his position in the family. He knew that his children were not anxious to be in his company. Sometimes they did not agree to see him. He felt that his wife was turning them against him and he knew they would continue to get along very well without him.

"So on that fatal morning he had no intention, in my submission, to return them at four o'clock, at five o'clock or to ever return them. If he had intended to bring back the children, he would not have taken with him that morning five pounds of meat. And he cannot now argue on the evidence, 'I just bought them that morning.' If everyone is really hungry on Sunday, they cannot eat more than a third of that quantity. Why does he take the rest?

"The 5:22 phone call is important in this case. 'I have decided you will never see the children again.' So he advises his wife he is making a decision. He has weighed this matter and come to a conclusion. He says very coolly and calmly without emotion. 'You will not see these children again.' He says, 'Seeing them like this is no good. It is better I don't see them at all, it is better nothing.'

"He goes on in his conversation and says, 'In any event, if I do bring them back now, you'll not let me see them again so I am committed to this course of action. I cannot return these children. I am locked in now, since I have taken this decision and told you about it."

Peter spoke about Al reacting so strongly when it was suggested by the RCMP that he sexually assaulted the kids, but showing no emotional response when they accused him of murdering them. He recounted how Al had proposed to deal the bodies of his dead children in exchange for a lesser charge.

"My Lord, I conclude my remarks by saying this. I say when a man kills two of his children, aged ten and twelve, and disposes of them without a trace, that alone tells us it is first degree murder."

John Bascom's response was a surprise. In his closing argument he stated that the children's death wasn't the issue. Legal observers thought it was a wise move to concede the point, because if he were going to try to tell the judge they weren't dead his other arguments would have been discarded. John made this concession so he could move away from first degree. Now the judge would be all ears.

He said there was lots of evidence to prove they were dead, but none regarding the circumstances of their deaths. Nobody knew. The only thing that the Court could find was an unlawful act in that Al took the children and had not returned them and that he had caused their death. But how? Who knows?

John debated that at most, it was manslaughter because for second degree murder, the Court has to be satisfied that the defendant intended to kill them, or cause them bodily harm that he knew was likely to cause death.

"My friend indicates with regard to the charge of first degree murder there must have been planning and deliberation because of what happened afterward. That, I submit, is not something the Court can rely on very heavily. What an accused person did after an offence is not, I submit, evidence of planning and deliberation." John cited a case from the Ontario High Court to back his argument up.

"With regard to the amount of meat, well, there is no evidence how long some of the meat was in the truck, except for one of the steaks."

Then he addressed Al's statement, 'I will have another surprise for you.' "We don't know what he meant. The wife of the accused understood that to refer to signing the offer for sale of the house. The conversations at 4:00 and 5:22 could also refer to signing the offer for the sale of the house."

John addressed the ambiguity of Ruth Lindmark's testimony. "Her first statement is that she saw one person in the vehicle. Later under hypnosis there was an indication there was another adult in the vehicle. This I would suggest is not possible if it is the same vehicle. It is quite clear from the evidence that there was no one in the vehicle except the accused. This vehicle was seen the next day a short distance down the exact same trail in the position where it was stuck. So if death ensued to the children, it would have to have occurred prior to that."

Bascom's argument was only five pages long. It was characteristic of John, concise and to the point.

How would the judge call it? Accident? Criminal Negligence? Manslaughter? Second degree murder? First degree murder?

On April 10, 1987, what would have been Paul's thirteenth birthday, Justice Sulatycky handed down his decision.

Sulatycky agreed with John that it was, "impossible to determine if the children were with the accused or not at the time that the accused was seen in his vehicle on the Sylvester Creek Trail by the Lindmarks." Then he said his research did not turn up any other case in which two persons had gone missing at the same time. "That gives this case a particular uniqueness, and it may well be unprecedented."

He agreed with both sides that the children were not alive. "Because they were old enough to act in their own self-interest and for self-preservation...and are not heard from again...I am satisfied with absolute certainty...that both children are dead."

Peter's argument that if you assumed the children were dead, it had to be first degree murder was rejected. The judge decided there was not enough evidence of planning and deliberation to satisfy him beyond a reasonable doubt. Of course, there was the fact he killed two people, so having killed the first, he had to kill the second. Tragically that would be the reality of this situation, unless he somehow held them both with one hand and killed both with one act.

The difficulty was, in order to convict on first degree murder, they had to know beyond a reasonable doubt which one he killed first. The first killing would be second degree murder. Then having killed the first child, he would intentionally decide to kill the second to remove a witness. That would make the second killing first degree murder. But who had been killed first? Only Al knew and he wasn't talking.

If it were an accident, then Al surely would have sounded the alarm and said, 'My children have been in an accident. They've fallen off a cliff or they've drowned.' It's such basic common behavior, you expect it from everyone. If it were anything else, like driving drunk and going off the road, you would still expect the same kind of behavior. He would say, 'I made a serious mistake, your honor. I caused the death of my children, but it was not intentional, not murder.' He would give an explanation.

"Any scenario which I can conceive of which would lead to the conclusion that the children died in some fashion other than at the hand of the accused, is irrational and unreasonable," Justice Sulatycky reasoned.

Then he pointed to Al's comments when he was in the custody of the police and told the story that he had taken the children back and had entered through an unlocked garage door. That was proven to be a lie.

"In my view, that false statement is the most compelling evidence in the accused's conduct after August 7, 1986." Justice Sulatycky said he had to conclude "that the second phone call was either notice of intention to do away with the children, or admission that such an unthinkable event had already occurred."

Then he considered telephone conversations Al had with Liba and said it's not possible to listen to her rendition of what Al said in those phone calls and think this was an accident or unintentional killing. The way he was talking, it was obviously an intentional act, but they were speaking to each other in Czech and though he trusted Liba's translation, it wasn't scientific.

"I just don't know when and how you killed your children so I cannot say positively it was planned and deliberate."

"Stand up Mr. Dolejs," the judge ordered. "I find you not guilty as charged on each count of first degree murder. I find you guilty of second degree murder on each count."

Liba watched Al's shoulders snap back, but felt no sense that justice had been served. She couldn't shake the fact Al got only second degree murder. She was convinced it was her fault. If only she had been a better witness, if she hadn't asked to consult her diary.

The judge could now sentence Al to anywhere from ten years to 25 years without parole. Sentencing was set for May 8th. The judgement had been eloquent and thorough.

At sentencing, Peter Martin came ready to ask for the maximum. He wanted Al put away for a very long time. He submitted that the details of the killing didn't matter.

"Suffice to say whatever happened, it was absolutely horrible," he contended. He spoke of Al's behavior after the killings. "As we speak now, the bodies of these children have still not been located. There is no suggestion or hint of any remorse on the part of the accused."

He asked the judge to impose the maximum penalty of 25 years without parole. "There is a principle in our law that the maximum penalty is reserved for the worst cases. We would be hard pressed, I say, to conceive of a worse case than this. And if this case does not attract the maximum penalty, My Lord, with respect, one wonders what type of case would it take to attract the maximum penalty?"

In defense, John Bascom cited a case where the appeals court had reduced the parole ineligibility for a convicted murderer from twenty to thirteen years because the justice placed too much emphasis on the fact his case was very close to first degree murder. John also argued it wasn't fair to penalize Al for not disclosing the location of the children's bodies.

"His actions are not necessarily the actions of a person who does not show remorse, but the actions of a man who is following the instructions of his counsel."

———————

Following the sentencing briefs, Justice Sulatycky handed down his sentence. "The accused previously threatened to either take away the children from his wife or implied to do harm to at least one of them. The children were with him for no other reason than their compassion for him. His abhorrent conduct towards them, resulting in their death, was nothing less than vengeance which he wished to visit on his wife.

"The concealment of the bodies of his children, which took place before he retained counsel is also an aggravating factor...He is, in my view, a person unable to show any remorse as he demonstrated from the moment of his apprehension and has continued until now. In short, the accused is a cool, calculating, cold-blooded murderer who is apparently fully pleased and content with the acts he has carried out, acts that are beyond the comprehension of any proper parent.

"I am of the view that the nature of the offence involving the killing of his two children, over whom he was in a position of responsibility, and to whom he owed the highest duty of protection and comfort, and his conduct both before and afterward which are most serious indicators of his real character, require that the maximum penalty be imposed on him.

"Stand up, Mr. Dolejs. You are sentenced to life imprisonment and you will not be eligible for parole until you have served 25 years."

As Al shuffled out of the courtroom and passed Liba, his eyes slid sideways toward her. She felt revolted, as if something disgusting had landed on her.

"Twenty five years,' she thought feeling some satisfaction. "Twenty five years before I'll ever have to think about him again, and perhaps he won't make it."

The overwhelming tragedy of the case was clearly felt by Peter. There was no joy in the verdict. He turned to Balfour Der, his young colleague.

"There is no victory after a case like this. We can only feel good about the job we have done. Here we have two young children who are dead, a mother who is grieving their loss and a man who will go to jail for the rest of his life. There is no cause for celebration."

But he was reassuring with Liba. "Keep in mind the result," he told her. "And the result is the same as if he were convicted for first degree murder. He could not have received a higher sentence. It's a distinction without a difference."

CHAPTER FORTY-FOUR

THE BODIES

After sentencing, Al approached Diane Rayburn, his placement officer with Corrections Services Canada. She was interviewing him as part of her routine prior to selecting the institution he would be assigned to. During the discussion, he told her he killed the kids using a knife that he threw away in the bush. He said the boy wasn't buried, but could be located under a pile of logs just off the road near the truck. He was relaxed and nonchalant, as if they were discussing a small business deal. He indicated he'd already let his lawyer know the location and, if he was sent to a prison out of the province, he'd give him permission to tell the police, that is unless the media found out.

Acting on the information Diane gave them, a small group of investigators were secretly dispatched to the McLean Creek area, but again found nothing. They didn't want to upset negotiations between Peter Martin and John Bascom on locating the bodies. Then on June 4th, the RCMP received a brief verbal description. They would find the bodies two hundred yards up the cutline off the Sylvester Trail, approximately two kilometers north of the truck. Once in the two hundred yard zone, the children would be found on the edge of a clearing. It would be fifty yards to the first body and another fifty yards to the second.

Within ten minutes of searching the area on foot, officers found Paul's skull in the underbrush. Minutes later they discovered his clothing under a rough pile of logs. The searchers soon located a dig suspected of being the second hiding place for a body. Squirrels, coyotes and bears, all carnivorous creatures, had eaten every bit of flesh from the bodies, leaving only their skulls and scattered bits of bone. However, all of their clothing was recovered, riddled with stab wounds. They also found Gabi's little pink glasses.

Liba was in Mexico on a massage course for four more days so the RCMP kept their find a secret until then.

When Patrick Nelson arrived at the airport to pick up Liba, he noticed Sandy Harder waiting too. He watched as Liba emerged from the gate and Sandy guided her to a waiting police car. Then he quietly drove home and waited for Liba to call.

———————

The day of the kids' memorial service, Liba stayed overnight at a friend's. Private invitations were issued to forty people. Liba specified she wanted her children united. They shared a room, ate together, played together and loved each other so much they should be buried together. At first she chose their favorite lullaby. She had the music, but in the end didn't give it to the organist because if it wasn't played just so, it would be too upsetting and Liba couldn't bring herself to rehearse it.

Then there was the issue of what toys to bury with the children. Maybe two toys each, but she couldn't decide. Vorisek? Winnie the Pooh? Pink Elephant? Brown bunny? Which would they have preferred? She couldn't bury one with Paul and two for Gabi. So she kept them all instead.

She remained stoic through Father Bastigal's English portion of the service. "Even though the children were not baptized in the Catholic Church, because God takes in all children just the same, that makes no difference. They died innocent and they died a senseless death," he spoke compassionately, "Despite their young age, they still left a mark on this world."

Then Father Kadlec, an old Slovak priest, conducted part of the service in Slovak. A few months before the children disappeared, Liba had read William Styron's book, *Sophie's Choice*. When Sophie walks into the concentration camp with her daughter and son, an SS officer approaches her and says, "Jesus said, 'Let the little ones come to me.' You may choose one child." She knows the other will be sent to the gas chamber. She has to make a choice which child to save and which to let die.

When Father Kadlec started his sermon, his opening line was, "Jesus said, 'Let the little ones come to me.'" Suddenly Sophie's agony became Liba's reality and she broke down for the first time in public and sobbed.

———————————

In the reception line afterward, Liba bent over to hug a little friend of Gabi's named Leisl. The weight of the girl's small body in Liba's arms was more than she could bear and she began sobbing again.

———————————

The next day The Calgary Sun newspaper carried a picture of Liba, obviously in deep mourning, getting out of her car in the cathedral parking lot. She felt violated once again.

CHAPTER FORTY FIVE

TODAY

Al was recently incarcerated at Warkworth Institute at Campbellford, Ontario, for 10 years. When he found out about this book he requested a transfer. He was moved to the crème de la crème of Canadian prisons, Fenbrook Medium Institution, in Gravenhurst, Ontario.

At Warkworth, he was a model prisoner, kept to himself and never got into trouble. His parole officer tried to talk to him about his crime, but he refused. What's done, is done, as far as he's concerned. He has never shown any remorse for his crime.

Up at six-thirty every morning for the past ten years, seniority earned him a private cell. He wore Corrections Canada blue jeans and favored a green work shirt over a white tee shirt. He purchased his own TV through the institution.

At Warkworth, breakfast is at seven. Some days, eggs, toast and cold cereal. Some days, pancakes. Once a week, inmates are served bacon. At eight o'clock, Al's workday would begin. As a senior carpenter, Al was on his own, doing repairs around the institution. There was no one supervising him. When he was sent to a certain building or location he was phoned through.

At twelve o'clock, he returned to his cell for the noon count. There are five counts a day. Morning, noon, supper, ten thirty and shortly after midnight. Al received the top prisoner pay level, $6.50 a day. He costs the prison institution $125 a day, plus his pay.

Warkworth is a medium security institution that opened in 1967. A double sixteen-foot chain-link fence topped with razor wire surrounds the buildings. There are 350 staff members and just under 600 inmates.

Although the guards wear uniforms, movement inside the institution is loosely controlled. It's a campus style facility sprawling over 200 hundred acres. There are thirty-one buildings, reception, hospital, administration, chapel, school, shop buildings and five cell blocks. The walls are mostly unpainted concrete.

After lunch Al would return to work until 4:15, then back to his cell for another count. At 5:00 he ate supper. Evening recreation involved anything from lifting weights and playing sports in the gym to watching TV or going to group activities. Social development groups included Alcoholics Anonymous, Bible study and special interest clubs, but Al was not big on these activities.

Most of the Warkworth inmates are in for relatively minor offenses, break and enter, theft, possession of stolen property, assault, impaired driving, fraud, but some were convicted of more serious violent offences, aggravated assault, assault with a weapon, drug trafficking and importing. Al had a small group of friends. They knew only that he was in for murder. None of the inmates or even the guards knew that he stabbed his two children to death.

Although Warkworth has psychologists and caseworkers on staff, they are there mainly to do assessments for parole board hearings. Al has basically gone untreated throughout his sentence. He was assigned a case management plan when he first arrived, but has long since finished his Alternative To Violence Program.

At 10:30 at night, Al was locked up in his cell where he turned on his TV. Crime shows are still his favorites, among them, Matlock, Law and Order and reruns of Murder She Wrote.

Cells are locked electronically seventeen at a time. Besides the crash of the cell doors clanging shut at once, it's generally pretty quiet. Al closed his cell himself. A guard goes cell to cell checking to make sure. Little lights go up the side panels that indicate the cell is locked, but the guard also gives each door a yank. It's been five years since the last escape. An inmate got out by concealing himself in a food truck.

Al's mother writes to him regularly. She and Pepa and Elunka still refer to the children's murders as "an unfortunate accident" and blame Liba for the breakdown in the marriage leading to Al's offence. They claim they will welcome him back home to live with them if he chooses when he is released. They scoff at the idea he may be dangerous. He has told his family he has gone back to God and they believe him.

His new home, Fenbrook Medium Institution at Gravenhurst, is considered leading edge among Canadian correctional institutes. Federal Solicitor General Andy Scott officially opened the facility in May, 1998. It's the first federal prison built in Ontario in 25 years.

Fenbrook is quite lovely. It looks like a collection of tiny villages set out to house 400 inmates. The unique landscaping and vegetation are highlights of its design. There are four apartment-style housing units in each village. Al and his fellow inmates are expected to cook their own meals and share communal housekeeping tasks. The institution also features private family visiting units, an industrial trade building, educational program building, chapel and health services clinic.

Programs emphasizing adult basic education and employment skills are the top priority. Wherever possible community standards have been mirrored in all operations including a satellite branch of the local library.

The institution's perimeter security is provided by a double twelve-foot-high chain-link fence that is wired with alarms and topped with coils of razor wire. The architectural design includes an environmentally sensitive fence and rock outcrops within the compound, which contribute to the overall atmosphere of normal community living. Security is augmented with 37 closed circuit cameras on the perimeter and another 12 throughout the facility.

There are few barriers and bars within the institution, but the positive interaction between staff and Al is expected to provide the best security until he gets out.

It turns out Al can apply for parole review through the Faint Hope Clause, Section 745 of the Criminal Code, that allows for early parole after 15 years of his 25 year sentence. In 1976, the Liberal government implemented a plan for prisoners with long sentences like Al's, to reduce their original punishments by ten years. Al's parole review date is August 6, 2001.

CHAPTER FORTY-SIX

PATRICK

Patrick's friends knew it was serious when, while out salmon fishing at Rocky Point in Nanaimo, British Columbia, there was a major run of fish going on and he was standing on the hottest fishing rock on the West Coast. Everybody was catching fish. He had eleven in two hours. Suddenly Patrick glanced at his watch and hurriedly began packing up his rod. His buddy looked at him as if he were crazy.

"Where are you going?" he asked in amazement.

"Gotta pick up my girlfriend. She's arriving at the airport in Victoria to join me fishing."

"Are you nuts? Call her and tell her to take the bus!" his friend urged.

"Naw. I better go get her." Patrick replied, heading for his car.

"She must be really something!" his friend called after him.

Patrick smiled. "She sure is."

Not long after, he bought a ring and brought it home, planning a romantic weekend with a candlelit dinner at the Chateau in Banff. He was going to propose on bended knee. Do it properly. Then Liba walked in the door and he didn't last five minutes. He told her how much he loved her and showed her the ring. Then he asked, "Will you marry me?" She said yes and it scared the pants off him.

"Those were the biggest words I ever heard," Patrick said. "And when you know you are saying them for once only, they are the biggest words you ever say."

They decided to elope during a salmon-fishing trip to Terrace, British Columbia. They were out on a 2000 pound steel jet boat with a guide on a raging river when it slammed into a stone wall and started sinking. The engine refused to start and they were swept sideways into rapids. The boat got high-centered on a rock so Patrick slipped into the deep river to rock it free.

It finally came loose and Patrick began fighting to pull himself back on board. As the boat swirled with the current, he got pinned by the water under the hull. Everyone was being knocked around and screaming for him to climb aboard, but he couldn't muster the strength. Then Liba grabbed the back of his chest waders and in one fell swoop hauled him in, just as the boat hit another rock wall. Two more seconds and he would have been cut in half. Patrick married her the next day.

Liba has her good days and her bad days, but with Patrick at her side, it makes everything a little easier. He provided a refuge from the media, a quiet escape. His calm and patient nature helped to balance the rest of her life. Their mutual love of outdoor adventure takes them to remote places ideal for soothing the soul.

She still feels Paul and Gabi's presence all the time. She even talks to them. Sometimes she worries she could have been a better mother. She feels sad when she thinks of how she should have been more patient with them, how she should have spent more time with them or when she may have been too strict.

Then she mentally talks to them about it and they reassure her, telling her it's okay and not to worry about such things. She still longs to see them and hold them, but at times they are almost a tangible presence. She smiles, reddening a little.

"I feel the touch, I feel the body weight. I feel the warmth from their bodies. Especially Paul's hand in mine and Gabi sitting on my lap."

She can conjure them most clearly when she plays certain pieces of music like the Easter Mass by Antonin Dvorak. Only recently she learned the piece was inspired by the vision of Mother Mary kneeling at the foot of the cross in front of her dying son.

CHAPTER FORTY SEVEN

REDEMPTION

With Al in prison, Liba needed to focus on something. She knew she would never want more children. They weren't replaceable like puppies. Besides, it would be unfair. She would be unfair. She would never let them out of her sight. She had to find something where she could be useful and she had to recover. She went back to her original passion, spending time in the mountains and outdoor pursuits.

It was terrible going to the mountains at first because she caught herself looking through the bush for traces of clothing or toys. It would take ten years for that feeling to leave her. Even driving past a playground, she would glance over expecting to see Gabi's rambunctious little form climbing the monkey bars.

But in time, the mountains proved cleansing. Three years after the kids died she was sitting atop Sentinel Pass on a glorious summer day, staring down at two sparkling mountain lakes and a pristine meadow valley amid ten peaks. Liba found herself talking to the clouds.

"How is it possible that the world is so beautiful and life in it can be so difficult?" Then she realized one doesn't contradict the other. One balances the other out.

Her competitive spirit reawakened. She began entering ten kilometer races and progressed to half marathons of thirteen miles, then eventually running a couple of marathons. She became an accomplished swimmer so much so that she was able to compete in triathlons, one third swimming, one third biking, one third running.

Patrick bought her a racing bike for a wedding present. Working out everyday, she got into great shape and as she became physically stronger her emotional state improved too. Her first race was horrible. Everyone else seemed fitter and faster so she decided to fix that.

At 41, five years after her ordeal, she tried out for the Canadian National Triathlon team and qualified for The World Triathlon Championship. In 1994, she was on her way to Wellington, New Zealand with 180 men and women in all age groups, juniors to 80-year-olds.

It was the most difficult race of her life. It was her first open ocean swim ever and she was terrified. The day began at 3:30 AM. She had gotten very little sleep. A horrendous storm had blown in from Antarctica and raged around the harbor for three days. The wind was so strong it was whipping water from the angry surface into the street. Everything was slick and wet. She knew she had to focus. She tried to block everything from her mind except her keen determination to complete the race.

She stood shivering on the parking lot near the rock wall where she was to begin her swim. She tried steeling herself against the cries from some of the competitors around her. No one wanted to wade into the whitecaps. She stared into the black waves and blocked out the chaos. A sudden realization descended upon her. After what she had been through, nothing would ever daunt her again. She zipped up her wetsuit and waded resolutely into the water.

She competed in Cancun, Mexico in 1995 and qualified again in 1996, but someone broke into her garage and stole her bike so she couldn't go. A tri-athlete's bike is an intregal part of her training, but Liba just shrugged. Material things mattered so little to her now.

"Maybe it wasn't meant to be," she smiled.

EPILOGUE

PROFILE OF A KILLER

According to some of his patients, Robin Reesal MD, Fellow of the Royal College of Physicians and Surgeons of Canada with accompanying certification by the American Board of Psychiatry and Neurology, is half psychiatrist, half clairvoyant. He runs the Center for Depression and Anxiety on the edge of downtown Calgary.

Robin looks amazingly young for forty-four. His skin is the color of café latte and unwrinkled, except for laugh lines around his large, expressive brown eyes. He has a lovely, warm smile, a quick wit and gentle manner. These tools come in handy dealing with patients in emotional crisis.

Robin obtained the highest standing in his medical school class for psychiatry at the University of Ottawa. He chose psychiatry due to his natural bent. Even as a teenager, male and female friends alike sought him out for advice. He listened, understood and always seemed to come up with a pragmatic solution. Robin is empathetic, but philosophical.

"Psychiatrists, like police and firemen, learn to diminish their emotional responses to what's going on, because it gets in the way of their objectivity and hinders their ability to help."

Twelve years after Al murdered Paul and Gabi, Liba was introduced to Robin.

She still had a lot of questions. Why did Al kill Gabi? Would the kids still be alive if she had handled things differently? Should she worry about Al getting out of jail someday?

Robin spent weeks with Liba, collecting the data he needed to form an opinion. Then he offered his best professional assessment.

At the beginning of their meetings, he told Liba he was going to go through the process of what he would normally do when he sees someone for a consultation. Only this time, he would do it by proxy. She would answer the questions he would normally ask the patient directly.

"You have a unique insight into the individual because you're the person who lived with him. The accounts by others are second hand. I put great value on what you say because you were there to experience it." But he added a caution.

"In this case, I cannot make a diagnosis of someone I have not examined. My opinions are meant to be general, applicable to anyone with a similar profile. Whenever I refer to Al, Paul, Gabi, Liba or to any of Al's parents or siblings, I am not referring to the actual persons, but to hypothetical individuals who possess the characteristics which you have described to me.

"First, we'll deal with the non-characterlogical psychiatric disorder. An individual like the one you describe would probably suffer from a mood disorder called dysthymia, a low-grade form of depression, dating back to his teen years.

"The criteria for dysthymia are changes in appetite, abnormal sleep patterns such as sleeping too much, low energy, poor self-esteem, lapses in concentration, feelings of hopelessness and a sense of not knowing who you are and where you belong in this world. Only two of these symptoms need to be present to diagnose the disorder.

"In the latter years, this quite possibly became a full-blown major depressive disorder. For that you need five of the following criteria and the first two are essential:

- a pervasive pattern of depressed mood
- a loss of interest or pleasure in most activity
- change in appetite, either eating too much or too little
- changes in sleep pattern, either wanting to sleep all the time or getting broken sleep

- becoming very slowed down and lethargic
- chronic fatigue and low energy
- changes in sexual interest
- poor concentration
- thoughts of suicide

Other symptoms typical in depression are:
- increased irritability
- poor sense of self
- inability to enjoy activities
- social withdrawal from others
- increased anxiety or over-representation of issues (the so-called making a mountain out of a mole hill)
- becoming more reflective of past patterns, in which one revisits the past and replays it over and over
- indecisiveness

Typically, depression comes and goes, but it's not unusual for a major depressive episode to be prolonged for years.

"Now we can look at the characterlogical structure of a person, how they think, how they process information and whether their means of looking at themselves and dealing with the world is leading to dysfunction. Usually the diagnosis cannot be made until after age eighteen because we believe character is essentially formed at that point in time. So we look for patterns beforehand and then follow-up.

"The person you describe may suffer from a mixed pattern, meaning there's a combination of three different patterns:
- anti-social personality disorder characteristics
- paranoid personality disorder characteristics
- obsessive/compulsive personality

"Let's start with the obsessive/compulsive component because it was prominent early in life.

"You have described a person who has a preoccupation with orderliness, perfectionism and inter-personal control at the expense of flexibility and openness with others. One way you can see this is in the job that a person picks. For example, a carpenter's job requires a lot of detail. The pieces of wood must be carefully measured and put together precisely. He also worked as an engineer, again a strictly ordered profession. In these jobs there is only one right way. Any other way is wrong. These individuals are black and white thinkers.

"Usually this type of personality is preoccupied with details, rules, lists and organization. There's a sense of perfectionism. They'll be very critical, constantly analyzing and reassessing their work and the performance of others.

"These personalities are very rigid, highly committed to a set of rules which may or may not be society's rules. Usually these people will be reluctant to delegate tasks. They can't trust anyone else to do it right.

"They often use a passive/aggressive style. He may be outwardly compliant and follow along, but privately harbor anger and resentment. For example, he may secretly resent doing a favor for a parent although he tells his mother he doesn't mind. Then he displaces the anger onto individuals who are more vulnerable, not on the parent who has more influence over his life because he fears rejection and repercussions. He withholds, withholds and then explodes. An inconsequential issue can serve as a spark to start the fire within. This is a generic pattern for individuals with this personality style.

"Now, add the component of paranoid personality disorder, a pervasive distrust and suspiciousness of others. These individuals constantly question the motive of others and give them a negative interpretation. They fear exploitation and deceit. This occurs even when objective evidence indicates otherwise. They are preoccupied with these thoughts and constantly question the loyalty and trustworthiness of friends, associates, co-workers and loved ones.

"The individual reads hidden meanings into remarks and activities. They see comments by others as demeaning or threatening. They're very big on grudges. They're unforgiving of what they perceive as insults or attacks, whether they actually occurred or not. They will harbor these resentments for months, even years. They constantly believe their character and reputation are under attack and will quickly respond with anger.

"Their suspiciousness can lead them to question the fidelity of their spouse. Therefore, they maintain constant vigil over their partner.

"So you have two elements, an individual who is very rigid and rule-oriented, together with paranoia. He is suspicious of all those around him, even his closest loved ones. That's already an unhealthy combination. Now you add the third component, an anti-social pattern of behavior. Usually in this pattern, there is a failure to conform to laws and a disregard for the rights of others. What the individual wants takes priority over what the rules say he is allowed to do. There's a pattern of deceitfulness, lying, a high degree of impulsiveness, irritability and aggressiveness.

"Anti-social personalities are often referred to as psychopaths or sociopaths. The more correct term is anti-social personality disorder. Traditionally, psychiatrists expect to see three things in their background: bed wetting, fire setting and cruelty to animals. When taking a history, we try to learn whether these behaviors are present.

"In this case, you have described an individual who doesn't follow the true pattern. I don't know whether he had a history of bedwetting. There's no evidence he set fires, but certainly, there was cruelty to animals in the case of the partridge chicks. That's why I'm saying this is a blend of different disorders. He's not the so-called true anti-social with a pattern of misbehaving from early in life. Stealing cars at age twelve, for instance.

But certainly the lack of regard for others, the breaking of rules, the constant deceit and the manipulation all fit the criteria.

"Look at the partridge chicks. You could say this was a precursor to the deaths of the children. What you had were twelve helpless animals. They were babies.This person made sure everybody knew that. He picked them because of it. Then progressively, it appears, bumped them off.

"The circumstances of their burial was similar to the death of the kids. Lie about what happened, but at the same time carry out the killing in a way the dead chicks will be found. He left them in the back yard and didn't bother to bury them. It matches the way the kids were discarded in the forest and left to be eaten by scavengers.

"The degree of cruelty to the action is significant. Most would say, 'How could you possibly take something that's so helpless as a child, that isn't going to harm anybody, and do such a vicious thing? How could someone be so callous, and have no feelings about it?' Well, it was all done before with the chicks. In exactly the same way.

"The idea of taking life wasn't novel. He'd rehearsed it with the helpless chicks. That barrier was broken. The ultimate gain of extinguishing life would override any emotions attached to cruelty. The final act of murder was really a culmination of a series of life events and life circumstances. It was an inevitability and just a question of time.

"Had Liba behaved any differently in the marriage, say, always being compliant and carrying out the dutiful roles of a housewife, it wouldn't have made any difference. If you apply the same principle to most people's lives, it works like this. There are days a person in the household is intent on creating conflict. Does the topic make any difference? No. Does the day make a difference? No. The disagreement will occur no matter what.

"There is a high level of manipulation which is part of the anti-social personality. Nothing is done for free. There is always a reason. He offered to locate the bodies in exchange for a lighter sentence. When that didn't to locate the bodies in exchange for a lighter sentence. When that didn't work out, he refused to divulge the location until the authorities gave second consideration to where he would serve his sentence.

"In society's eyes this person has committed the most heinous of crimes, but he continues to be able to use that situation to his advantage. The bodies of his own children have been reduced to mere bargaining chips. There is no remorse, no sense of a conscience.

"The nature of this aggressiveness is demonstrated by the gruesome choice of stabbing the children to death. Stabbing is a slow, painful and violent way to die. It requires a fierce level of anger.

"Also typical of anti-socials is the refusal to accept responsibility for repeated failures. 'It's not my fault. I had to do this.' There are always justifications for acts. 'I killed the children because you wouldn't let me see them when I wanted to. It's really your fault.'

"This brings us to what we call the dynamic formulation, adding color to the basic structure, using what we know of this person's history to develop a hypothesis as to how they came to be the person they are today. Essentially, we have a gentleman born into an Eastern European culture who may have belonged to a matriarchal family in which the power lay with the mother. We do not know if she was a rigid, controlling lady who dominated the household and intruded into the lives of others.

"The father was apparently passive in nature, did not seem to challenge his wife in the household, yet had a tremendous amount of skill and was well-respected as a lawyer. The family was upper middle-class with education as a major priority. So you have education, financial stability and the presence of both parents. It goes to show how money and education do not offset the possibility of having a psychiatric disorder.

"He is the second child of three. His older sister carries the same name as her mother and may have developed many of her characteristics. Now you have a man growing up who may perceive women as controlling and intrusive. He may feel they impose their thoughts and ideals upon him.

"It would be interesting to know if he lived in fear of his parents. Even when he was an adult in Canada and his mother came to visit, he apparently tried to change his behavior to conform to her desires.

"The brother seems to have recognized something was terribly wrong so he responded differently. Maybe he realized there was no use in playing the family game where the rules were stacked against him. His attachment to his in-laws was the only means of escape.

"Part of the frustration for our man is everybody in the family except him had the opportunity to become educated and have some choice of career.

"My feeling is he would have felt inadequate. In a family like the one Liba has described, a child's thoughts and ideas are struck down. The child must listen to what is said.

"As a result, a child will soon learn not to argue or challenge authority. So they don't do it verbally, they do it through behavior, through acting out and through passive/aggressive measures. For instance, if I say, 'You're going to do ten pages of homework tonight, you can't challenge me,' then what you'll do is say, 'Fine, I'll do the ten pages, but I'm going to take my time because you cannot control that.'

"When one uses position-power, which many parents and bosses do, you then end up with a very angry person who may dream of revenge. He thinks, 'One day I'm going to be free of this.'

"Some people step away and say, 'This is what was done to me, therefore I don't want to continue this pattern into another generation.' But if they are not insightful enough, they may choose to say, 'That's the way I was raised and that's the way I'm going to raise my kids.' We don't have much history of his early adulthood until his marital relationship. If his army service was mandatory, in his mind this would be another example of authority figures telling him how to live his life. The army can be like another parent. It has rules. It has its own culture. You can't buck the world is. Their perception is, 'I never get a say. I'm always told what to do. People only do what's in their best interest and never look out for me.'

"This is how some of the paranoia comes into play. He is described as someone who believes his welfare is never looked after. Not in the home or outside of it.

"He goes into the marriage carrying these preconceptions. Lo and behold, he is with somebody who has a good level of character strength, who is capable of taking care of herself, who knows what she wants out of life and he thinks, 'I'm stuck with another controlling person.'

"Unconsciously, many people choose patterns they're used to because they know the rules of that game. In this case it's a pattern he loves to hate. It allows him to carry on a battle against an authority figure. He thinks the world is against him. 'My wife won't allow me freedom. Here's another person who's going to try to emasculate me. I have to fight against this and preserve my manhood.'

"This brings up the relationship with his daughter and son. The daughter is initially seen as a good friend. He can influence her until she reaches the age she can start thinking for herself and start questioning some of his thoughts. That is unacceptable. Now she's becoming just like all the other authority figures. 'How dare she question me? You don't idealize me anymore. You're just like every other woman I've met.'

"Essentially, he is stuck in the past. In his mind he may feel women have always been unpleasant to him and controlling. To him his daughter represents another controlling figure. Now is his chance to create the relationship he always wanted. This is about regaining power and control. The reality is he has had trouble with authority figures be they men or women.

"The situation at school when she takes his hand and says proudly,

"The situation at school when she takes his hand and says proudly, 'This is my Daddy!' was very telling. She idolized him. He was the king. This kind of person is living out the ideal of what he always wanted. Power and control over women and authority figures. His wife representing all the lousy components of women and his daughter representing how he would like women to be. His daughter allows him to be in total control, she idealizes him, he can do no wrong and he gets to make all the decisions.

"When he first got together with his wife, she was vulnerable and he was helpful. But the contract changed as she developed her individuality. With his daughter he wanted the unconditional adoration to continue forever. The only problem is people grow up and relationships change. The daughter at some point would develop a mind of her own and see him differently.

"You have to realize he doesn't think the way most of us do. We would ask, 'If you love somebody so much how could you possibly harm them?' For him, it's not so much a question of loving the person, but loving the relationship of power versus vulnerability. He didn't want to end that relationship. He wanted to preserve the way things were. The hero lives forever. In some ways it was more important for him to kill Gabi, than Paul.

"By killing Gabi, he could preserve and maintain his power over his daughter forever.

"It's ironic the daughter ends up being the child that shows the greatest level of strength and independence. He could most likely tell that from a young age, so she's really growing up with the very qualities that he will learn to hate. Yet that's what he knows and that's what he loves. So you can see the paradoxes.

"Poor Paul had the misfortune of being born to a father who saw the parts of himself that he hated when he looked at his son. He saw Paul as a vulnerable child, a boy who wouldn't stand up for himself, a sissy who allowed the world to dictate to him, who allowed people to stomp all over him. He was emotional. He wasn't tough. These are all the features he hated in himself because he was so powerless as a child.

"Paul was in a double bind. If he did try to assert himself, his father would make sure that he got batted down. It would not be acceptable for another male to show strength in the household. That would make his father feel more inadequate. It wasn't Paul, the individual, he hated. It was what he represented. There was no way to please his dad. And that sadly is the way Liba described Paul's relationship with the father.

"So you have a person who tries to be aggressive, to be very strong, to appear in control and you have his child who represents every quality the father hates in himself.

"And now we come to the end, 'I hold the card to where these children are and you can jump as high as you want, you can shout, you can scream, you can jail me, you can kill me, but you know what? There's only one way you're going to know where they are and that's if I tell you. And so I'll dictate how high you jump, I'll call the shots. The control is back in my hands.'

"While Liba has not been able to fully verbalize to others what she's afraid of, that is exactly what it is. One day this person will get out of jail. He has a very sinister component, is looking for revenge, looking to regain control and punish the world that he feels has been out to get him for many, many years.

"This type of individual can put aside the emotional component when he wants. This blended behavior is more ominous because the anti-social individual, who started from a young age, usually goes through what we call a burnout in their mid-forties. They no longer have the desire to carry out anti-social acts and are not quite sure why they wanted to do them in the first place.

environmentally entrenched. You're not going to get rid of that anger against authority figures. You're not going to get rid of the frustration that was caused over the years by not being allowed to do what you wanted to do. You're not going to get rid of the suspiciousness toward others.

"This man's suspiciousness is not to the point of delusions or hallucinations. He doesn't think people from outer space are chasing him. He does not have overt psychiatric symptoms that would cause people to be wary, but he can be very cunning. He has already shown that.

"While a person like this is in jail, time has passed, but his frame of mind is probably the same. It was only fate that saved Liba and her mother. Had he not dropped the car keys in the mud while he was out in Bragg Creek, he could have come home and quite possibly done them in.

"Is it fair to say that the person is a continued risk? Yes. He needs to have somebody to hang his misfortunes on and she likely will continue to be his scapegoat.

"In terms of human nature, not by legal definition, I would say that at the time he committed these crimes, he knew what he was doing. Whether he decided that morning or the day before, or the week before, I don't know. But he had many chances to change his mind along the way. He had to start at home. He had to drive out to the secluded place he picked. Then he had to decide how he would carry out his actions.

"It is doubtful he had been in some kind of trance. His story that his mind went blank doesn't hold up. The act was too long, too many details were involved and the direction he took too consistent.

"People have asked, 'Well couldn't Liba have seen this coming? She must have been naive.' When you use the word naive, it implies somehow she was deceived. This comes back to trust. In a marriage, when trust is misused, there's no defense. By definition, trust implies that no matter what you see, regardless of the facts, you continue to trust your partner.

what you see, regardless of the facts, you continue to trust your partner. That is what trust is all about.

"It's very common to hear people say in retrospect, 'Oh you know, Robin, all the signs were there, why didn't I pick up on it? Why didn't I do something earlier?' But it is difficult to ignore the previous level of trust and to forego a strong commitment to the institution of marriage. As a mother, Liba thinks, 'I would like my kids to have a family and the family consists of a mother and a father. Regardless of my poor relationship with my husband, I would like to ensure as much as possible that I give my kids the ideal family.' So when you decide to leave, you're saying, 'Gee, I'm going to have to throw all that away.'

"It's not fair to go back and say, she should have picked up on this. The idea that anyone could have seen this coming is very unlikely. That means she would have to have in the back of her mind, 'I married somebody who I live with on a day-to-day basis, who is the father of my kids, and this person is going to go out and try to bump us all off.' Who would ever think this of their spouse and come to that conclusion? In fact I don't believe anyone in his own family could have known or should feel responsible for his actions.

"Sometimes there are no answers and there are no explanations. Things were going to go down that pathway. Unfortunately sometimes you hook up with somebody bad and you cannot escape them. I think this is one of those scenarios. What took place did not happen because of the kids, Liba, or his parents. None of it made any difference. This person was sooner or later going to reach a breaking point.

"Once people get to that point, I find it hard to trust them again. I don't believe any treatment is effective for these individuals. That intensity of cruelty with that end result will always be a possibility in the future. A definition of psychosis is losing touch with reality. Whether he did or didn't during that time I don't know, but you wonder how an individual can end their own child's life by stabbing them to death.

"When you look at the use of slow death, knives rather than guns, and ensuring the victims are suffering, there's something morbid about that choice. For the safety of others I would assume he has not changed."